FRIENDSHIP

MERIDIAN

Crossing Aesthetics

Werner Hamacher

& David E. Wellbery

Editors

Translated by
Elizabeth Rottenberg

Stanford
University
Press

———

Stanford
California
1997

FRIENDSHIP

Maurice Blanchot

Originally published in French in 1971 under the title
L'Amitié

© 1971 Editions Gallimard

Assistance for this translation was provided by the French
Ministry of Culture

Stanford University Press
Stanford, California

Printed in the United States of America

CIP data are at the end of the book

Contents

"My complicitous friendship: this is what my temperament brings to other men."

". . . friends until that state of profound friendship where a man abandoned, abandoned by all of his friends, encounters in life the one who will accompany him beyond life, himself without life, capable of free friendship, detached from all ties."

—Georges Bataille

FRIENDSHIP

§ 1 The Birth
of Art

It is certainly true that Lascaux fills us with a feeling of wonder: this subterranean beauty; the chance that preserved and revealed it; the breadth and scope of the paintings, which are there not in the form of vestiges or furtive adornment but as a commanding presence; a space almost intentionally devoted to the brilliance and marvel of painted things, whose first spectators must have experienced, as we do, and with as much naive astonishment, the wondrous revelation; the place from which art shines forth and whose radiance is that of a first ray—first and yet complete. The thought that at Lascaux we are present at the real birth of art and that at its birth art is revealed to be such that it can change infinitely and can ceaselessly renew itself, but cannot improve—this is what surprises us, what seduces us and pleases us, for this is what we seem to expect of art: that, from birth, it should assert itself, and that it should be, each time it asserts itself, its perpetual birth.

This thought is an illusion, but it is also true; it directs and propels our admiring search. It reveals to us in a perceptible manner the extraordinary intrigue that art pursues with us and with time. Lascaux should be both what is most ancient and a thing of today; these paintings should come to us from a world with which we have nothing in common, the barest outline of which we cannot even suspect, yet they should nonetheless make us, regardless of questions and problems, enter into an intimate space of knowledge. This surprise accompanies all works of past ages, but in the valley of the Vézère, where, in addition, we are aware that the age is one in which man is just beginning to appear, the surprise surprises us still more, while confirming our faith in art, in that power of art that is close to us everywhere, all the more so that it escapes us.

"When we enter the Cave of Lascaux, a strong feeling takes hold of us that we do not have when standing before the glass cases displaying the first fossilized remains of men or their stone instruments. It is this same feeling of presence—of clear and burning presence—that works of art of all ages have always excited in us." Why this feeling of presence? Why, furthermore—naively—do we admire these paintings? Is it because they are admirable, and also because they are the first, works in which art visibly and impetuously emerges from the night, as if we had in them, before us, proof of the first man, for whom we are searching with an inexplicable curiosity and an untiring passion? Why this need for the origin, and why this veil of illusion with which all that is originary seems to envelop itself—a mocking, essential dissimulation, which is perhaps the empty truth of first things? Why, nonetheless, does art, even when it is engaged in the same illusion, let us believe that it could represent this enigma but also put an end to it? Why is it that in speaking of "the miracle of Lascaux" Georges Bataille can speak of "the birth of art"?

It should be said that the book he has devoted to Lascaux is so strikingly beautiful that we are persuaded by the obviousness of what it presents.[1] Of what we see and of what it invites us to see—in a text that is assured, scholarly, and profound but that, above all, does not cease to be in an inspired communication with the images of Lascaux—we can only accept the affirmation and recognize the joy. It seems to me that one of the great merits of the book is that it does not do violence to the figures it nonetheless tears from the earth: it endeavors to shed light on them according to the brightness that emanates from them, a brightness that is always clearer than anything that explanations can offer us in order to clarify them. It is indeed important for us to know that the procession of animal figures, figures that either compose each other or become entangled with one another, a procession that is solemn at times and exuberant at others, is related to magical rites, and that these rites express a mysterious relation—a relation of interest, of conspiracy, of complicity, and even of friendship—between the human hunters and the flourishing of the animal kingdom. Ceremonies with which we are not familiar, but which specialists nonetheless try to imagine by evoking what they do know of "primitive" civilizations today.

What we have here are vague but serious interpretations. From these interpretations there arises a world that is heavy, dark, complicated, and distant. Yet if the world of Lascaux is thus a world of obscure savagery, of mysterious rites and inaccessible customs, what in fact strikes us, on the contrary, in the paintings of Lascaux is how natural they are, how joyful and, under cover of darkness, how prodigiously clear. With the exception of the scene hidden in a well and aside from the slightly disguised figure called the Unicorn, everything comes into a pleasing contact with our eyes, a contact that is immediately pleasing with the only surprise being caused by the familiarity of beautiful things. Images without enigma in a style that is refined, elaborate, and yet bursts forth, giving us a feeling of free spontaneity and of an art that is carefree and without ulterior motive, almost without pretext, and joyfully open to itself. There is nothing archaic about them; they are less archaic even than the first forms of Greek art, and there is nothing that could be more dissimilar to them than the contorted, overburdened, and fascinating art of primitives today. Indeed, had eighteenth-century men descended into the cave of Lascaux, they might have recognized, along the dark walls, the signs of the idyllic humanity of the earliest times—happy, innocent, and a little simple—so often encountered in their dreams. We know that these dreams are dreams. However, although it is less naive than they, the art of Lascaux seems to provide them with a guarantee of its inexplicable simplicity—disorienting us—yet by its nearness and by all that renders it

immediately readable to us, mysterious as art but not an art of
mystery nor of distance.

~

An art that thus comes to our encounter from the depths of
millennia, in the lightness of what is manifest, with the movement
of the herd in motion, the movement of the life of passage animat-
ing all of the figures, and in which we think we touch, through an
illusion that is even stronger than theories, the only happiness of
artistic activity: the celebration of the happy discovery of art. Art is
present here as its own celebration, and Georges Bataille, according
to the thinking that has distinguished his research, shows that the
paintings of Lascaux are probably linked to the movement of
effervescence, to the explosive generosity of celebration when man,
interrupting the time of effort and work—thus for the first time
truly man—returns to the sources of natural overabundance in the
jubilation of a brief interlude, to what he was when he was not yet.
He breaks the prohibitions, but because there are now prohibitions
and because he breaks them, he is exalted far beyond his original
existence; he gathers himself in this existence while dominating it,
he gives it being while leaving it be—this is what would be at the
root of any movement of artistic "designation." It is as if man came
to himself in two stages: there are those millions of years during which beings with names as formidable as *Australanthropus,
Telantropus, Sinanthropus,* whose descendants often resulted in
things other than men, stand erect, use a tibia in combat, break the
bone in order to make use of its fragments—until it is stones they
break—make tools of things and later tools with things, thus
distance themselves dangerously from nature, destroy nature, and
learn to recognize destruction and death and to make use of them.
This is the infinite time in which the pre-man, before being a man,
becomes a worker.

We are of course ignorant of the "feeling" experienced by that
worker, when, by means of prodigious innovations, he began to
occupy a place apart and to separate himself from other living
species. We are tempted to attribute to him some movement of

pride, of power, of disquieting cruelty that is nonetheless superb. Perhaps such was indeed the case. However, everything seems to indicate that man retained a memory of distress and horror of his first steps into humanity. Everything forces us to think that latent man always felt himself infinitely weak in everything that made him powerful, either because he sensed the essential lack—which alone enabled him to become something completely other—or because, in becoming other, he experienced as a mistake everything that led him to fail what we call nature. This void separating him and the natural community is, it seems, what revealed destruction and death to him, but he also learned, not without pain or misgiving, to use this void: to make use of and deepen his weakness in order to become stronger. The prohibitions, which Georges Bataille assumes man used to draw a circle around human possibility from the very beginning—sexual prohibitions, prohibitions about death, and murder—are there as barriers preventing the being who goes beyond himself from coming back, in order to force him to continue along the dangerous, doubtful path, a dead end more or less, and thus to protect all forms of activity that are tedious and against nature, and that have taken their final form in work and through work.

In this way we arrive at the Neanderthal man, from whom, as we know, we are not directly descended and whom, according to a plausible hypothesis, we would have destroyed. He is a being about whom one speaks without affection, although he is a hard worker, a master of tools and weapons, perhaps even the organizer of workshops; he is aware and respectful of death, thus probably surrounded by obscure defenses and in possession, therefore, of the key to humanity's future, of which he cannot avail himself. What is he lacking? Perhaps only the ability to break the rules with which his strength and his weakness protect themselves in him, with a movement of levity, of defiance, and of inspired power: that is to say, of knowing the law by sovereign infraction. This final transgression alone is what would have truly sealed the humanity in man. If one could, musing on the schemata that are proposed by scholars, use an approximate language, one could say that there

occurred during this legendary walk two leaps, two essential moments of transgression.[2] In one, pre-man *fortuitously* does violence
to the natural givens, stands erect, rises up against himself, against
the nature in himself, becomes an animal raised by himself, works,
and becomes thus something not natural, as far from what is
natural as are the prohibitions that limit what he is in order to
benefit what he can be. This first, crucial transgression seems,
however, not to have sufficed, as if the separation between man and
animal were not sufficient to make a man that could be our fellow
creature. Another transgression is called for, a transgression that is
itself ruled, limited, but open as if resolute; one in which, in *an
instant*—the time of difference—the prohibitions are violated, the
gap between man and his origin is put into question once again and
in some sense recovered, explored, and experienced: a prodigious
contact with all of anterior reality (and first with animal reality)
and thus a return to the first immensity, but a return that is always
more than a return, for he who returns, although his movement
gives him the illusion of abolishing millions of years of bondage, of
submission, and weakness, also becomes tumultuously conscious
of this impossible return, becomes conscious of the limits and the
unique force that allows him to break these limits, does not simply
lose himself in the dream of total existence but instead affirms
himself as that which is added to this existence and, more secretly
still, as the minute part that, at a distance and through an ambiguous play, can become master of everything, can appropriate it
symbolically or communicate with it by making it be. It is the
consciousness of this distance as it is affirmed, abolished, and
glorified; it is the feeling, frightened or joyful, of a communication
at a distance and yet immediate that art brings with it, and of which
art would be the perceptible affirmation, the evidence that no
particular meaning can attain or exhaust.

"We put forward with a certain assurance," Georges Bataille
says, "that, in its strongest sense, transgression exists only from the
moment that art itself becomes manifest, and that the birth of art
coincides, more or less, in the Age of the Reindeer, with the tumult
of play and celebration proclaimed in the depths of the caverns by
figures bursting with life, a tumult that always exceeds itself and

fulfills itself in the game of death and birth." There is something joyful, strong, and yet disconcerting in this thought: that man does not become a man through all that is human in him, strictly speaking, and through what distinguishes him from other living beings; but only when he feels confident enough in his differences to grant himself the ambiguous power of seeming to break away from them and of glorifying himself, not in his prodigious acquisitions but rather by relinquishing these acquisitions, by abolishing them, and, alas, by expiating them—it is true, also by overcoming them.

~

Art would thus provide us with our only authentic date of birth: a date that is rather recent and necessarily indeterminate, even though the paintings of Lascaux seem to bring it still closer to us by the feeling of proximity with which they seduce us. Yet is it truly a feeling of proximity? Rather of presence or, more precisely, of apparition. Before these works are erased from the history of painting by the ruthless movement that brought them to the light of day, it is perhaps necessary to specify what it is that sets them apart: it is the impression they give of appearing, of being there only momentarily, drawn by the moment and for the moment, figures not nocturnal but rendered visible by the instantaneous opening up of the night.

This strange feeling of "presence," made up of certainty and instability, scintillates at the edge of appearances while remaining more certain than any other visible thing. And it is this same feeling, it seems to me, that is to be found in the impression of first art, an impression with which the paintings of Lascaux fascinate us, as if, before our eyes, art were lit up for the first time by the torches' glow and asserted itself suddenly with the authority of the obvious, which leaves no room for doubt or alteration. And yet we know, and we feel, that this art, beginning here, had already begun a long time before. Lascaux is unique, but it is not alone; it is first, but it is not the very first. For thousands of years man had been sculpting, engraving, drawing, coloring, and scribbling; sometimes he even represented a human face, as in the figure of Bassempouy, which is already strangely open to feminine beauty. In some ways we are very well informed about the first movements of artistic activity. Sometimes it is the bear who invents art, by scratching on walls and leaving furrows, which his human companion (if it is true that the bear was then the majestic domestic friend of man) demarcates with surprise, with fear, and with the desire to give them more visibly the mysterious feature he finds in them. Sometimes, like Leonardo da Vinci, man looks at the stones and the walls, recognizes in them spots that are figures, that appear through slight modification. Sometimes he lets his dirty fingers drag along the surface of the rocks—or on himself—and these traces please him, and the mud is already color. Sometimes, finally, the one who breaks the bone or the stone with which to arm himself, also breaks it apart for his own delight, perfects these useless fragments, believes he makes the pieces more effective because of certain happy features he inscribes in them or even because of the strange impression he gets in modifying hard things and turning them into "fragments." We have evidence of all this, or at least vestiges with which we put together our own evidence, and this took place long before Lascaux, which dates back to as early as 30,000 years ago, or as late as 15,000 years ago (which is almost today). Lascaux itself, with the power of its complex work, a work that is vast and complete, reveals that there were already centuries of painting behind the paintings we see, that the paintings of Lascaux were elaborated through contact with traditions, models, and uses, as if they were on the inside of that particular space of art that Malraux has called the Museum. It would barely be an exaggeration to say that there already existed at the time real workshops and something like an art market: signs of these were found around Altamira, and there is the little bison engraved on a stone, of which the large painted bison of Font-de-Gaume, 300 kilometers away, is the exact reproduction: as if some errant artist had wandered from one place to the other with his little stone and, responding to the demand, either on the occasion or the obligation of his sacred function, had decorated the privileged sites or conjured up in very singular ceremonies the images that fascinated men then and continue to fascinate us today.

Thus it is true that what is indeed a beginning at Lascaux is the beginning of an art, the beginnings of which, let it be said, lose themselves in the night of all ages. There is a moment where there is nothing, and then a moment where signs multiply. It does not seem that the Neanderthal man, as Georges Bataille insists, had even the faintest idea of artistic activity, and this is troubling. This indeed leads us to think that in the very place where what we call work (turning things into objects, into weapons, and into tools) was discovered, the power of affirmation, of expression, and of communication was not necessarily grasped, the power of which art is the realization. It is possible that in other lineages, no less ancient, from which we are thought to have descended more directly, men were already, at the same time, both workers and artists. This is even probable; it simply pushes back the first ages. But the example of Neanderthal man is no less significant, he for whom the skillful handling and the competent manufacturing of objects were not sufficient to put him in touch with an activity more free, demanding freedom itself and the force obscurely set on breaking prohibitions, in which art was then embodied. As if the division of human possibilities, the analysis of the fundamentally different ways in which man can stand on the inside or the outside of being as non-presence, were in some sense determined by an exigency having little to do with the movement of evolution (without one being able, moreover, to conclude anything relative to the respective values of these possibilities, but only to draw from them the thought that they do not necessarily go together, that they are not always born at the same time, and that sometimes one—art—is missing, as happens later in the Neolithic Age, a disappearance all the more dangerous because it leaves man intact, lacking only the unbound levity that, while putting him in touch with everything he has ceased to be, also allows him never to be simply himself).

~

Teilhard de Chardin has remarked that beginnings escape us and that "if we are not able to see a beginning, it is due to a profound law of *cosmic perspective*, a selective effect of absorption by time of the most fragile—the least voluminous—portions of a development, whatever it may be. Whether it be a question of an individual, of a group, of a civilization, the embryos do not fossilize." Thus there is always a lacuna: as if the origin, instead of showing itself and expressing itself in what emerges from the origin, were always veiled and hidden by what it produces, and perhaps then destroyed or consumed as origin, pushed back and always further removed and distant, as what is originally deferred. We never observe the source, nor the springing forth, but only what is outside the source, the source become reality external to itself and always again without source or far from the source. "The humanizing mutation," Teilhard de Chardin continues, "will always defy our expectation." Not, perhaps, because it is missing but because it is this very missing itself, the gap and the "blank" that constitute it: because the mutation is what could not occur without already having occurred and with the power to throw far back what was just behind it.

This mirage, if it is one, would be the truth and the hidden meaning of art. Art is intimately associated with the origin, which is itself always brought back to the non-origin; art explores, asserts, gives rise to—through a contact that shatters all acquired form—what is essentially before; what is, without yet being. And at the same time it is ahead of all that has been, it is the promise kept in advance, the youth of what is always beginning and only beginning. Nothing can prove that art began at the same time as man; on the contrary, everything indicates that there was a significant lapse in time. However, the first great moments of art suggest that man has contact with his own beginning—is the initial affirmation of himself, the expression of his own novelty—only when, by the means and methods of art, he enters into communication with the force, brilliance, and joyful mastery of a power that is essentially the power of beginning, which is also to say, of a beginning-again that is always prior. At Lascaux, art is not beginning, nor is man beginning. But it is at Lascaux, in its vast and narrow cave, along its populated walls, in a space that seems never to have been an ordinary dwelling place, that art no doubt for the first time reached

the plenitude of initiative and thus opened to man a unique abode
with himself and with the marvel, behind which he had necessarily
to remove and efface himself in order to discover himself: the
majesty of the great bulls, the dark fury of the bison, the grace of
the little horses, the dreamy sprightliness of the stags, even the
ridiculousness of the large jumping cows. As we know, man is
represented—and then merely by certain schematic features—only
in the scene at the bottom of the well: there he lies, stretched out
between a charging bison and a rhinoceros that is turned the other
way. Is he dead? Is he asleep? Is he feigning a magical immobility?
Will he come to, come back to life? This sketch has challenged the
science and ingenuity of specialists. It is striking that with the
figuration of man, an enigmatic element enters into this work, a
work otherwise without secret; a scene also enters into it as a
narrative, an impure historical dramatization. Yet it seems to me
that the meaning of this obscure drawing is nonetheless clear: it is
the first signature of the first painting, the mark left modestly in a
corner, the furtive, fearful, indelible trace of man who is for the first
time born of his work, but who also feels seriously threatened by
this work and perhaps already struck with death.

§ 2 The Museum, Art, and Time

There are times when one regrets that Malraux's books on *La Psychologie de l'art* did not receive more rigorous planning: one finds them obscure not in their language, which is clear—and a little more than clear, brilliant—but in their development. Malraux himself, at the end of his essays, seems to wish that their composition were stronger. Perhaps Malraux is right, but his readers are surely wrong. It is true that the ideas he develops have their quirks; they are quick, sudden, and then they remain without end; they disappear and return; because they often assert themselves in formulas that are pleasing to them, they believe themselves thereby defined, and this accomplishment suffices for them. But the movement that abandons them calls them back; the joy, the glory of a new formula draws them out of themselves.[1]

This movement—this apparent disorder—is definitely one of the appealing sides of these books. The ideas do not lose their coherence in this movement; it is, rather, their contradictions that they escape, although these contradictions continue to animate them and keep them alive. One must add: it is not ideas, exactly, that would be out of place here. Someone—perhaps Valéry—has written: "One must always apologize for discussing painting." Yes, an apology is in order, and he who discusses a book that discusses painting is no doubt in need of a double apology. Malraux's apology is not in the passion he devotes to the art he discusses, nor even in the extraordinary admiration that he bestows upon it (for perhaps art does not always wish to be admired; admiration also displeases art), but in this exceptional merit: that the thoughts, although they tend toward an important and general view of art according to their own exigencies, succeed, in their risky dialogue with works of art, with the images these works accompany, in illuminating themselves, without losing their explanatory value, with a light that is not purely intellectual; in sliding toward something that is more open than their meaning; in carrying out, for themselves—and for us who are destined to understand them—an experience that imitates the experience of art more than it explains it. Thus the ideas become themes, motifs; and their somewhat incoherent development, about which some complain, expresses, on the contrary, their truest order, which is to constitute themselves, to test themselves through their contact with history by way of a movement whose vivacity and apparent wandering make perceptible to us the historical succession of works of art and their simultaneous presence in the Museum where culture today assembles them.

Malraux no doubt does not think he has made a discovery when he shows that, thanks to the progress of our knowledge and also as a result of our means of reproduction—but also for reasons more profound—artists, every artist, has universal art at his disposal for the first time. Many critics before him have reflected on this "conquest of ubiquity," including, to mention him again, Valéry, who speaks of a very near future rather than the present when he writes: "Works of art will acquire a kind of ubiquity. Their immediate presence or their restoration of any period will obey our call. They will no longer be only in themselves but they will all be wherever someone is." And from this he concluded: "One must expect that such great novelties will transform the whole technique of art, will thus affect invention itself, will perhaps go so far as to modify, marvelously, the very notion of art." Marvelously, but Valéry resisted this marvel, which, moreover, he did not want to perceive except in the light consciousness of a half-dream. No more than he readily accepted history did Valéry like the museums that

Malraux called high places but in which Valéry saw only polished solitudes having in them, so he said, something of the temple and the salon, the school and the cemetery: in these houses of incoherence, he seemed only to perceive the unhappy invention of a somewhat barbaric, unreasonable civilization, although even his disavowal was light, was not insistent.

Not only is Malraux insistent, but with persuasive force he makes of the Museum a new category, a kind of power that, in the era at which we have arrived, is at the same time the purpose of history—as it is expressed and completed by art—its principal conquest, its manifestation, and still more: the very consciousness of art, the truth of artistic creation, the ideal point at which this truth, at the same time that it realizes itself in a work, cites, summons, and transforms all other works by putting them in relation to the most recent work that does not always challenge them but always illuminates them in a different way and prompts them to a new metamorphosis that it does not itself escape. To recall it more quickly, *Le Musée imaginaire* points first to this fact: that we are familiar with all of the arts of all civilizations that devoted themselves to art. That we are familiar with them practically and comfortably, not with an ideal knowledge that would belong only to few, but in a way that is real, living, and universal (reproductions). That, finally, this knowledge has its own singular characteristics: it is historical, it is the knowledge of a history, of a set of histories that we accept and receive without subjecting them to any value other than their own past. But at the same time this knowledge is not historical; it is not concerned with the objective truth of this history, its truth at the moment of its occurrence; on the contrary, we accept and prefer it as fiction. We know that all ancient art was other than it seems to us to be. The white statues deceive us, but if we restore their colored coating to them, it is then that they appear false to us (and they are false, because this restoration disregards the power, the truth of time, which has erased the colors). A painting ages; one ages badly, the other becomes a masterpiece through the duration that decomposes its tones, and we are familiar with the fortuitousness of mutilations: this Victory to which only the flight of time could give wings, the heads from Bardo, of mediocre craftsmanship, that the sea has resculpted, has made fascinating. Moreover, the very means of our knowledge transform almost at will that which they help us to know: through reproduction, art objects lose their scale; the miniature becomes a painting, the painting separated from itself, fragmented, becomes another painting. Fictive arts? But art, it would seem, is this fiction.

Other, more important results occur: one must further add that these results are not simply still and inanimate effects but the very truth of the Museum, the active meaning that permitted it to develop, while at the same time art became more consciously connected to itself, to the freedom of its own discovery. The Museum assists in the contestation that animates all culture. This is not immediately clear so long as the Museum, incomplete, glorifies a single art, sees in it not one art but perfection and certainty. Thus Greek art and the art of the Renaissance are evidence that the artist can emulate, but even if he equals them, he does not bring them closer to his time; he makes himself lasting, he takes his place outside of time by their side. This is why the only Museum is a universal one. Then the "all has been said," "all is visible" signifies that the admirable is everywhere, is precisely this "all" that triumphs only when the incontestable has disappeared and the eternal has come to an end. On the other hand, as soon as the Museum begins to play a role, it is because art has agreed to become a museum art: a great innovation, and for many the sign of great impoverishment. Is art poor because it is simply itself? This is open to discussion, but the evolution is obvious. Plastic art is first in the service of religious sentiments or invisible realities around which the community perpetuates itself; art is religion, says Hegel. At this stage one finds it in churches, in tombs, under the earth, or in the sky, but inaccessible, invisible in a way: who looks at Gothic statues? We do; the others invoked them. The consequence of the disappearance of prayer was to make monuments and works of art appear, to make painting an art within reach of our eyes. The Renaissance begins this evolution. But the visible that it discovers absorbs it. Certainly it is not content with reproducing appearances, or even with transforming them according to a harmonious understanding that it calls the beautiful. The whole Renaissance did not take place in Bologna, for who, more than the Florentines, disregarded charm, the pleasure of mere detail, and even the delight of color so as better to grasp the meaning of forms—a prejudice they do not owe to antiquity but one that is in them like the passion for a secret? It remains that the Renaissance, if it makes art real, present, seems, through its success and the ambiguous nature of its success, to link this presence to the ability to represent. Whence the misunderstandings, which have still not come to an end—but in the final analysis excellent misunderstandings, given that so many great works arise from them. These great works continued to belong to churches, however; they were at home in palaces, where they sometimes played a political role; they had powerful ties to life, which sought to make use of them. A portrait in the home of the one it figures remains a family painting. But when all of these works really or ideally enter the Museum, it is precisely life that they renounce, it is from life that they agree to be separated. Artificial places, one says of museums, from which nature is banished, the world constrained, solitary, dead: it is true, death is there; at least life is no longer there, neither the spectacle of life nor the sentiments and manners of being through which we live. And what else takes place? What was a god in a temple becomes a statue; what was a portrait becomes a painting; and even dreams, that absence in which the world and the images of the world were transfigured, are dissipated in this new brightness that is the broad daylight of painting.

In this way the transformation, the contestation that is specific to art is momentarily at an end. Modern art, in the Museum, would become conscious of its truth—which is to be neither in the service of a church, nor of a history or specific event, nor of a figure—its truth, which is to remain ignorant of immediate life, the furnishings of appearances, and perhaps all of life in order to recognize itself only in the "life" of art. The painter serves painting, and apparently painting serves no purpose. The strange thing is that from the day he makes this discovery, the artist's interest in his art, far from diminishing, becomes an absolute passion, and the works that signify nothing seem to incarnate and reflect this passion. Why? One may well ask oneself this.

~

Malraux himself asks the question and supplies various answers. But first, one must see more precisely what this evolution expresses, this revelation caused by history, which affirms itself in these two forms: the imaginary Museum and modern art. It will not escape one that in many respects Malraux's views apply to the plastic arts, inspired as he is by the discoveries of our time, the movements of a thought whose principles reside with Hegel. There are certainly many differences, but the analogies are interesting. When one indicates that today, for the first time, art has doubly unveiled itself, the words "for the first time" have an obvious authority: they indicate that a conclusion has been reached, and this conclusion, if it does not bring time to a close, nonetheless permits the observer who speaks in the name of this first time to speak of time as of a closed truth. It is clear that for Malraux, and no doubt for each of us, our era is not—at least for what concerns the plastic arts—an era like any other: it is the radiating world of the "first time." For the first time, art has unveiled itself in its essence and in its totality: movements that are intimately connected. Art abandons everything it was not and extends itself to everything it has been; it reduces itself to itself, it is deprived of the world, the gods, and perhaps dreams, but this poverty leads it to acquire the wealth of its truth and subsequently the wealth of a whole array of works it was prevented from reaching, and was brought to underestimate, to disregard, or to despise because art was not yet conscious of itself. The imaginary Museum is thus not only the contemporary of modern art and the means of its discovery; it is also the work of this art—one might say its masterwork, were it not also necessary to say, to an extent that is half secret, its compensation. That art should be nothing but its passionate contestation, the absolute brilliance of the single moment when art, denying all the rest, is affirmed marvelously in itself—this might not be tolerable were it not

everything, were it not that art slid through the time and civilizations of the world like purity at daybreak, and made suddenly
visible, with all of its works, this marvelous event of our art being
universal, which means that all works of all times are also our work,
the work of our art, which, for the first time, reveals them to
themselves, unveils them as they are.

Perhaps we are going a little further than Malraux's formulas
would permit. But if today, for the first time, art has arrived at a
consciousness of itself (a consciousness that is above all negative:
painting no longer imitates, no longer imagines, no longer trans-
figures, no longer serves values that are foreign to it, is no longer
anything—and here is the positive side—but painting, its own
value, which, it is true, is not yet easy to grasp)—if, in addition, this
consciousness, far from placing art in a timeless place, is linked to
duration, is the meaning of this duration, which at a certain
moment takes form and makes itself absolutely manifest—then it is
true that this moment is indeed privileged, that it has the power to
turn back on all the other moments, and because it is absolute
transparency for itself, it is also the transparency of all the others,
the light in which these moments show themselves in their purity
and their truth. No doubt things are not so simple. Art is perhaps
not a comet whose brilliant point or shimmering head—modern
art—would lead and illuminate the more muted and more obscure
beauty of its immense orbit. And what is more, if the works of
today help us to become the "heirs of the entire world"—and we
must add, more than heirs, the creators and conquerors of all
possible works—they themselves depend in turn on this conquest,
this creation. This dependence is not one of dry causality but a dialectic to which Malraux gives the name—perhaps insufficiently rigorous or too evocative—metamorphosis. Art—and by this should
be understood the entirety of works and that which makes each one
a work of art—is in essence anxiety and movement. The Museum is
in no way made up of immutable afterlives and the eternal dead.
Statues move; we know this, just as Baudelaire was frightened to see
unreal images subject to a surprising development. With each
decisive work of art, all the others shudder and some succumb, a

death that is the resurrection of tomorrow; and this movement is in appearance infinite, for if, as Schiller said, "what lives immortally in song must die in life," what this immortality maintains, conveys, and sustains is this death itself become work and negative creation. At the end of his three volumes, Malraux writes, "The first universal artistic culture will no doubt transform modern art, by which it has been oriented up to this point." Modern art is thus destined, promised, or condemned to the power of metamorphosis from which it springs, but more than this: of which it seems to be the purest form, the expression of an instant reduced to this expression alone. The unknown is its future. But in the meantime, and because there is no one moment that is like any other, but only this privileged moment that at once revealed and multiplied the power of metamorphosis, it seems possible to search, through modern art, for the meaning of the question to which all the arts are the answer and for the reason why this answer is equally valid and decisive. This is the problem of artistic creation to which Malraux has devoted the second of his books, the book some may prefer, in which civilizations become works of art, in which works of art are composed and accomplished according to the secret of their own completion, which they make perceptible to us as if by transparency and as if this transparency were precisely their secret. This impression, it is true, is but the joy of an instant, and what we will have to say about it is rather the unhappiness that follows, the obscurity that closes in on this fleeting day, for art, having become a problem, is also an infinite torment.

~

The plastic arts are strangers to nature: we know this, but Malraux shows it with an energy and perseverance that are sometimes surprising, as if this truth continued to be threatened. It is because he wants to show a little more. When he writes, "Any art that claims to represent implies a system of reduction. The painter reduces all form to the two dimensions of his canvas, the sculptor all virtual or represented movement to immobility," the reduction he is speaking of still seems to refer the artist back to nature. Would the painting of a landscape be a landscape reduced, transformed by the recourse to technique, thus turned over to the disinterestedness of art? Not at all, for the purpose of painting would then be the search to reduce this reduction, since, as is obvious, many schools have attempted it, not to their credit. In reality, if "art begins with reduction," this means that the work of art is never constituted except on the basis of itself, on the inside of the artistic universe in perpetual becoming—history made art—which the imaginary Museum symbolizes for us, but which, however limited and poor, has always been presupposed by an artist's eye. Art does not begin with nature, were it even to deny it. The origin of a painting is not always another painting, or statue, but all of art, as it is present in works admired and intuited in works scorned; and the artist is always the son of other works, the works of others that he passionately imitates until the moment when he rejects them passionately. Why is Malraux so unyielding in his affirmations, affirmations that force him, for example, to hold in low regard the drawings of children, for the child, if he draws a dog, perhaps does not draw the dog that he sees, but neither does he draw a dog of Tintoretto (and perhaps one should say so much the better)? It seems he needs to put the artist in a place apart, sheltered from the world and beyond the world, just as the Museum is a universe that leads nowhere, a solitary duration, the only free duration, the only one that is a true history, equal to the freedom and mastery of man. The imaginary Museum, plus the new artist who shuts himself away in it to be free—such is art; in it are found gathered all of the givens of artistic creation. How did Giotto discover his vocation? By looking at Cimabue's paintings and not the sheep whose shepherd he is. How does any vocation develop? By way of imitation, copy, until the moment when, through the passionate imitation of masterly forms, the nascent artist becomes the master of the plastic secret of works and little by little, sometimes very late, sometimes without ever achieving it except in the margins, experiences, creates, distinguishes his own plastic secret, what Malraux calls the "initial schemes" of his art. These "schemes" are first powers of rupture, intentions in which is expressed—not abstractly or aesthetically but plastically—a will to surpass, to transform the art and the style through which the young creator found himself one day introduced into the Museum, and thus made free, although a prisoner, still, of his masters. To rediscover, to describe these schemes is to rediscover the progression, the discoveries, the metamorphoses: in a word, the specific experience that has meaning only in the works and that one betrays the least—but one still betrays it—when one describes it in its most concrete and technical aspect. The most persuasive pages that Malraux has written show, in terms that are extremely evocative and nonetheless precise, what the itinerary of El Greco might have been starting out from Venice, or that of Tintoretto also starting out from Venice, or that of La Tour starting out from Caravaggio, or that of Goya starting out from himself, from that other artist who until the age of forty was called Goya unbeknownst to him. And to return to El Greco, it is not the moving pages on Toledo, the solitude, the somber twilight with which the artist surrounds his own vision, that would bring us closer to this mastery, but everything that makes the central point of his discovery perceptible to us, which can be expressed thus: to maintain the baroque drawing of movement—the turbulence of all lines—while eliminating that from which it arose: the quest for depth (the distant).

Malraux seems irritated when he hears mention of an artist's "vision." This antipathy to vocabulary is remarkable. Just as he energetically excludes from art the idea of representation, so does he seem to exclude from artistic genesis the notion of image. This is logical up to a certain point (one might say that painting is a struggle to escape vision); it is in any case the consequence of formulas that he willingly repeats: "Plastic art is never born from a way of seeing the world but of making it." And this banishment of vision holds for imaginary vision as well, for interior fiction, for everything that might reduce painting to the passive, subjective expression of a resemblance, be it one of an invisible form. In his three books, Malraux grants only one line to surrealism, and this is to brush it aside. This distrust, which is strong but instinctive—it is obvious that Malraux uses terms according to his own pleasure, which is authoritarian, and it would be a malicious game to take him at his word—this distrust of the word *vision* and of the imaginary tends above all to separate everything from plastic art that might make its function, its creative activity, less obvious. The painter is a creator of forms and not a visionary who would passionately copy down his dreams, and the conception is nothing outside of the painting in which it does not suffice to say that it expresses itself, for before the painting there is nothing but an intention that is already pictorial, given that it is in its contact with other paintings that it took shape, trying itself through imitation. Painting is an experience in which a specific power affirms or seeks itself, which is valid only for that art and makes sense only in relation to it, a power that must nonetheless be defined, or at least named, and that Malraux calls style. What is art? "That by which forms become style." But what is style? The answer can be found, and from a certain perspective—it should be said—is surprising: "All style is the giving of form to the elements of the world that help orient the world toward one of its essential parts."

~

There would be reason enough to imagine that *La Psychologie de l'art* is uniquely concerned with restoring to art the experience that belongs to it, the world that belongs to it, this Universe of the Museum (monad without windows), which the artist creates and elicits into the infinite of time, perfectly self-sufficient, self-ordered, oriented toward itself alone, animated by the duration of its metamorphoses, a solitude worthy of all passions and all sacrifices, in which the one who enters knows that he goes before the greatest danger, because what he seeks is the extreme. Yes, one can imagine that Malraux's investigations might have taken such a turn, and one can tell oneself that such a turn might not disagree with "one of [his] essential parts," that part which bound him to painting and to the plastic arts with true passion. But for this, Malraux would perhaps have had to be a painter himself, would perhaps have had to be interested in painting in order to continue it and not to justify it, in order to make it and not to see it. Still, the more one advances in the investigation of a problem, the more difficult it becomes not to express it from the point of view of all the questions to which one is vitally bound. Malraux is interested in painting, but, as we know, he is also interested in man: to save one through the other, he was not able to resist this great temptation. A temptation all the more imperious in that the problem itself leads us to it, for one must indeed reflect on this strange Museum in which we dwell and on this even stranger history into which it introduces us. What do we see in it? What we prefer—and what we prefer are those works, which, like our own, are ignorant of appearance, do not submit to it, create a world that is other and whose power and victorious strangeness fascinate us. But these works (those, for example, of Byzantine style, to take the best-known works) and this refusal of appearance, this rupture they express—we are forced to recognize that it is not the search for form, it is not at all the search for a style that has produced them: it is, rather, those values alien to the world, those to which we owe all of our gods, those from above and those from below. Striking observations, but not unexpected. If art is defined and constituted by its distance in relation to the world, by the *absence* of world, it is natural that everything that puts the world into question, what one calls, in a word—a word whose usage has become so unrigorous— transcendence; everything that surpasses, denies, destroys, threatens the body of relations that are stable, comfortable, reasonably established, and anxious to remain; all of these powers, be they pure or impure, proposed for the "salvation" of man or his destruction, insofar as they shatter the validity of the common world, work for art, open the way for it, call it forth. Gods thus become, in the greater part of the Museum, the surprising illusion that has permitted the artist, in consecrating himself to their cult, to consecrate art. Art is at this moment religion, that is to say, a stranger to itself, but this strangeness, being what tears it away from profane values, is also what brings it closest to its own truth without its knowledge, although this truth is not manifest. In this sense, one could say that gods were only the temporary substitutes, the sublime masks—but without beauty—of artistic power for as long as this power, through the dialectic of history and of metamorphoses, could not achieve, in the artist finally reduced to himself, the consciousness of its autonomy and solitude. The Pantocrator waiting for Picasso.

And now? Now art is perhaps called Picasso, but it seems that it is Picasso's duty to continue the Pantocrator, not only because the demiurgic task of being a creator of forms and a creator of everything that is the life of the Museum falls to him alone, but also in bringing painting into harmony with this "essential part," this superior aim, the level of the eternal, which was represented for men of the first centuries by the golden image of the absolute. For modern art and for Malraux's aesthetics this is a turning point, a difficult moment. It is true the complicitous gods have disappeared; they have reentered the profound absence, this realm above or below the world; it seems that it was formerly their task to make this absence appear or, more precisely, to offer it to art as the bold place—the void—in which art could become master of itself without, however, knowing itself. Absence, depth, destined to divert the gazes of the "real," to challenge appearances, to substitute the conquering power of a style for representation. But from the moment that art gained consciousness of its truth, that it revealed itself as the refusal of the world and the affirmation of the solitude of the Museum, this absence, this depth, reconquered by painting, in which the gods lived in order to accustom the artist to managing without life—must it not in turn disappear in the painting, be painting—and nothing more; be the fact that painting has *worth* as painting—and nothing else? Yes, it seems it must, and yet if one returns to Malraux, this absence does not permit itself to be thus mastered by art and it still claims under more or less glorious names—the human quality, the ideal image of man, the honor of being human, in a word, "the essential part of the world"—to be the exemplary power, the divinity that art cannot leave unexpressed without losing itself. The arts of the past certainly had a relationship with the gods. The arts intended, by expressing the gods, to make present that which is not seen, does not express itself, does not make itself present; and through this superb pretension, art found itself not led astray toward the invisible or the formless but, rather, on the path of pure visible presence and form as it alone affirmed itself purely. Impressive results. However, the invisible remained. It was not really mediatized. More must be said, because for Malraux painting is not "image," is not the pictorial conquest of this *absence*, which, before any technical reduction, brings that which is seen back to the stupor of a "this is not," "this cannot be seen," because, in addition, he does not want to reintroduce the invisible as fiction (although he makes a place for "poetry" in his third book), the invisible, which is not pictorialized, can but wander dangerously around the painting under the name of the ideal and the values of culture.

This reorientation does not occur in a deliberate way; it is a stirring debate that Malraux seems to pursue with the different parts of himself. To what end do the evolution of time and the metamorphoses of the Museum lead? To a painter who would be only a painter: to Cézanne, who, compared with Goya, is painting liberated from metaphysical passion, from the dream and the sacred, who is painting that has become a passion for itself and creation of itself alone. Malraux confirms this to us: modern art imposes the autonomy of painting, autonomy with regard to all tradition and even culture. Painting that has become culture is a stage, a moment: a bad moment, and this moment corresponded to the intervention of intellectuals who could see in the plastic arts only what was most visible in the arts: a harmonious fiction, the transfiguration of things, the expression of values, the representation of a human and civilized world. But can painting, when its representative function has disappeared, when it is only bound to the pursuit of its own values, still serve as the guarantor of a culture? "An art of great Navigators," yes, says Malraux. "But is a culture of great Navigators conceivable?" Elsewhere doubt becomes the answer: "Picasso succeeds Cézanne, the anguished questioning supplants annexation and conquest. But a culture of questioning alone cannot exist."

This is probably true. But should one not conclude that art, the impassioned questioning, has nothing to bring to this stationary ideal, this body of recognized values, public truths, and established institutions that one calls civilization, just as it has nothing to receive from it? The painter, the artist, as we are made to see him, is certainly a being who may be called divine, and we are not surprised by this, since he has taken the place of the gods; but more than this: he is the truth of which the divinity was only the mask, its necessary caricature. "The gestures with which we handle the paintings we admire . . . are those of veneration. The Museum, which was a collection, becomes a kind of temple. Of course, a still life by Braque is not a sacred object. And although it is not a Byzantine miniature, it belongs, as does the latter, to another world and is part of an obscure god that one wants to call painting and that is called art." Malraux adds, expressing a repugnance that we share with him: "Religious vocabulary is irritating here, but there is no other. This art is not a god; it is an absolute." An absolute, but one whose truth it is to be closed in on itself, whose truth it is to have its excellence and its signification in itself—and what is outside of itself one can only call insignificant. This, at least, is what Malraux's views on modern painting seemed to invite us to think. The god is called painting, and painting, in the past, so as to escape the temptations of aesthetic realism, was in need of a metaphysical or religious realism, which is why it liked the gods. But today, when the gods have become paintings, when it is a matter of the "creation of a painting that wants to be only painting," metaphysics must also disappear in the painting and must be nothing more than *this* painting, for fear of transforming it into metaphysics—of restoring, consequently, another form of realism or, worse yet, of appearing above the painting as the duty, the purely moral obligation to save civilization and protect man.

⁓

However, this obligation becomes more and more urgent in the course of the third book, and it seems that art also assumes this obligation more and more willingly: what one could call its idealizing function, its ability to "sustain, enrich, or transform, without weakening, the ideal image of himself that man has inherited." An aim that is perhaps urgent, perhaps inevitable, but the result is that the whole perspective in which the Museum, the world, and the artists appeared to us, changes. The Museum seemed to be the artist's own universe, not the history of art but art as the freedom of history, the expression of a specific duration (which we would still have to question), the manifestation of a time *sui generis* that the idea of metamorphosis shed light on. All works of art were present in the Museum, and because modern art expresses, without mediation or travesty, the truth (the language that needed all of these works in order to be heard), one could say that in effect these works formed a totality and consequently that they were, from a certain point of view, one and the same work whose true meaning—whose pure plastic merits—could be perceived and admired in the past only through a pretense of anecdote, fiction, and sacred values, but whose clear and manifest truth we are able to see today with a gaze that is finally competent. Of course, we know that Byzantine art was not an art for itself and that it wanted to make things attain a sacred universe, but our role is to replace what Byzantine art was to itself with what Byzantine art is to art, that is to say, first a system of forms (as Malraux writes in *Le Musée imaginaire*: "But for us Byzantine art is first a system of forms; any art that is reborn undergoes metamorphosis, changes signification; it is reborn without God"). In the same way, if so many disparate works today are a part of what we prefer, if we are able to enjoy both Negro art and Poussin, it is, it seems, because we are able to discover the elements common to art in works without community, it is because painting must appear to us as a specific language, a language that is present in a manner that is more or less expressive and more or less manifest, whatever the representation, suggestion, and historical travesty to which this language is linked.

But in reality this is not the case, and we were deceiving ourselves about the Museum. "This place that gives one the highest idea of man" cannot be only the Temple of images; it is the Temple of civilizations, religions, historical splendors. And the Museum we should enjoy is not such as it is revealed to us by Cézanne—a museum of art that wishes to be only painting, negation and authentic refusal of all content, of any part of the world—but, if it may be said, the museum of contents, the museum of histories and times. "Our time," says Malraux, "seemed at first to want to found the unity of the arts it recognized on the kinship of forms alone. But a great artist who knew, besides contemporary works, only the specifically plastic qualities of past works, would be a superior type of modern barbarian, one whose barbarity was defined by the refusal of any human quality. Our culture, were it limited to the extremely acute culture of our sensibility to colors and forms, and to what expresses this in the modern arts, would not even be imaginable. But our culture is far from being limited in this way, for a culture without precedent is being established." And this artistic culture, as Malraux has just warned us, cannot be, must not be, *purely* artistic; moreover, as soon as art becomes culture, is the means, the instrument of a culture, it can no longer belong to itself; it falls prey to travesties and servitudes: the wheel of values and knowledge.

However, Malraux does not intend to put into question so easily that which appeared to him to be the meaning of modern art. The affirmation of painting as negation of the world and all values (other than itself) does not even appear to him to be incompatible with the service imposed on it, which is to save the quality of man and his values. This is one of the thorny points of *La Psychologie de l'art.* To understand it, one must try to understand the situation of the Museum better in relation to history and the situation of art opposite time. When we are in a museum—but perhaps, then, we are there as "spectators" and no longer as "artists"—it is indeed true that our admiration and our interest are also for the past that these works represent to us, for the past not as it may have been but as it is present and as it shines forth ideally in these works. Is it Greece that is there, is it Sumer, Byzantium? No, not at all. Our historical vision is an illusion; it is a myth, but this myth has an extreme "spiritual wealth." This illusion represents what is eternally true, that part of truth which there is in an afterlife that stays present to us, remains accessible to us, moves us, fascinates us, belongs to us, as if this afterlife found life in us, and we, survival through it. "The dialogue that links our culture to the ephemeral absolutes transmitted to it by resuscitated arts, reestablishes, with the past it shapes, the link between Greek gods and the cosmos, between Christ and the meaning of the world and the numberless souls of the living and the dead. Every Sumerian work of art suggests the kingdom of Sumer, in part ungraspable, in part possessed. The great museums satisfy in us an exoticism of history, *give* us a vast domain of human powers. But the long trace left by the sensibility of the earth in these museums is not the trace of history. It is not dead societies that art resuscitates: it is often the ideal or compensatory image that these societies had of themselves." One can therefore say of art that it perpetuates the spirit, that it plays, in relation to history, the role that, for Hegel, history plays in relation to nature: it gives it a meaning, it assures, beyond the perishable and across the death of duration, life and the eternity of meaning. Art is no longer the anxiety of time, the destructive power of pure change; it is bound to the eternal; it is the eternal present, which, through vicissitudes and by means of metamorphoses, maintains or ceaselessly re-creates the form in which "the quality of the world through a man" was one day expressed. A power that Malraux never tires of celebrating in striking terms: "In whatever way an art represents men, it expresses a civilization as this civilization conceives of itself: it grounds the civilization in meaning, and it is this meaning that is stronger than the diversity of life." "On Judgment Day, let the gods raise up the army of statues in face of the forms that were living! It is not the world that they created, the world of men, that will testify to their presence: it is the world of artists. . . . All art is a lesson for its gods." And this revealing line: "The obscure relentlessness of men to re-create the world is not in vain, because nothing becomes *presence* again beyond death, with the exception of re-created forms."

But where does this privilege, if it is one, come from? For it could be that it is also a curse and the darkest failure of art, of which art is perhaps only today becoming conscious. Where does this exceptional power come from that seems to make the artist the sole torchbearer, the sole master of the eternal? Malraux notes it more than he proves it. But one can nonetheless perceive the reasons that underlie his thinking. The main reason is that the artist is par excellence a "creator." He is one because he is never subject to nature, neither when he seems to imitate it nor when he impugns it in order to submit himself to the gods. With regard to the gods themselves, he is free; he is perhaps ignorant of this freedom, but his work affirms and exercises it. It sometimes happens, even today, that he allies himself with the nocturnal powers and, like Goya, with monsters, with horror, with the night; or, like those "primitives" that haunt us, with the fascination for the formless and for chaos: a disturbing dependency that seems to signify a possession more than a mastery. But herein lies the wonder: through the work of art, possession becomes the power to possess; servitude wakes up emancipated. "Although the expression of archaic sentiments, even when it is indirect, gives the masterpiece a particular resonance, the recourse to darkness remains in the service of a royal accent: no monster in art is an end in itself. Always mingled in our admiration are the feelings about the deliverance of man and the mastery of the work." Goya's solitude is great, but it is not without limits, for he is a painter, and if "the painting is for him a means of reaching the mystery . . . the mystery is also a means of reaching painting" and thus of coming to light, of becoming the freedom and the brightness of the day. Van Gogh is mad; his paintings are a superior lucidity and consciousness. The artist is never dependent on his time, or on his personal history, no more than his paintings depend on the common vision. We now understand why, from his birth to his death, he has been represented to us within the sole existence of the Museum: this is because he is free only in the Museum, because his freedom is to belong to art that belongs only to itself, although art is always, when it is creative, that which transmutes existence into power, subordination into sovereignty, and death itself into a power of life.

~

It seems that for Malraux, it is the artist alone who saves us from absurdity and contingency, he alone who transforms what would otherwise be only the formless ruins of a duration without memory, the disgusting rot of the cadaver of time, into a radiant, intelligible, and salutary present. When in the passage we have cited he writes, "nothing becomes *presence* again after death, with the exception of re-created forms," he indeed invests art with this exorbitant privilege, seemingly without asking himself whether all vestige of human labor has not the same power of becoming historical and, through history, of taking on and keeping meaning, of constantly being enriched by a meaning that is always new. And yet this is the question one would be tempted to ask oneself: if so many remote works attract and fascinate us as if they were highly aesthetic, it is because remoteness can substitute itself for art; it is because the retreat, the movement of history—on the condition that they escape all proximity with our world—have in themselves a value of creation that can be compared with that of the artist. But perhaps this remark helps us to recognize where Malraux's assurance comes from. It is very likely that he is aware that fragments of polished stone are just as moving and carry just as much human meaning as does Praxiteles' smiling *Hermes*. If, however, he puts art beyond comparison, it is because his discovery of the Museum and his feeling of wonder before works of art have made him sensitive to the paradox in which time causes any work of art to slip. It is true that there is something strange in the manner by which duration opens into this figure of Praxiteles, for example. This has often been commented upon: I can approach the canvas or the marble, but not the "images" in which the artistic intention is incarnated, and no more than their nearness puts them within my reach, does the passing time move them from themselves or seem to have any hold on them. Why? Could one say that this presence is an emancipation of duration, a marvelous equivalent of the eternal? Classical aesthetics believed this, and perhaps a part of Malraux himself remains classical. The idealization of figures, the search for perfection and beauty, are supposed to maintain this endless presence, to liberate absolutely the unique moment that the statue symbolizes and affirms from time. The ideal of the beautiful is but the theoretical elaboration of this exceptional situation. Subsequently it was thought that a figure would last eternally if it was beautiful; but this was because it was first felt that, beautiful or not, it did not pass away, or else that it had always already passed away. Of course, the value attributed to this eternal present of the figure (artistic immortality) itself depends on the times and on histories. Even today, one seems to forget that the survival of images has often been valued very little or cursed outright, and one forgets, furthermore, that it is the survival that is condemned and not the image. Civilizations of the eternal are perhaps the only civilizations, but man is also aware that if eternity shelters him from what makes him dangerous and what exposes him to danger, then eternity is the illusion that takes from him his one chance at truth.

Art, it is evident, plays a role in the faith in this illusion. In humanistic civilizations, it is immediate life, ephemeral time that it is called on to transmute, to eternalize by placing it under the seal of a resemblance. Resemblance is not a means of imitating life but of making it inaccessible, of establishing it in a double that is permanent and escapes from life. Living figures, men, are without resemblance. One must wait for the cadaverous appearance, the idealization by death and the eternalization of the end for a being to take on the great beauty that is its own resemblance, the truth of itself in a reflection. A portrait—one came to perceive this little by little—does not resemble because it makes itself similar to a face; rather, the resemblance only begins and only exists with the portrait and in it alone; resemblance is the work of the portrait, its glory or its disgrace; resemblance is tied to the condition of a work, expressing the fact that the face is not there, that it is absent, that it appears only from the absence that is precisely the resemblance, and this absence is also the form that time seizes upon when the world moves away and when there remains of it only this gap and this distance.

What does one call this time? Perhaps it does not matter. To call it *eternity* is consoling but misleading. To call it *present* is no more exact, for we know only one present, the present that fulfills and realizes itself in the active life of the world and that the future ceaselessly raises to itself. It is just as tempting to see in it a pure and simple absence of time. The critics tell us this: Praxiteles' *Hermes* smiles from the depths of its mystery, and this smile expresses its indifference to time, the mystery of its freedom in relation to time; this is why all of these smiles of art that touch us as if they were the human secret par excellence, the smile of Rheims, the smile of Saint Anne, affirm the defiance with which the expression of the ephemeral—grace and freedom of an instant—challenges duration by enclosing itself within the unreal.

But the absence of time here signifies only the absence of the world in which we act and work (that of the possible, which constantly denies being in order to transform it, through work, into livable reality). The absence of time that art would designate alludes only to the power that we have of putting an end to the world, of standing before or after the world—that space of practical life but also of truth as it is expressed, of culture and significations— a power that is perhaps a sovereignty but that also asserts itself in all situations in which man gives up mastering himself and accepts that he will not recover himself. This is why art is tied to all that puts man in danger, to everything that puts him violently outside the world, outside the security and intelligence of the world to which only the future belongs. Thus in Goya blood, anguish, death are the work of art. Thus also the child who is almost completely ignorant of the world and the madman for whom the world has almost been lost are "naturally" artists. All of them, through anguish, heedlessness, already belong to this absence—which could be called nothingness, but a nothingness that is still being, being about which one cannot grasp anything or do anything, where nothing ever begins and nothing ever ends, where everything is repeated ad infinitum because nothing has ever truly taken place. The eternal, perhaps, but if so, the eternal recurrence.

～

Just as the world of art is tied to absence, so the time of art is related to eternal repetition. However, it would be difficult not to see it: this absence to which art tries to be equal and in view of which, but also by means of which, it tears all things from the measure and truth of the world; art must *realize* it, and this reality can lead to the rehabilitation of the "world." This is unfortunate, because it involves playing with misunderstandings; it also paradoxically gives art the duty to perform, through its submission— the submission to appearance—its task, which is to achieve absence; not simply the absence of the world, but absence as world. In any case, under whatever form it may be and according to whichever means, absence tends in turn to become world, reality—but, as modern art teaches us, a reality all the more "authentic," all the more worthy of absence the more it fulfills itself according to the exigencies of this art, in terms that give this art a full existence and give full existence to it alone. One might ask oneself whether formalism does not threaten an art that is so close to itself. The threat is certain; any art is always threatened by what appeases it. But this would be, however, to forget that art is perpetually unequal to what it seeks; that it constantly betrays what it seeks, the closer success brings art to it; and that this dissatisfaction, this infinite contestation—unable to be expressed except through the experience of plastic art—can only render vain all attempts to give it theoretical limits (for example, by reducing it to a purely formal question).

Yet more needs to be said: the canvas or statue perhaps aspires to solitude, not in order to become the sole masterpiece capable of erasing all others but in order to remove itself from the society of masterpieces and thus to maintain a *remoteness from everything* that it must make manifest. This aspiration to remain alone is the hopeless truth of all works said to be authentic, but in general this desire is in vain. And this means not only that the painting must enter into the world as a pleasant spectacle and a commercial value, but also that it must take its place *outside* the world, in the imaginary space, in the life freed from life to which Malraux has called our attention under the name of Museum. The Museum is not a myth, but this necessity: that the condition of being outside the world, which the work of art seeks to maintain, nonetheless puts it in relation to a group, ends up constituting a whole, and gives rise to a history. The Museum, as Malraux has taught us, moreover, is not a place but a history. This history is certainly not a celestial history, without relation to the history of the "world"; however, one cannot deny that a specific form of duration and a particular dialectic are realized in it. The term *metamorphosis* has made us sensitive to this dialectic. Any great artist takes form in the Museum, by submitting to it, and then by submitting to its mastery. Any great work of art transforms all others. And there is a labor specific to duration that disturbs the canvases and awakens or puts to sleep the statues. Torsos are complete because time has broken their heads. The crushed face of Saint Elizabeth of Bamberg gives her a nocturnal likeness that she was obviously expecting. Colors decompose, and this dissolution is the reward of art, thus reconciled with absence. What does all of this signify? First, that it is not true that Praxiteles' adolescent smiles in an eternal present. This smile took form in the unreal, but the unreal is also a form of time, a time that is the work of forms and the destiny of images. Even if the marble has preserved this smile, the figures who do not smile—the *Daughter of Euthydikos*, the *Head of an Ephebe*, with which time, our time, puts this smile in relation—have changed it, have disdainfully erased it, by making it too visible, too "worldly." It would not be enough to say that we see the smile differently; the smile is truly other. It is no longer the smile of absence, it is the presence of a smile, an interesting witness but one that interests culture and that the artist barely notices anymore.

Classical aesthetics did not seek to idealize forms or to make them pure so much as it tried to idealize the moment, to make it an absolutely pure present, capable of being repeated without growing faint. Out of the obscure malediction of eternal recurrence—this time-space that takes hold of us when the world moves away—this aesthetics made the glory and joy of a repetition that nothing seems able to prevent from always being new. Remarkable goals. And sometimes it achieves them by means of a stylization that keeps life at a distance without compromising it, while at other times it achieves them through a desire to fuse with the living moment, to grasp it and make it ungraspable. But classical aesthetics cannot, be that as it may, do without the representation of appearance. Why? For many reasons (the most obvious is that it aspires to the world:

art, insofar as it is closely bound up with nothingness and absence, is a curse that must be overcome by great humanist activity) and for the following reason, which is no less pressing: namely, that the image, when it becomes *representative*, gives the most vivid idea of a *presence* that seems able to repeat itself, removed from the pain of becoming. This repetition is affirmed in the doubling of resemblance; the similar, which is then in the safekeeping of the painting, refers eternally to the similar. Praxiteles' adolescent will eternally resemble itself in its smile, because this resemblance, detached once and for all from the life from which it is presumed to have been borrowed, is protected, by the force of the sculpture, from the marble—in some sense behind the marble, which is solid but not eternal—as it is also protected from the sculpture. When appearance disappears or moves away from works of art, this demonstration of a present that is always capable of repeating itself—an unreal Mona Lisa always ready to smile behind unreal colors and lines—singularly loses some of its obviousness. When a work decides to identify itself with its canvas, its spots, and its material ingredients, without dissimulating anything or promising anything behind itself, then the pure present collapses, the ideal instant has perished, the power of beginning again that the work brings closer to us is also brought closer to it and assures the work neither a true present nor a certain future, dooming it to the fascination of evanescence and to the call of metamorphoses.

The classical ideal strives to shelter the image and the moment that carries it forth from perishable things, canvas and stone—those things that, however, allow us to grasp them: canvas deteriorates and marble cracks, but the image is incorruptible and the moment repeats itself without completion (consequently, without exhausting itself). The Museum teaches us that such is not the case. It is perhaps disturbing for us to recognize that the truth of a painting is not at a distance from the painting but is inseparable from the painting's material reality, from its "means"; that its glory resides in this presence of pure matter arranged in such a way as to capture absence; and that it is tied to the fate of this matter. One could not say, however, that the painting is entirely in what *is there*—the

canvas, the spots, the shuddering become thickness—for the painting is entirely in the assurance that it is not there and that what is
there is *nothing*; assurance that it communicates to us in greatest
intimacy, in the *fascination*, that gaze that would like to make itself
nothingness, which is contact and no longer vision, the shattering
possession by something that has slid outside of all meaning and all
truth.

The duality of the painting thus persists in modern art, with the
difference that its essence can no longer be divided: it is always
essentially pure matter, pure material presence, and pure absence,
passion and desire for this absence, which is also the absence of
itself; it is essentially that which contradicts itself and that which
posits itself at the same time in this contradiction that it nonetheless cannot accommodate and that it does not want to appease. But
the result is also that time works according to this duality. Sometimes wearing away the stone, decomposing its tones, a wearing
away that most often has an aesthetic value, just as what is very
ancient has an aesthetic value, in the gap that is thus revealed to us.
And this work is not an accident; what is altered is also not the
inessential outside of the work of art, as the classical age had hoped,
but its intimacy, its truth, which has it that the statue is only stone
and Leonardo's fresco is doomed to erasure, an erasure that he had,
in some ways, premeditated. At other times—and this is what is
most important—time turns this absence, which is also the essence
of the work, into a principle of change, the anxiety of metamorphoses, a powerful and powerless dialectic. The work is tied to
this absence, and this absence tears it from itself, makes it slip
outside of itself. For the classical age, the work eternally repeated
itself (that is, did not repeat itself or did not reproduce itself in
the always first identity of its essence), because it was connected to
the unreality of the moment whose notion of the similar, of the
inexhaustible reflection, provided, as it were, an obvious translation. Thus the work did not fear anything from others, nor from
itself. It was not protected from time; it was the protection of time,
and in it lay the absolute fixity of a present preserved, which we
believed we were admiring and wanted to admire. But the work is

its own absence: because of this it is in perpetual becoming, never complete, always done and undone. If, through an image, one were to make perceptible to oneself the dimension that the work acquires in its relation to absence, one can consider the Museum to be, in its imaginary totality, this absence realized, a realization that supposes a certain completion, that completion precisely which modern art would give it. At the heart of this absence, works of art are in perpetual dissolution and in perpetual motion, each one being but a marker of time, a moment of the whole, a moment that would like desperately to be this whole, in which absence alone rests without rest. And because this wish is impossible, the work itself, as it becomes more and more conscious of this impossibility, always reaches further to assert itself as a pathetic sign, a fascinating arrow, pointed in the direction of the impossible.

~

From Malraux's remarks on metamorphosis, one of the possible conclusions that he might have reached is the idea that the masterpiece is no longer very meaningful, is always more threatened. He alludes to it quickly when he questions himself regarding an "absolutely free art." "A symptomatic element, which no painting had ever known before, begins to develop in our art. Let us call it, for lack of another word, a spot. A spot that is not connected to the structure of the canvas nor to its composition in the traditional sense; which is not, furthermore, an accent in its construction, nor as in Japan an accent of its representation.* On the contrary, the spot seems to be the canvas's reason for being, as if it only existed through the spot. . . . In Miró, as formerly in Kandinsky, sometimes in Klee, all subordination has disappeared; one is tempted to speak of an art of one dimension. But this spot seems to push the painter to destroy the painting in the same way as the writing of certain Picassos [does]. . . . We touch the provisionally extreme point of our painting." This extreme point (if, as Malraux says, "every major discovery is projected onto all of the past") thus warns us that since there is the Museum, there can no longer be true works, real repose (nor perhaps any Museum), and that all masterpieces tend to be but brilliant traces of an anonymous and impersonal passage, which would be that of art as a whole, orienting and dispersing itself toward the spot. There can be no doubt that works of art attract us less in themselves than as the dazzling marks that make the passionate development of an artist visible to us, the movement expressing his specific contestation and, through it, the contestation of art having become stability and repose—and every artist appears to us in turn as the trace, not destined to endure but perhaps to be erased, a trace that art has left in search of its extreme point. This is why it is difficult to make out the difference that Malraux, who is concerned with culture, energetically maintains between savage or crude art and the art of masterpieces. For him, the drawings of children or "madmen" do not belong to art, because they manifest a possession and not a mastery. "The child is artistic but is not an artist in that he is possessed by his painting, in that the artist finds support in a work—be it his own—which he seeks to surpass, something the child never does. Furthermore art is not dreams, but the possession of dreams." Which also brings him to write the following: "We would not, without remorse, dare to describe as a masterpiece anything but those works that make us believe, as secretly as it may be, in the mastery of man." This may be, but then one must give up the Museum, the perspective without perspective of the Museum, which is itself, alone, the sole true artist, which is just as capable of making one perceive the essence of artistic creation in the drawing sketched by the chance of a hand—in the fortuitously happy mark of an artist who had not intended it—as a great creator is capable, as Kandinsky said, of transforming into painted work the residues that the disorder of tubes has marvelously thrown upon his palette.

Art is no longer to be found in the "perfection" of *a* work; it is *nowhere*, and if the Museum has meaning, it is because it seems to be this "nowhere," the anxiety and the powerful negation of which it conveys. Certainly we want to admire masterpieces; we even become attached to each one of them through a fascination that willingly excludes all others. And it is also true that the work of art, before it destroys or proudly offers itself to the erasure of metamorphosis, would like to eternalize itself for a moment and, for a moment, become equal to all of art. But to become equal to art is already to return to absence, and absence alone is "eternity." The image, we feel, is joy, for it is a limit beside the indefinite, the possibility of suspension at the heart of a shifting movement: through it, we believe ourselves to be the masters of an absence become form, and the dense night itself seems to open itself to the resplendence of an absolute clarity. Yes, the image is joy—but close to it lies nothingness; nothingness appears at the limit of this image, and all the power of the image, drawn from the abyss in which it is founded, cannot be expressed except by calling to nothingness. Citing a famous line from his last novel, Malraux turns it into the song of glory of artistic creation: "The greatest mystery is not that we were thrown by chance between the profusion of matter and the profusions of the stars; rather, it is that in this prison we drew from ourselves images so powerful as to negate our nothingness." But perhaps one must add that the image, capable of negating nothingness, is also the gaze of nothingness upon us. It is light, and it is immensely heavy. It shines, and it is the diffuse thickness in which nothing reveals itself. It is the interstice, the spot of this black sun, a laceration that gives us, under the appearance of a dazzling brilliance, the negative in the inexhaustible negative depths. This is why the image seems so profound and so empty, so threatening and so attractive, always richer in meanings than those with which we provide it, and also poor, null, and silent, for in it this dark powerlessness, deprived of a master, advances; it is the powerlessness of death as a beginning-again.

§ 3 Museum Sickness

I draw the following remark from one of Curtius's essays: "The possibility of always having Homer, Virgil, Shakespeare, Goethe completely at our disposal shows that literature has a different manner of being than art." A striking remark, at first almost obvious. However, we quickly realize that this is falsely obvious. Curtius seems to be writing at a time in which there are no long-playing records, no audiovisual means of communication, no museums, and certainly not the "imaginary Museum," which the improvement in the technology of reproduction continues to enrich with prodigious generosity. That art and all of art can be brought to each person, at any moment, is the considerable event that Malraux has made perceptible to us and from which he drew a new outlook and seemingly a new exigency for artistic creation. We cannot forget this. But we are aware that this change could not have occurred by accident. Technical advances give us art, just as they give us the earth; they give us possession of everything and access to everything through a power of domination that scares some and drives others but can be stopped by no one. Let us not linger on this fact, which is of the first order, and let us take another look at Curtius.

He would perhaps say to us (if he could still speak to us), I doubt that a work of art is reproducible, when, in fact, it is the characteristic of great literary works to be transmitted without loss of substance and without alteration, indefinitely. This is what surprises us, and, in truth, how can he say that we have Homer, Dante—I would also add Mallarmé, René Char—completely at our disposal? The word *completely* is provocative. On the contrary, we know that no work, be it a literary one, be it the most immediately contemporary one, is at our disposal, for we must make ourselves receptive to it. We know that we have almost nothing of the *Iliad* and almost nothing of the *Divine Comedy*. We know that these works, even if they are transmitted without error, escape us and are estranged from us by the reading that makes them accessible to us. Everything separates us from them: the gods, the world, the language, what we know and what we do not, but above all our knowledge— our knowledge of Homer and our always more precise knowledge of what to attribute to the civilization of Homer. Here, familiarity succeeds only in making the strangeness of books go unnoticed— even by a mind as subtle as that of Curtius. It is very difficult to understand why he who denies that the work of art is reproducible, perhaps rightly so, accepts the indefinite transmission of literary works as a given, their power of communication that would bring them to us without harm and, while remaining themselves, would be marvelously enriched by our ignorant and learned reading of them.

~

This debate has a long history. It is not a question of printing but of writing. What Plato says against writing (such a surprise that Plato should still be free to denounce in the written exigency a dangerous and ruinous innovation) is just about everything that Georges Duthuit formulates with vehemence against the Museum and the facility of reproduction.[1] Plato, it is true, is not concerned with literature but with thought. What is this speech, he says, that is spoken by no one, that only knows how to repeat what it says, that never responds to the one who questions it, no more than it defends itself against the one who attacks it; a speech that no one speaks and yet lets itself be spoken by anyone, without discernment or preference or refusal, appallingly abstract, having been torn from the place and life that conceived it, that thus wanders without authority, without name, here and there, with a blind vagrancy; a dead language that is capable of making us dead without memory, because it is, henceforth, written speech that will remember in our place, will think in our absence?[2]

This severity of Plato's (a protest made, with a first and deceptive appearance, in the name of a reasonable "humanism," that of Socrates, for whom there must be, behind every speech, a living man intending to vouch for it, to affirm it, and to affirm himself in it) cannot be seen as vain for having been unable to do anything against manuscripts, nor later against books. Today still, Heidegger is very close to seeing Socrates—who did not write—as one of the last men of thought: "And since Socrates, all thoughtful meditation has but led to books." Why this disdain for written things? It is undoubtedly linked to the idea that writing is second in relation to speech (as if one wrote only in order to relate, restore, and make oral communication last), just as the hatred of images, capable of repeating the singular work perfectly, is linked to a judgment made about technology. Mechanical production is essentially capable of reproduction: this is the meaning of the machine. What it produces, it reproduces indefinitely, identically, with a power that is carried out as if outside of duration. A power of the strongest, but a power that has always been feared, not only because it promises us monotony but perhaps for a reason more profound. One might say that the possibility of reproducing and of being reproduced reveals to us the fundamental poverty of being: that something could be repeated means that this power seems to presuppose a lack in being, and that being is lacking a richness that would not allow it to be repeated. Being is repeated, this is what the existence of machines means; but if being were an inexhaustible overabundance, there would be neither mechanical repetition nor mechanical perfection. Technology is thus the penury of being become the power of man, the decisive sign of Western culture.

On the contrary, art and works of art seem to affirm and perhaps restore the dignity of being: its richness escaping all measure, its force of renewal, its creative generosity, and everything that the

words *life, intensity, depth, nature* call forth. Art tells us of the being
that is not repeated, that is always other; the brilliance of the
beginning, the first light. How could the artistic work, about which
one already speaks inaccurately when one says that it is produced,
not be opposed to everything that tries to make of it something fit
to be reproduced? How could there not be an essential opposition
between the solitude of the work, its existence that is always
momentary, its uncertain certainty, its light all the more clear that
it may go out at any moment, and the particular mode of reality
assured it by the techniques of reproduction? At issue here is not a
conflict between the one and the many, between the painting
jealously preserved by a narrow-minded admirer and the right to be
seen by the greatest number. Something else is at stake. In the case
of art, the power to reproduce, in being carried out, changes the
meaning of what is reproduced. It is not that the work escapes this
power and that the copy always allows what is singular in the work
to be lost. One could very well accept a picture taking the place of
the original perfectly, a representation completely replacing presence. But what would the result be? More than an invisible destruction of the work: a destruction of art, the proof that what we
thought was linked to the infinite overabundance of life is so poor
as to lend itself to repetition and not be betrayed by the empty
permanence of mechanical reproduction. To which one will answer
that the painter, when he paints, continues to attest to the ability of
painting always to begin anew, without repetition, without disruption, without consequence, and that the mechanical diffusion of
the work does not prove anything against the singular movement of
discovery that has for its place the painting. But is this so certain?
Do we not sense that if the work were intimately associated only
with the nonrepeatable essence of being, then its exact reproduction could never be carried out, no more than a superior life form
could, until further notice, reengender itself identically? It is thus
art in its very heart that is affected, perhaps compromised by this
multiple presence of the singular painting, a presence that makes
certain possibilities appear and ruins many others: henceforth there
is no *original,* no organic link between the work and the painter;

soon perhaps there will hardly be a painter at all, but instead an anonymous, impersonal power of "creation." There is no one who does not obscurely feel—to deplore it or to delight in it—the dominant influence that the machine's new role in diffusing the work of art will soon exert upon the work's creation. So many temptations and so many vicissitudes. Hence, perhaps, the anxious thoughts that have led Duthuit to write his important book against Malraux, a book that is enormous but also moving, for it is the sign of a certain despair in the face of this disorientation of art, the perilous nature of which the experience of the imaginary Museum has caused us to neglect.

$\sim$

However, this danger is neither obscure nor new. One has but to enter any place in which works of art are put together in great number to experience this museum sickness, analogous to mountain sickness, which is made up of a feeling of vertigo and suffocation, to which all pleasure of seeing and all desire to let oneself be moved quickly succumb. Of course, in the first moment, there is shock, the physical certainty of an imperious, singular presence, however indefinitely multiplied it is. Painting is truly there, in person. But it is a person so sure of herself, so pleased with her prestige and so imposing, exposing herself with such a desire for spectacle that, transformed into a queen of theater, she transforms us in turn into spectators who are very impressed, then a little uncomfortable, then a little bored. Surely there is something insuperably barbarous in the custom of museums. How did things come to this? How did the solitary, exclusive affirmation that is fiercely turned toward a secret point that it barely indicates to us, lend itself, in each painting, to this spectacular sharing, to this noisy and distinguished encounter that is in fact called a show? There is also something surprising about libraries, but at least we are not obliged to read all the books at once (not yet). Why do artistic works have this encyclopedic ambition that leads them to arrange themselves together, to be seen with each other, by a gaze so general, so confused, and so loose that the only thing that can ensue, it seems, is the destruction of any true relation of communication?

A lugubrious state of affairs, but one for which I doubt Malraux is solely responsible. Manifestly, one must suppose that this pro-digious development of the museum, almost universal today—one that coincides with the moment at which art attempts to make itself visible for itself, no longer an affirmation of the gods or the divine, no longer the expression of human values, but the emer-gence into the day of its own light—answers to a decision whose course we cannot suspend, whose meaning we cannot reduce because of our own personal tastes. In works of art, we already sense the infinite diversity of the conflict that divides them, exalts and ruins them: the need to be alone and always closed in on them-selves, visible-invisible, without sight, and, as Rilke says, separated from us by a void that pushes us away and isolates them; but also a need to be in relation to each other, a need to be, each in itself and yet all together, the manifestation of art, to be unique, self-sufficient, but also to be merely the moment of a greater becoming while making perceptible to us, real and already complete, the space in which this becoming is endlessly carried out.

The Museum is an allusion to these diverse forms of communi-cation. Real museums, those palaces of the bourgeoisie where works of art, having become national property, give way to rivalries and to conflicts of interest, have all that is needed to degrade art by confirming its alienation in order to profit a certain form of econ-omy, culture, and aesthetics; in this sense, the disclosure by the image is far from being a greater debasement. But is the imaginary Museum, as Malraux has made us conscious of it, merely the sum of real museums, completed by the images of those works that cannot be exhibited? Is it the museum become library? It is imagi-nary: this means that it is never given, nor present, but always in question in every new work, and always affirmed and shaken by it at the same time. I do not know if I am distorting the conception that animates *Les Voix du silence*, but it seems to me that in naming and describing the imaginary Museum with inspired vivacity, Mal-raux has given us, above all, an image of the particular space that is artistic experience: space outside of space, always in motion, always to be created, and time always absent that does not really exist but exists only in the eyes of the work still to come that is always searching for itself in the artist. The word *experience* here is the most important, understood as that which escapes the reality of what is lived through. The Museum is thus not the receptacle of erudite contemplations, nor the ordered inventory of the discoveries of culture. It is the imaginary space where artistic creation, struggling with itself, ceaselessly searches for itself in order to discover itself each time as if anew, a novelty repudiated in advance.

It is true that Duthuit would undoubtedly have been no less hostile to this form of experience, and I think he would have tried to use the qualifier *abstract* in just such a polemic against it. Because it tears the works from their origin, separates them from their world, deprives them of what one very confusedly refers to as their aura, the Museum is indeed the symbolic place where the work of abstraction assumes its most violent and outrageous form. To this space that is not one, this place without location, and this world outside the world, strangely confined, deprived of air, light, and life, Duthuit opposes, in a way that is most impressive, a simple, living space, the reality of which the great Byzantine edifices still allow us to grasp, in which a relation of communion and inner harmony is established between the many and the one, between works of art and everyday existence, between beliefs, feelings, things, and their transfiguration by art. A space that Riegl calls *absolute* or *without limit*, that Worringer calls a *perpetual space*, one that is in relation to the infinite, but that Duthuit, although he makes use of their analyses, wishes only to call *real*, in order not to separate it from life, in accordance with the movement that inspires his aesthetics. A real space thus, a "space of rites, of music and of celebration," but real where? On the earth of Byzantium or in the heaven of Plato, for he asserts the following on the subject of this space: "which, had it been otherwise converted and without trace of coercive theology this time, would still have been that of everyone today; there is no reason to deny it, however deprived of it we are, hounded by trucks, surrounded by the architecture of a hygienic penitentiary and neon lighting that is decapitating our neighborhoods one by one, while they have promised us, in a manner of compensation, to turn our cities into trash cans with illustrated portulacas." What is here called *real* is thus only ideal and, I fear, terribly abstract, for it forces us, by means of an exclusive violence, to set aside the reality of the world that is ours, with all of the living forces that assert themselves in it, and to retire into the nostalgic memory of a remote past.

~

The person who wishes to fight abstraction—and the struggle is hopeless, though honorable—should first take on time as it gives itself to us through the suspension of the end of times. It is time that separates, tears, divides. Whether we encounter the mosaics in Damascus itself, at the Mosque of the Umayyads, or in the exhibit that offered us a first reconstitution of them a few years ago, in both cases they come to us just as mutilated, just as removed from their "real" space, and almost equally abstract. We may be grieved by this, and it is in fact very sad, but the museum is not only situated at the Louvre, it is also at Saint Sophia or at Saint Philibert of Tournus. The very fact that we speak of art in reference to them is enough to subject them to the rape of the archaeologists and to turn us momentarily into so many satisfied Lord Elgins. Malraux often speaks of resurrection, but what is it that is reborn? Our illusion, the mistaken belief that what is there, is there as it was, whereas it is there at most as having been: that is, as an illusion of presence. However, there is also something else, as we know, and this is the experience specific to our time. What was formerly world and presence of a world, asserts itself today as the nonpresent presence of what we call, perhaps in all ignorance and awkwardness, art. In the past, in the furthest reaches of time and in all times, works were invisible as works of art, hidden in their place of origin where they had their shelter. Once their universe had crumbled, they came to us through the historical movement of other worlds that elicited from them a presence that was otherwise hidden. These works offer themselves to us now for the first time, visible as works, in their fugitive manifestation, their radiant solitude, the secret essence of their own reality, no longer sheltered in our world but without shelter and as if without a world.

In a certain way, the Museum expresses this lack, this destitution and admirable indigence, which is the truth of art without refuge and which Hölderlin was the first to recognize. However, and this must be added at once, if the Museum expresses this lack, it is in a very equivocal way and also by affirming the opposite. For it is precisely in the museum that works of art, withdrawn from the movement of life and removed from the peril of time, are presented in the polished comfort of their protected permanence. Are the works of the Museum deprived of the world? Are they turned over to the insecurity of a pure absence without certainty? When the term *museum* signifies essentially conservation, tradition, security, and when everything collected in this place is there only to be preserved, to remain inactive, harmless, in this particular *world*— which is that of conservation itself, a world of knowledge, of culture, of aesthetics, and which is as far from the questioning of art as the archival work that assures the life of a poem is far from the poem itself. This equivocation is not fortuitous. It is no accident that what gives itself as "pure presence" is immediately frozen and stabilized in a permanence without life and in the rotting eternity of a solemn and indifferent void. And if Duthuit is right to be surprised by and even despairing of the extreme favor received by the imaginary Museum, it is because the idea supporting this figure is necessarily so ambiguous that it is always ready to respond to our own questioning of art: either by expressing and realizing the need for inventory and the concern for recapitulation, for which our time can only vary the pretext, or else by affirming the new experience of literature and art, its essential *reversal*, which we all feel is the task of our days and our responsibility—sometimes saying *art* as if it were no longer anything but the grouping of all works of all times, art of the past and belonging only to the past, or, on the contrary, speaking of art as its unceasing metamorphosis, its endless becoming, its always future advent, its power to be, at every moment, a singular beginning and first appearance, but *at the same time*, divested of itself by that which affirms it from the eternal beginning-again.

§ 4 The Time of
Encyclopedias

1. If one expects anything from an encyclopedia today—and naturally one expects everything, and more than everything—it is because an encyclopedia offers us knowledge, the historical paths as well as the theoretical routes of knowledge, but more still: in the entity that it forms, it offers us a kind of interior becoming, the invisible and incessant circulation of truths, of probabilities, of uncertainties, of all that is stated and all that is kept silent. This movement alone is capable of making the small library of 50 volumes, in which our reading is all too tempted to seek an immobile order, into a living cosmos. Circular knowledge is the justification of any encyclopedia, a knowledge that is all the more rich and all the more beautiful the more shifting it is and the more it can respond to all of the complexities of circular figures, such that what one knows finitely nevertheless partakes of this infinite move-ment, which, were it even possible to know everything, and every-thing about everything, would still ensure the eternal renewal of knowledge.[1]

In the Encyclopedia of the encyclopedists, it was alphabetical randomness, corrected in an often very subtle way, that was cause for dissatisfaction and made the systematic mind weary—that cer-tainty of a logical order, perfectly assured and reasonable, which the seventeenth century had finally substituted for theological cer-tainty. Diderot does not believe in a nature that could be *naturally* divisible into layers of knowledge. He has a fantastical idea of nature, though perhaps a little murky, that calls to mind universal motion and unceasing vicissitude, the prodigious power of transformation that allows nature to be grasped only in a form it has already brought to ruin. This idea pushes the Encyclopedia forward as a living creation, preventing it from being merely a bookish reality, but would have prevented it from ever taking form had d'Alembert, whose mind was very different, not had a rigorous dryness of spirit and a concern for order that made him look for principles in each science and for a momentary ordering in the whole of science where the supreme mapping of the human mind could be expressed in its diversity but also in its aspiration to unity.

2. An encyclopedia, if it is not written by a single person, cannot be conceived of today in a single language. We need this change of perspective. One of the concerns of the Encyclopedia of the Pléiade is "to leave plenty of room for the contributions of extra-European cultures" and "to restore Oriental literatures their dignity." A commendable concern. This is indeed what we expect from such an undertaking: not only should it teach us that there were other cultures besides our own, but it should allow us to know this in such a way that it renders us somewhat other in relation to ourselves. Is there a reader so unenlightened today as to be ignorant of the plurality of worlds, the plurality of traditions, the plurality of styles, and not to know that there is, at all times and in all languages, often much more to admire than what we docilely admire close to us? Yet is there a reader so enlightened as to be capable, beyond this banal theoretical knowledge, of truly feeling, concretely in experience, the prodigious encounter of these separate works, the movement that carries them toward each other, and the monstrous communal place that, it seems, they attempt to form together, in some strange spirit called on to greet them all at once, perhaps only to notice that each one is weightier, more important, and more real when it is alone than when it has been added to all the others?

This singular, and certainly barbarous, yet inevitable and thus desirable, encounter must at the very least be made manifest by the encounter of languages, countries, methods, and centers of research. An encyclopedia is not just a simple bookstore phenomenon. When it is prepared with all of the intellectual and material resources that have been working on the elaboration of the Pléiade, it challenges the many forces that seek to come together and to bend the imaginary whole of our preoccupations and inventions back to a center. If it is true, as Teilhard de Chardin says in his mythical and very approximate language, that we are at a moment in which our physical, social, intellectual, and artistic universe is changing its curvature and in which the forces of distention and divergence are also becoming forces of compression and of concentration, then the Encyclopedia is not a negligible moment of this structural transformation.

First, because the Encyclopedia is essentially a collective work, it ensures the "interconnection between researchers" and forms something like an immense impersonal reflection where every particular knowledge enters into contact in order to follow a direction that is still necessarily not well known. But it is also important in that it tests the possibility of what it wants to realize. Today, at this moment of the modern age, is an encyclopedia possible? Naturally, it is, and in many ways, just as it can fail in many ways while still being successful. Our age is certainly capable of adding a small library to all of those in which we can shut ourselves away in order to learn and unlearn. However, to the extent that it tries to collect itself around what it knows, is it still prepared to find this kind of very general presentation, a knowledge in the form of books and the kind of unity it assures, important or even valid? For example, it is well known that researchers work collaboratively more and more, that they form communities among themselves that are sometimes visible, sometimes invisible, but centered around a knowledge so specific and so hard to separate from its technical aspect, that it is only with great difficulty that such a knowledge could lend itself to the general form of an encyclopedia. Here, it is not only the specialization but the importance of the technical, that is, of an almost instrumental knowledge that has no meaning outside of its practice, which challenges the seriousness of books. Soon, each person will be able to know only with a mechanical or completely formalized knowledge; at a moment when the resources of a different speech and another vision provide us with the wealth of a culture that is altogether new, the Encyclopedia comes as an almost archaic way of assembling knowledge.

In other words, even with all of its rich twentieth-century material, does the Encyclopedia not still belong more or less to the eighteenth century, dating it thus from the moment of its greatest success? And will it not always be behind, in a disturbing way, by privileging its form over its content, or by the necessity of formulating a knowledge in a language that this knowledge has already quit or set aside?

3. In the pages written to present the project of the Pléiade, Raymond Queneau says in his first sentence: "The growing use of robotics, the use of atomic energy, the achievement of autonomy in their civic and industrial life by Asian or colonized peoples are the three most recent reasons for Western man to think that he is perhaps at the beginning of a new era." He adds, "Is it not necessary to consider these problems, posed on a global scale and announcing profound revolutions in cultural and social forms as well as in morals, to their full extent and to emphasize their connection with those problems with which man has been struggling up to the present day? What exactly are the possibilities of science?" This indeed shows that the Encyclopedia of the Pléiade does not intend to limit itself to a minor pedagogical work. It knows that it is capable, in its exposition of science, time, power, things, and men, of circumscribing everything possible, perhaps of saying it, and thus of putting it into question to a certain extent. It should therefore be essentially "philosophical," even if it means assuming a place behind philosophy in the slow funeral procession that philosophy leads, not without pleasure, to lay itself to rest. Philosophical: no encyclopedia can fail to be it, and an encyclopedia is worthwhile to the extent that it does not lose sight of the

exigency it represents, whereas it is not worth anything, whatever its particular merits, if it hides the implicit affirmations that its very existence presupposes behind an alleged objectivity.

4. The Encyclopedia is tied to a certain form of culture. What is this form, and what is it worth? What does it force us to lose, to forget, to be, not to be?

There is the answer of the skilled technician for whom all knowledge is knowledge only in action (but encyclopedic culture, being the universal speech, claims to be able to speak of science in the language that allows it to say everything, and not only according to the mode of being of a particular science).

There is the answer of the Marxist, for whom this culture will necessarily be alienated as a whole, even if it remains legitimate in this or that of its parts. And it should be said that this is one of the difficult problems that the Encyclopedia must face. Queneau wants to show that "Western man is no longer the only representative of the human race worthy of consideration," the Encyclopedia having thus for its task to enlighten us from those great regions of time and space that, in all respects, represent the most distant. But when one speaks of Western man, of whom is one speaking? Is he not fundamentally divided? Is he not more distant with respect to himself than the Orient is with respect to the West? Surely, an encyclopedia can speak to us correctly of Marxism, but this is not enough: Marxism must also be able to speak to us from the encyclopedia as a whole and as one of its centers. There is thus a choice to be made here that challenges the possibility of a coherent discourse valid for Western cultures as a whole: unless it makes the *discordance* that divides them the horizon of its search and a question that is renewed at every moment—which would perhaps be extremely desirable.

There is Alain's answer: "When I hear of a Library of General Culture, I run to the volumes, expecting to find in them exquisite texts, precious translations, all the wealth of the Poets, the Politicians, the Moralists, the Thinkers. But not at all: instead I find very educated men, in all likelihood cultivated, informing me of their culture. Yet, culture cannot be transmitted and cannot be summarized."

Rabelais and Montaigne had already voiced their reservation: "It doesn't cultivate." "It is not ripe for human meditation." General culture would like to make *to know* a verb without an object: it is a matter of knowing in a way that is absolute and substantial, not of learning what one does not yet know. So be it, but one must still learn something; the measure will be arbitrary: a little of everything, a mere nothing about anything. Tradition fixes this measure. Alain believes that what is too new, what has not been thought and rethought with the effort of great time, wounds and surprises the average mind—ours—but does not form it. He himself always kept his door closed to Einstein and held fast to Euclid. A moving resolution, even admirable, but one that only a man who is alone, and who has, in some sense, already thought everything, can make for himself.[2] Today the tradition is Einstein; we can do nothing about it, and the tradition is also the distrust with respect to tradition, its loss of authority, its disruption, and finally it is the substitution of general culture—the rich cream of knowledge that has long made for unctuous and well-nourished minds—and it is the necessity of also drinking the sharp, sour whey of knowledge, which the agitation and acceleration of the ages no longer let rest. The necessity of knowing everything, not individually but collectively, as a result of the greatly multiplied relations of men and human groupings, as a result also of the very firm consciousness of the interdependence of all forms of knowledge: this is what still justifies the encyclopedia today, the image of the living human community collecting itself in an almost organic way around itself, around the community, the learned, knowing, and ignorant community that it also is for itself.

5. But let me return to Alain's answer. It cannot be gotten rid of so easily. And I think the following question is in fact a preliminary one: In the universal speech in which everything is said, and in which everything is said by adopting the language that only allows one to say everything, could there ever be room for literature, if

literature is first the affirmation or the play of a speech that is altogether *other*? And would literature not disappear in it necessarily and essentially, in such a way that literature could not be spoken about otherwise than through misunderstandings? We already know that the relation of literature to history creates a problem that is very difficult to master and more difficult still to reconcile with the encyclopedic exigency. And there is something else. In the world of culture, it is necessary and it is good for us to have both Mallarmé and Victor Hugo, Goethe and Hölderlin, Racine and Corneille, to take just a few "great incontestable names." But there is a point at which it is necessary for Goethe to remain deaf to Hölderlin, to reject Kleist, and at which we, too, cannot open ourselves to Hölderlin and to Goethe at the same time. This point is located outside culture, and culture must be ignorant of it: Could one imagine and even conceive of an Encyclopedia that would have this point for its center, for one of its centers?

6. There can be no encyclopedia without translation. But what is translating? Is it possible to translate? Is not translating, that singular literary act, what not only enables the encyclopedic work but at the same time prevents it, threatens it? Translating, the bringing into "work" of difference.

§ 5 Translating

Do we know all that we owe to translators and, even more, to translation? We do not properly know. And even when we are grateful to the men who valiantly enter into the enigma that is the task of translating, when we salute them from afar as the hidden masters of our culture, tied to them as we are and docilely subject to their zeal, our recognition remains silent, a little disdainful—owing to our humility, for we are in no measure able to be grateful to them. From one of Walter Benjamin's essays, in which this excellent essayist speaks to us of the task of the translator, I will draw several remarks on this particular form of our literary activity, this original form; and if one continues to say, rightly or wrongly, Here are the poets, and there the novelists, indeed the critics, all of whom are responsible for the meaning of literature, then one must in the same way count the translators, writers of the rarest sort and truly incomparable.[1]

Translating, I would remind the reader, was, for a long time, regarded as a baneful pretension in certain regions of culture. Some do not want anyone to translate into their language, and others do not want anyone to translate their language; and war is needed in order for this treachery, in the literal sense, to be carried out: to hand over the true language of a people to a foreign land. (Let us remember Eteocles' despair: "Do not wrench from the earth, prey of the enemy, a city that speaks the true language of Greece.") But the translator is guilty of greater impiety still. He, enemy of God, seeks to rebuild the Tower of Babel, to turn to good account and profit, ironically, the celestial punishment that separates men in the confusion of languages. In the past, one believed it possible thus to return to some originary language, the supreme language that one needed only to speak in order to speak truly. Benjamin retains something of this dream. Languages, he notes, all intend the same reality, but not according to the same mode. When I say *Brot* and when I say *pain*, I intend the same thing according to a different mode. Each language, taken by itself, is incomplete. With translation, I do not content myself with replacing one mode with another, one way with another way, but instead I make a gesture toward a superior language, which would be the harmony or the complementary unity of all these different modes of intention and which, ideally, would speak at the place where the mystery of all languages that are spoken by all works is reconciled. To each translator thus his own messianism, if he works toward making languages grow in the direction of this ultimate language, attested to in every present language by what each language contains of the future—and which the translation seizes upon.

The above contention is clearly a utopian play of ideas, for one supposes that each language has but one, same mode of intention, always with the same signification, and that all of these modes of intention could become complementary. But Benjamin suggests something else: every translator lives by the difference of languages; every translation is founded upon this difference even while pursuing, or so it appears, the perverse design of suppressing it. (A work that is well translated is acclaimed in two opposing ways: "It is hard to believe it's a translation," one says; or else, "It is truly the same work," one finds it marvelously identical. In the first case, however, one effaces the origin of the work to benefit the new language; in the second case, in order to benefit the original work, one effaces the originality of both languages. In both cases something essential is lost.) In fact translation is not at all intended to make the difference disappear—it is, on the contrary, the play of this difference: it alludes to it constantly; it dissimulates this difference, but

occasionally in revealing it and often in accentuating it; translation
is the very life of this difference; it finds in this difference its august
duty, and also its fascination as it proudly brings the two languages
closer by its own power of unification, a power similar to that of
Hercules drawing together the banks of the sea.

But more remains to be said. A work has acquired the age and
dignity to be translated only if it contains this difference in such
a way as to make it available, either because it originally makes a
gesture toward *another* language or because it assembles, in a
manner that is privileged, the possibilities of being different from
itself and foreign to itself, which any spoken language has. The
original is never immobile, and all that a language contains of the
future at a particular moment, all that there is in the language that
points to or summons a state that is other, sometimes dangerously
other, is affirmed in the solemn drift of literary works. Translation
is tied to this becoming; it "translates" and accomplishes it. Translation is possible only because of this movement and this life, a life
it seizes, sometimes in order to deliver it cleanly, other times to
captivate it with effort. As for classical works of art, which belong to
a language that is not spoken, they demand to be translated all the
more because they are, henceforth, the sole depositories of the life
of a dead language and the only ones responsible for the future of a
language that has no future. Only translated are these works alive;
moreover, in the original language itself they are always as if
retranslated and redirected toward what is most specific to them:
toward their foreignness of origin.

The translator is a writer of singular originality, precisely where
he seems to claim none. He is the secret master of the difference of
languages, not in order to abolish the difference but in order to use
it to awaken in his own language, through the violent or subtle
changes he brings to it, a presence of what is different, originally, in
the original. It is not a question here of resemblance, Benjamin
rightly says: if one wants the translated work to resemble the work
to be translated, there is no possible literary translation. It is much
more a question of an identity on the basis of an alterity: the same
work in two foreign languages, both because of their foreignness

and by making visible, in their foreignness, what makes this work such that it will always be *other*, a movement from which, precisely, one must find the light that will clarify the translation by showing through it.

Yes, the translator is a strange man, a nostalgic man, who feels, as lacking in his own language, all of what the original work (that he cannot, moreover, fully attain, for he is not at home in it; he is the eternal guest who does not inhabit it) promises him in present affirmations. From this statement there follows the testimony of the specialists, according to which the translator, in translating, is always in greater difficulty in the language to which he belongs than he is confused by the one he does not possess. This is not only because he sees all that is lacking in French (for example) in order to rejoin the given, dominant, foreign text, but because the translator henceforth possesses the French language according to a privative mode—rich, however, in this privation—which he must fill with the resources of another language, itself rendered other in the unique work in which it gathers for a moment.

Benjamin cites the following, rather surprising quotation from a theory of Rudolf Pannwitz: "Our translations, even the best ones, proceed from a wrong principle. They want to germanize Sanskrit, Greek, English instead of sanskritizing, hellenizing, anglicizing German. Our translators have a far greater reverence for the usage of their own language than for the spirit of the foreign works. . . . The basic error of the translator is that he preserves the state in which his own language happens to be instead of subjecting it to the violent impulse of the foreign tongue." This statement or claim is dangerously seductive. It implies that each language could become all other languages, or at least move without harm in all sorts of new directions; it assumes that the translator will find enough resources in the work to be translated and enough authority in himself to provoke this sudden mutation; finally, it assumes a translation free and innovative to such an extent that it will be capable of a greater verbal and syntactic *literality*, which would, in the end, make translation useless.

Nonetheless, to fortify his views, Pannwitz is able to draw on the strength of such names as Luther, Voss, Hölderlin, George, none of whom hesitated, in every instance in which he was translator, to break the framework of the German language in order to extend its boundaries. The example of Hölderlin illustrates the risk that is run, in the end, by the man fascinated by the power of translating: the translations of *Antigone* and *Oedipus* were nearly his last works at the outbreak of madness. These works are exceptionally studied, restrained, and intentional, conducted with inflexible firmness with the intent not of transposing the Greek text into German, nor of reconveying the German language to its Greek sources, but of unifying the two powers—the one representing the vicissitudes of the West, the other those of the Orient—in the simplicity of a pure and total language. The result is almost frightful. It is as if one were discovering between the two languages an understanding so profound, a harmony so fundamental, that it substitutes itself for meaning, or succeeds in turning the hiatus that lies open between the two languages into the origin of a new meaning. The effect of this is so powerful that one understands the icy laughter of Goethe. At whom, indeed, was Goethe laughing? At a man who was no longer a poet, nor a translator, but who was recklessly advancing toward the center in which he believed he would find collected the pure power of unifying, a center such that it would be able to give meaning, beyond all determined and limited meaning. One understands that this temptation should have come to Hölderlin through translation. For with the unifying power that is at work in every practical relation, as in any language, and that, at the same time, exposes him to the pure scission that is always prior, the man who is ready to translate is in a constant, dangerous, and admirable intimacy—and it is this familiarity that gives him the right to be the most arrogant or the most secret of writers—with the conviction that, in the end, translating is madness.

§ 6 The Great Reducers

Literature and Revolution

I can see why the book of Trotsky that has recently been translated into French—which, like other important books, we owe to the series "Lettres nouvelles," edited by Maurice Nadeau—is well liked by traditional critics, by which I mean all of us, at those moments of fatigue or leisure during which we identify literature and culture and, inheriting from ourselves, are happy with our own past. The meaning of this enterprise of recuperation, the distinguished flight by which we take hold of the resistant great works by making them similar to us, should be studied more closely along with its mechanism: why is assimilation inevitable, why is it not complete, and, not being complete, why does it always make possible this work of unification and identification, which is carried out in many forms? Thus, even the irreducible helps to maintain the activity of the great reducers, the powerful collective machinery that silently and imperceptibly, day and night, pursues its task. There were, fortunately there still are, points of resistance: politics, the play of desire, poetry, thought. These points have grown weak but have not given way. Perhaps the forms of censorship themselves change. There is a period in which one condemns Baudelaire, another in which he is drawn into the Académie; a period in which Trotsky inspires fear and in which he has no other companion in literature except André Breton, then a period in which, as revolutionary, he might still inspire fear yet he is welcomed with reverence into the Pantheon of writers, where he is reassuring in his role as a man glorious and peaceful when dead.

We should not think, however, that our society or our literature or even our culture is able to withstand everything: there are always prohibitions, there is a structure of exclusion, an obscure reference to limits and, as it were, an outside in relation to which and in opposition to which we come together and take refuge in our apparently limitless freedom. However, these limits are less visible and less fixed; the outside—what we reject without knowing it—is not determined once and for all, and our manner of excluding is at work precisely in our will to assimilate everything, there precisely where we glory in our gift of universal comprehension.

~

We understand everything. Understanding everything (not superficially but really), we turn away from what is not this grasp of the whole and we forget the radical distance that, when all is understood and affirmed, still leaves open the space and time for a questioning (the most profound question) conveyed by speech. It is up to literature—to poetry—to put forward an experience of this space and this time that no longer belong to the whole of comprehension, an experience such that we are put to the test of the absolutely other, of that which escapes unity. But in our time, as in any other time, because the work of unification is far from being completed, because every society and every culture cooperate in this effort by trying to seize it for their benefit, any literary work is also turned—thus legitimately turned away from itself—toward unity: the circumstantial unity, which is that of the dominant society, and the unity to come, which is, dialectically or utopianly, in play in the search for a universal society without difference. Every writer, as we all know, is a monster with many heads and often without a face, the just traitor of whom Hölderlin spoke, the one who always turns away, but whose turning away may serve the maneuvers of a particular domination. What is it today that appeases us in a Trotsky who is respectable? The answer is easy: he is a writer with style, a man of letters of a very high class (and thus the word *class* is rehabilitated); better yet, a critic who knows how to speak of literature as a professional. I remember the happy surprise of one of our most famous literary men upon discovering, when he read the autobiography of Trotsky, that the terrible revolutionary was a true man of letters: how reassuring it was and what happiness to be able for an instant to feel that one was also the intimate of Trotsky. And it is by chance that the one—who, with Lenin, brought about the October insurrection and who, before Lenin, drew all of the consequences from the declaration of permanent revolution already proposed by Marx, who was an inflexible leader of a revolution that was anything but gentle—agrees to grant us "a total freedom of self-determination in the realm of art." The term *freedom*, even when it is given its most forceful meaning by Breton and Diego Rivera, in accordance with Trotsky's "everything is permitted in art," is one at which the critics rejoice and which they are always ready to put in their heritage, because, for them of course, a free art means an art whose ideal of freedom can be used against the communist exigency, a use that, it is true, immediately reduces the alleged freedom—the power of non-employment that they claim for art—to nothingness. But the contradiction disturbs no one.

～

   There is an immense disdain for literature in this manner of conceiving it and in this way of being reassured, when, dreading to find a revolutionary, one also discovers a writer. As if writing were not what is most innocent, that is to say, most dangerous. This is because, for the masters of culture, to write is always to write well, and to write well is thus to do good, to recognize the good even in the bad, to be in agreement with the world of values. Sartre realized this when his book *Les Mots*, praised almost unanimously by the traditional critics, was made hostage of, and provided them with the evidence that this unorthodox writer was becoming redeemable. And why was this? Because it was a brilliant book. I remember, around 1946, a conversation with Maurice Merleau-Ponty. He was asking himself, asking me, why Camus was well received by the critics and why they hated Sartre; I answered without very much thought that Camus reassured them with his style, whereas Sartre did not have a writer's good manners. With *Les Mots*, they felt that a rapprochement was close: a beauty of form that was studied, a lighthearted and spiteful style; this was a part of our best traditions, all the more so that, for once, the spitefulness was directed against Sartre himself, or in any case against the young Sartre, whom everyone, every good soul, had to pity and to protect, telling the author, "But you weren't a deceptive child at all, you sincerely loved your mother and your grandfather; look at this heartwarming passage on the Jardin du Luxembourg," and so on. Obviously, everything was not agreeable in the book; there were reflections that were immoral, grating, bothersome. However, one got used to it; this is the merciless fact. There is a moment at which the writer, if he has an important reputation, can do almost nothing against it; he has become an institution, and the regime annexes him without taking any account even of his opposition, certain that his glory will serve it more than his powerful hostility will harm it. This explains, it seems to me, the recent Swedish episode. It was as if the objective were to punish Sartre with the Nobel Prize for his too brilliant book, in all ingenuousness yet not without malice. (Just as Sartre was right to refuse it. Just as this refusal was simple and true. A writer cannot accept distinction, he cannot be distinguished; and to accept such a choice would have been to accept not only a certain form of culture and social establishment, but more: it would have been to accept a certain conception of freedom, thus making a political choice.) To punish him, that is, to reward him by having him enter the elite of writers, by making him accept the idea of an elite in which the truth of writing, which tends toward an essential anonymity, is lost.

The Consciousness Industry

Such an industry, as Hans-Magnus Enzensberger remarks in an interesting essay,[1] is particular in that the exploitation it pursues is principally immaterial. Certainly the works, whether they be books or other artistic forms, are products, but what is produced is not only wealth in the most general sense but opinions, then values, then forms and the obscure power to give or to refuse meaning, the speech to come. We will simplify the situation to make it clearer. According to the practices of traditional capitalist exploitation, it is only a question of seizing the labor force and nothing else. With the new practices that technical progress permits, the power to judge and to decide is what must be used, yet without seeming to force the power, or even to restrain it: by allowing it to have the indispensable appearance of freedom. The consciousness industry could not exploit consciousness except by preventing itself from appearing to destroy it. The big networks of information, of diffusion, and of pressure that are, directly or indirectly, controlled by power have the greatest need not for docile producers but for unusual works and for refractory thoughts. The operation is doubly advantageous. By disseminating works that are aesthetically rebellious, one gives oneself the appearance of being without prejudice, as is proper for the important patrons of culture; one secures oneself the collaboration of the intellectuals of the opposition whose untimely political declarations one would refuse, but whose literary cooperation is always harmless. One is thus supported by them, and with the backing that they innocently provide, one increases the effectiveness of the work of persuasion, just as one increases the authority of official statements. The more a cultural service is tied to the political, the more it is in its interest to present itself as literarily and artistically debonair. But this is still only a crude game.

The game becomes more subtle and more perverse when the object is to neutralize the works themselves. The consciousness industry, controlled by the power of the State, runs a risk in helping to diffuse certain troubling works: what is at stake is the ability to maintain control of consciousness without appearing to weaken it; the risk is to expand it, and in expanding it, to make it too lively by multiplying its contradictions.[2] In the same way, the object is not to enslave the writer—a writer who has been won over is no longer a useful ally, he is useful only when he is used while remaining the adversary—but to let him be free, to employ his freedom, secretly to make an accomplice of the infinite power of contestation that is literature. At the end of a day of television, a skillfully elaborated series of programs (and those who do the programming have only a very confused consciousness of what they are doing, because they are working on the inside of a system, and it is the system that is conscious), if, after listening carefully to the clever interview of a writer who thinks it good to speak about what he has written without noticing that he thereby makes it inoffensive; after hearing a political commentary discreetly or indiscreetly oriented; after watching, one after the other, a daring work and an insignificant work, the viewer goes to bed telling himself that the day was a good one but that, in the end, nothing happened, then the result is achieved. There should be interesting events and even important events, and yet nothing should take place that would disturb us: such is the philosophy of any established power and, in an under-handed way, of any cultural service. But it is absolutely necessary for turbulent works to be able to cooperate in this result in order that the turbulence itself be pacified and transformed into a cause for interest, into a subject of distraction.

Literature is perhaps essentially (I am not saying uniquely or manifestly) a power of contestation: contestation of the established power, contestation of what is (and of the fact of being), contestation of language and of the forms of literary language, finally contestation of itself as power. It constantly works against the limits that it helps fix, and when these limits, pushed back indefinitely, finally disappear in the knowledge and happiness of a truly or ideally accomplished totality, then its force of transgression becomes more denunciatory, for it is the unlimited itself, having become its limit, that it denounces by the neuter affirmation that speaks in it, which always speaks beyond. It is in this sense that any important literature appears to us as a literature of final daybreak: disaster is awake in its night, but a receptiveness is also always preserved in it, an inclemency of the not-I, a patient imagination at arms that introduces us to that state of incredible refusal (René Char). Which means that literature is always vanquished, vanquished by itself, vanquished by its victory, which only helps, enriching the immense secular deposit, to enrich culture. But culture is not nothing. On the contrary, culture is everything. And if poetry takes place only where a power to exclude and to be excluded is still marked out, at the limit of all limits, culture, which is the work of inclusion, is necessary to poetry to the very extent that it is fatal to it.

Paperback Literature

Let us consider a small phenomenon of our literary life. Hubert Damisch, in an excellent article from which I borrow many of the following reflections, calls it "paperback culture."[3] In truth, I think the only importance we should accord it is a transitory one. French publishers, who are very timid because they are very traditionalist as a whole, always frightened by what changes their habits, have recently discovered this process—that is, much later than their American and German counterparts—and are amusing themselves with it as they would with a clever invention that is very profitable. And, of course, one must rejoice at such success. How could one not want something that increases the diffusion of major (and minor) works? How could one not be aware that if there is a power of conformity and a rule of compromise in a humanistic culture— be it only through the work that continually makes a content appear where there was a form—one does not limit it with shots from a revolver but, on the contrary, by developing it, by pre- cipitating it, in such a way as to transform the stop-and-go system that founds it into an explosive process? Let us thus rejoice, but let us not be altogether naive. Paperback literature functions like a myth, a little, obtrusive, and profitable myth. This myth, in con- formity with the analyses of Roland Barthes, is organized in such a way that, under cover of an obvious signification, an implicit and doubtful supplementary meaning is at work. What is a paperback? A book that is inexpensive. What could be better? Who could be against it? But inexpensive books have existed for a long time. What matters here is not the difference in price (which, moreover, is often very little, and shrinking more and more), but rather the systematic character one gives the book and the political conclusion that one wants to awaken in us: namely, that "our society works so well that it guarantees free access to culture even to the poorest person." This is an obvious mystification, for it is not the great popular masses who benefit from this diffusion but a very particularized and always well-off public; an enriching and comforting mystification for those who organize it, because it consists, of course, in a profitable enterprise, and this profitable enterprise passes itself off as a good deed by pretending, philanthropically, to put the privileges of culture at the disposal of everyone. What is particular to the paperback, thus, is that it dissembles and imposes a system. There is an ideology to this literature, whence its interest. The book proclaims (1) the people henceforth will have access to culture; (2) it is the totality of culture that is brought within reach of everyone. This second affirmation is only implied, and although one is wary of tending toward so highly improbable a result, one would still have us believe it: hence the sophisticated mix (as Damisch himself puts it) with which, at the same time, one offers the old classics, the writings of Mao Tse-tung, a volume from the Presse du Cœur, the Gospels, the works of the "New Novel"; one goes so far as to publish (and this is the subtlest subtlety) an innocent excerpt from Sade, but quite obviously it is not in order for it to be read but rather to proclaim it: See, we publish everything, we have published the unpublishable Sade.[4] However, there are economic imperatives with an altogether different end that correspond to this claim of totality. The paperback publisher ensures his profit not by selling many printings of any particular book but by procuring a large market for the entire series. Here we detect cheating: the series must reach the most varied public; it must therefore be made up of many things, heterogeneous, superficially broad, of a deceptive eclecticism and without any unity aside from its presentation—the colorful cover whose scintillation attracts the gaze and gives the buyer a luxurious pleasure: a luxury and quality within the reach of everyone. But the paperback series (unlike series in traditional publishing) has its own commercial necessities. Damisch formulates them as follows: "The sale must be quick; stocks cannot be left to accumulate; on the contrary, the publisher hopes to see the stocks run out as quickly as possible." The books show themselves, then disappear: here I am forced not only to accept but, more insidiously, to "desire what is offered to me right at the moment"; tomorrow it will be too late, tomorrow they will move on to something else, and I will no longer be offered Beckett, but some submissive production of literature that I, naively faithful to the enchantment of the series and confident in the certainties of culture, will welcome with an equally respectful spirit. Duration, the time of maturation and patience, which up until now, rightly or wrongly, we took to be necessary for any cultural transmission, tends thus to be abolished. "Thus paperback culture works to destroy the means of a specifically cultural diffusion of works in order to replace them with technical mechanisms that are efficient in other ways."

Nothing can be said against the technical. But what is striking in its employment is once again the ideology that it masks and that provides the paperback with its most basic meaning, its morality: the technical regulates all problems, the problem of culture and its diffusion, like all other problems; there is no need for political upheaval, and even less need for changes in the social structures. It suffices to reproduce works, in a flattering manner and at what appears to be a modest price, for them to have free rein, and it suffices for them to appear to have free rein (nonetheless within the very determined limits of the capitalist market) for everyone to be able to assimilate them, appropriate them in what they have that is unique (of course, one does not deny that the reader must be introduced to these often difficult works; whence the use of scholarly or obscure prefaces, which are no less difficult than the book itself: this is because they are not there to make reading easier but rather to confirm the educational nature of the enterprise, its value as "high culture"—a culture at a low price but not discounted).

The Improbable Heresy

The invention of the paperback—which is harmless in any event, which only deceives us in a harmless way and simply alerts us to other, more advanced inventions—does us the favor, because of its simple mechanism, of helping us to better understand the reductive power that is difficult to dissociate from any culture. The title *pocket book* already says just about everything: it is culture in the pocket. A progressive myth. All works are available, accessible, and, better yet, immediately ours, received and as it were absorbed by a simple contact: the furtive gesture of the buyer. This assumes (1) that culture, the great impersonal force, acts as a substitute for each person and accomplishes, in each person's place, the slow work of assimilation through which works, reduced to values, are already understood in advance, already read, already heard, and reduced to the man of universal comprehension whom we are supposed to be and who in truth we are necessarily; (2) that the work's *irreducible* distance, the approach of which is the approach of a remoteness and which we grasp only as a lack—a lack in ourselves, a lack in the work, and a void of language—the strangeness of the work, the speech that can be spoken only a little beyond itself, is reduced to a happy familiarity, commensurate with possible knowledge and utterable language. Culture is substance and full substance; its space is a continuous, homogeneous space without gap and without curvature. Indeed, it grows and continues indefinitely; this is its power of attraction. Culture progresses; thus it has some emptiness in the direction of the future, but if it is in motion, it is also immobile by order of this motion, because its becoming is horizontal. The ground upon which it raises itself and to which it refers is still culture; its beyond is itself, the ideal of unification and identification with which it merges. It could not be otherwise. Culture is right to affirm it: it is the labor of truth, it is the generosity of a gift that is necessarily felicitous. And the work of art is but the sign of the ungrateful and unseemly error for as long as it escapes this circle (which is always expanding and closing itself). Will this doom the writer—the man who puts off speaking—to the impractical lot of having no other choice but to fail by succeeding or to fail against success itself? I will first ask the question of René Char. And here is his response: "To create: to exclude oneself. Who is the creator who does not die despairing? But is one despairing if one dies lacerated? Perhaps not." And I ask the question of Trotsky, who develops the utopia of the happy future with sumptuous simplicity: "Man will seriously amend nature, and more than once. Eventually he will remodel the earth according to his taste. There is no reason to fear that his taste will be poor. . . . The average man will reach the stature of an Aristotle, of a Goethe, of a Marx. And above these heights there will rise new summits." But what does he say of art? "The new art will be an atheistic art." This does not simply refer us back to the calm horizon of the absence of God, but also invites us, shaking off his yoke, to repudiate the principle in which God is but a support, and to attempt to leave the circle where we remain and have always remained enclosed in *the fascination of unity*, under his protection and under the protection of humanism—in other words, to leave (by which improbable heresy?) the enchanted knowledge of culture.[5]

§ 7 Man at
   Point Zero

As historians, scientists, thinkers, and even aestheticians have
long since explained to us, we have entered the final and critical
stage in which economic, technical, ethical, scientific, artistic, and
spiritual expansion carries humanity "to the heart of an always
accelerated vortex of totalization upon itself," as Teilhard de Chardin puts it in his ingenuous way. Thus one must be interested in
everything, recognize oneself in everything, and appropriate everything. The words *world civilization, universal domination, planeti-
zation, collective cerebralization* are expressed or inferred in everything that we say and think. Each person sees himself as master of
the entire earth and of all that has existed on earth.

Claude Lévi-Strauss should not have been surprised, therefore,
by the great success of his book,[1] of his books. No doubt he did not
rejoice at the success, other than to find in it some confirmation of
the dangerous force of attraction exerted on the margins of science
and against science by the general talent, thanks to which one
always risks being praised and admired (and critiqued) somewhat
wrongly. But why this difficulty of passing at the same time for a
man of science, a man of thought, a man of writing, without one or
the other of these activities disavowing itself? (The same question
today about Jacques Monod.) Here, aside from misunderstood
reasons concerning scientific technicity, one must take into consideration the dominant features of an age that is coming to an end

73

and that authorizes what is written only as auxiliary to culture,
culture itself being only a manner of mediating and holding a place
between knowledge and the silent caste of scientists. This is because, for scientists, the more withdrawn they are into the narrow
specialization within which they work, the more united they are to
the collectivity of researchers who are equally limited, and the more
compelled they feel to speak for everyone about what makes sense
only in the extremely particularized—formalized—language of
their knowledge. The result is often very disappointing. On the
one hand, the researchers know that their minute problem puts
everything into question; they know that there would be a great
interest in thinking about what they have discovered, introducing
it into thought and translating it into the language of thought. But
this is almost impossible. The leap that must be made in order to
pass from one language to another, from the rigor of instrumental
precision to the rigor of what is imprecise, disturbs them all
the more because they are always ready to believe that what they
know but cannot grasp is immediately translatable. When Einstein
speaks to us, he moves us, and we listen to him with friendly
respect, not because of what he says to us but because we believe—
naively—that if he could really speak to us, what he would teach us
about ourselves and about the working of our mind would be
shattering. In the same way, when Oppenheimer tries to improve
our "common sense," he only makes us think by way of the
contradiction between the force, the seriousness, and the authenticity of his science and the insignificant conclusions he elicits from
it for the benefit of popular thought.

~

Is it because ethnography is a very specific knowledge, concerned
almost directly with men, that Lévi-Strauss's reflections seem much
more important to us than the reflections of those scientists with
whom he could, with good reason, be compared? Or else is it that
Lévi-Strauss, having begun by teaching philosophy, abandoned
philosophy because he disliked having to teach it repeatedly, and
perhaps because he disliked philosophy, which is certainly the best

way of liking it and of staying loyal to it? What is striking is that the problems with which he struggles are obviously very close to those with which the popularization of modern science has made us familiar, but which, in his case, immediately affect the researcher and force him, beyond his research, to ask himself about the value and the meaning of what he does. The ethnographer sets out to study men who belong to societies that still exist but belong to a space other than ours and, as it were, in another time. Ethnography is not something that belongs to the present. It is as ancient as the great voyages that displaced the axis of the Old World. Conquerors, missionaries, utopianists have always practiced it, without knowing it, and with remarkable effectiveness. But it was established as a science only very late, at a moment when its object was apparently becoming scarce and when it could almost no longer find peoples to study who were truly foreign, and whose discovery remains the great ambition of the beginning ethnographer.

This is the first paradox that plagues the researcher. One cannot say that it is the paradox of all science. The astronomer always has at his disposal the entire sky and all that is unknown of the sky, which his discoveries only help to widen. In order to become curious about men who were formed outside great historical civilizations and capable of studying them without prejudice, the ethnographer has to be brought to the ends of the earth by means of the dominant success of the modern world, which enables him to observe unknown portions of humanity while taking hold of them, that is, while destroying them or transforming them. The ethnographer is the uneasy companion of imperialism, which with one hand gives and with the other hand takes from him his science and the object of his science. One admires Bonaparte for having brought scientists along with him to Egypt, scientists who did much for Egyptology. Every researcher feels that he is the fraudulent servant of a Bonaparte who is more or less visible. Unhappy situation. What is more, this Bonaparte always ends up destroying graves, cities, civilizations, and, naturally, killing men. Consequently a disastrous and absurd situation. But there is another problem.

The scientist regrets being a part of the baggage of an army or of a business enterprise. Like the missionary, he can console himself by thinking that science is not responsible for the errors of the conquest but must take advantage of the conquest for the good of humanity (a very uncertain reasoning, because science is linked to the development of the will to power, to which we owe conquests and destruction). Yet this concerns the scientist and only the scientist; even the ethnographer, who is the most anxious to succeed in his task without disturbing—through his methods and his way of life—those communities that are not familiar with his science and about which his science is concerned most particularly, is certain to exert upon these groups a destructive or disruptive influence. Wherever modern man penetrates, there occurs a profound alteration in traditional cultures and in the groups that protect these cultures. Wherever a scientist still has the chance to enter into contact with an unknown and original little world, he knows that this contact will modify the world and wipe out its originality. Here, in particularly simplified form, science is able to experience its power of volatilization, which does away with its object of study by studying it, and in this case it is not a matter of particles or germs, but of men or cultures whose value is irreplaceable.

Naturally, ethnography does not disappear as a result of this. It is no less interested in the changes that occur in these communities, which had been preserved until then, under the action of external influences or of its own influence. The bric-a-brac of composite formations, where an appalling mix of ancient and modern upsets the traveler, is also a choice subject for ethnography. Impurity is simply another problem. So be it. But the dream of encountering great and intact cultures nonetheless remains at the heart of ethnography. Lévi-Strauss is candid enough to tell us that he would have liked to live in the time of true voyages, "when a sight that was not yet ruined, contaminated and accursed offered itself in all of its splendor." He also tells us: "There is no vision more exalting to the ethnographer than that of being the first white man to enter an indigenous community. . . . Thus I could relive the experience of the ancient voyages and through them that crucial moment of modern thought where, following the great discoveries, a humanity that thought itself complete and finished was suddenly struck by something like a counterrevelation, the news that it was not alone." A decisive experience, but is it one that can be begun again today? Lévi-Strauss recognizes its deceptive side. He quickly denounces the illusion that makes him want to be Bougainville with the eyes and the curiosity of Lévi-Strauss, to have the innocence of the sixteenth century and the knowledge of the twentieth. He also knows that the encounter with debilitated and crippled groups such as the Pimenta-Bueno Indians cannot be compared with the sudden appearance of those accomplished, superior, and radically distant civilizations that offered a revelation of the plenitude of the unknown to the adventurers of four centuries ago. He knows, finally, that he carries with him a fatal germ in the very fact that he desires in vain to surprise such a civilization in the freedom of its intact life—a sad knowledge not easily reconciled with the enthusiasm of research, and whose sadness has settled in his book, in the very title of his book.

~

However, vocation is the stronger, and it is vocation that communicates to Lévi-Strauss's work that which one finds so enthralling in it: a brisk energy, an alert quickness, and the pleasure of always moving forward, an impatience that perhaps lacks contentedness but also avoids the exhaustion of a satisfied happiness. What is, then, the meaning of this central experience that so powerfully turns the ethnographer away from the civilization to which he belongs in order to carry him far from himself, into regions where he can at most hope to encounter a few decayed communities without wealth, without writing, without power, and about which he tries to grasp the minute particularities that are barely different from the ones already known? One must put aside personal reasons, however interesting they may be: the desire for the faraway; the discontentedness with one's world; the need to escape books and libraries, to make research an experience lived while thinking in the open air, in the depths of forests and natural solitude; or else the need to engage oneself truly and physically in work that requires one's days and one's nights, a true engagement, but one that always consists in disengaging oneself from one's time.

Why this movement? Is it destined only to make possible a confrontation of customs and worlds by forcing us to recognize that there are other ways of seeing besides our own, a contestation constantly being made by Montaigne, Pascal, and particularly by the eighteenth century, but one that must, no doubt, be rediscovered again and again? It seems that the ethnographer has something more to confess to us, and it is one of the merits of Lévi-Strauss that he does not mask with erudition the true attraction that he felt, which is the attraction of beginnings, an interest in what is first, the search for originary possibilities of which human societies are the constant implementation. When the author of *Tristes tropiques* speaks to us of the ambition of the ethnographer, "which is always to return to the sources"; when he writes "Man really creates only in the beginning; in whatever the realm, only the first process is wholly valid"; when finally he turns to Rousseau, to whom he would like to dedicate, with great fervor, every page of his book, we indeed sense that he is approaching here what is essential to him, and a problem that is also perhaps primordial.

It is not that the study of societies said to be primitive gives us any hope of encountering natural man, who is good and innocent, in whom Rousseau never believed, knowing that the societal state is necessary and inevitable; it is not even that such societies are closer than we are to what is or might be "originary in the nature of man," as Rousseau says (if indeed the word *originary* makes sense here); it is, rather, that they allow us hypothetically to construct this idea of a beginning or of a "theoretical model" of a society close to this force of beginning, which we will certainly never encounter anywhere in realized form, which one must even refrain from considering as a correct theoretical ideal—rather, one must see it as a working hypothesis, a product of the laboratory, constructed fictitiously in order to help us to see clearly into the complexities of existing societies.

"The ambition of the ethnographer, which is always to return to the sources." This expression calls for reflection. What might such a return signify? Why this passion for the origin? This search for first forms, which is analogous to the search for the first man or for the first manifestations of art, which we nonetheless know to be ungraspable, if it is true that in one sense there never was a beginning, not for anything nor at any moment? In the past, the navigator who crossed "the line," the zero parallel, was under the impression that he found himself at an exceptional moment and at a unique point, a sacred zone, the passage over which symbolized a crucial initiation. An imaginary line, a point that was geographically null, but one that represented, precisely by its nullity, the degree zero toward which one could say that man strives, out of a need to attain an ideal landmark from which, free of himself, of his prejudices, of his myths and gods, he can return with a changed expression in his eyes and a new affirmation.

∼

This search for point zero is necessarily ambiguous: it lends itself to all misrepresentations and encourages all simplifications. There are those who see only its destructive side, under the name of nihilism, recognizing in it the dark appeal of nothingness hearkened to by a weary civilization or, more precisely, a civilization in which man has lost hold of himself, no longer able to measure up to the questions that are being asked him by the answers of technical development. Others find in it an alibi, believe that this search is an alleviation, a return to archaic forms, a denial of modern tasks, a denunciation of what one calls progress. Naturally it is very easy and very tempting to confuse first and primitive, beginning and starting point, then origin and beginning; to believe that when a painter is inspired by savage arts, he artificially seeks an art without artifice; to believe that when a philosopher turns to the pre-Socratics, he asks them for truth because, being more ancient than Plato, they would have expressed a thought not yet elaborated. It is also easy—and perhaps useful—to denounce the illusory character of this search for point zero. Not illusory, however, but imaginary, almost according to the meaning given this word by mathematics:

imaginary is the reference to a man without myth, as is *imaginary* the reference to the man dispossessed of himself, free of all determination, deprived of all "value," and alienated to the point where he is nothing but the acting consciousness of this nothing, the essential man of point zero, whose theoretical model certain analyses of Marx have proposed and in relation to whom the modern proletariat discovers itself, defines and affirms itself, even if it does not truly satisfy such a schema.

When the issue is ethnography and when one sees a scientist, as if by vocation, turn to the study of social forms that might be called elementary, and live among men who are indifferent to everything that seems to make up the meaning and value of our civilizations, one is still much more inclined to make a mistake and to think that the "ambition . . . always to return to the sources" is, in this case, only the nostalgia for a humanity, not only different but simpler, more naked, closer to nature, and escaping the denaturation that technical power tirelessly pursues. I would not say that Lévi-Strauss is entirely free of this nostalgia, and although he, better than anyone, knows that "there are no existing child peoples," that "all are adult," that "all human societies leave behind them a past that is approximately of the same order of magnitude," it nonetheless happens that, by force of the brotherly compassion he has felt for certain distant peoples, we are taken in by the mirage of the word *primitive* and are ready to find in it not the hard and rich necessity—the impossibility—of a beginning, but the joy of the carefree and the purity of an age of man free of seriousness and of the boredom of maturity.

We remember the pages of his travel diary in which he tells us about the Nambikwara. It is night. The campfires are aglow. Around him, the most impoverished humanity, protected only by a few palm trees and without any riches save the poor objects that can fill a basket. What could be more wretched? "But this misery is animated by whispers and laughter. Couples embrace as if nostalgic for a lost unity; the caresses are not interrupted by the passing of a stranger. One imagines that they are all possessed of a gentleness, a profound lightheartedness, a naive and charming animal satisfaction, and if one were to join these different feelings, something like the most moving and the most truthful expression of human kindness." Ten years later, another observer encounters the same indigenous group and describes them as subhuman, ravaged by sickness, by ugliness and meanness: "One need not spend much time with the Nambikwara to recognize their profound feelings of hatred, of distrust and despair." This change comes no doubt as the result of contact with white men, but it is also inscribed in the truth and beauty of the lightheartedness, which, free of the weight of the future, is, because of this, also without future. He who chooses the lightness of the carefree and achieves it for an instant, knows (or does not know) that he chooses for the next instant the weight of a ravaged life.

~

It is certain that a reader who is not content with our time will find in *Tristes tropiques* many pages in which to nourish his dream of living far from the present, and far from the future, in small, brotherly villages, cursing the folly of human invention. In Lévi-Strauss one finds a man who is not ready to regard Western civilization as something perfect, nor even to believe that the advent of a world society, impelled by the technical development and social transformations that will result from it, will lead to a solution that is necessarily satisfactory. He is certainly protected from the prodigious optimism of Teilhard de Chardin, who leaves it to a double providence—biological and spiritual—to promise humanity, collected in a spiral around itself, a superhumanity, master of all problems and infinitely superior to all that we can foresee of it.

In this same book, however, Lévi-Strauss praises Marx no less than he does Rousseau. To forget this would be not only to distort his thought but to fail to see what is most interesting in it, and also to fail to see that his search for the beginning is not tied to the mirage that the word *primitive* sometimes conjures up in him and in us, the illusion of our deserts. Just as he is tempted to unite the liberation proposed to us by Buddhism thousands of years ago when it separated us from all activity, and the liberation that Marxism seeks to accomplish through a total affirmation of the activity in labor, so we understand that even if he crosses the line geographically, it is not in order to escape the beginning, of which our time would be the perilous realization, but to awaken in himself, through the appropriation of what is other and the assimilation of the foreign, the knowledge of the *violent gap* that is required by any point of departure, any initial procedure, and one that the impression of familiarity constantly—when it is a question of our civilization—causes us to lose.

We do not know that what is close to us is not close to us. We necessarily forget that the security—be it a frightened one—in which we live and which gives us the certainty of being, in our time and in our language, at home, deceives us. Certainly the declamations against technical advances are always suspect, but no less suspect is the kind of appeasement we are ready to find when we affirm that technical developments will suffice to put the solution of all the difficulties they create into our hands. There is no chance of this, of course, and one might even add: fortunately. For if societies born of technology have an advantage over other societies, it is to be found not in the bountiful material resources with which they endow us, but in the state of crisis to which they clearly bring us, thus baring us before the leap of the future.

It is therefore, in some sense, the poverty of the world of technology that is its truth, and its great—intellectual—virtue is not to enrich us but to denude us. A barbarous world, without respect, without humanity. It empties us horribly of everything we love and love to be, drives us from the happiness of our hideouts, from the semblances of our truths, destroys that to which we belong and sometimes even destroys itself. A fearsome test. But this contestation, precisely because it leaves us destitute of everything except power, perhaps also gives us the chance that accompanies any rupture: when one is forced to give up oneself, one must either perish or begin again; perish in order to begin again. This, then, would be the meaning of the task represented by the myth of the man without myth: the hope, the anguish, and the illusion of man at point zero.

§ 8 Slow Obsequies

I will pose what will be an obviously naive question: Is there for intellectuals a good and a bad way of entering into the preliminaries of Marxism, a good and a bad way of departing from them? I will remark that the reasons for these two movements are often the same. One (almost everyone) approaches Marxism for the moral reasons that oblige one, at some point, to move away. Surrealism comes to Marxism in the name of poetry and withdraws immediately as a result of this same exigency of poetry—perhaps the most surprising move. That of Henri Lefebvre is as irregular as it is remarkable: a philosopher, but in no way Hegelian, close to Nietzsche, to Pascal, to Schelling; in tormented contestation with religion; it is the revolutionary romanticism of Marx that attracts him, in its aspiration in which he recognizes his own (total revolution, the absolute it represents in its project to put an end to the State, to the family, and to philosophy, liberating the individual in view of his limitless possibilities). But it is also Marx's effort to overcome such romanticism, to order and protect it, that, for the thirty years that Lefebvre represented—all too officially—Marxist certainty in France, kept him in agreement with Marx's thought. This is because both of these moments are in him: the romantic spontaneity and the need to see clearly; individual affirmation, but also the coherence that organizes this affirmation by putting it in relation to the social entity and even the cosmos.

Having entered a romantic, Lefebvre exits a romantic. We may note that the practical discipline and the control of the apparatus do not exhaust the initial inspiration. The original questions do not lose their momentum; their force is less mastered than it is dramatized, rendered more intense by "terror," by which I mean the absolute exigency with which any living and thinking person, working in the shadow of what we call "Marxism," is necessarily in some relation, an exigency that also manifests itself by an external constraint. It may be that the irrational side—in the case of a romantic adherence to the Party, and when the man in question is concerned with coherence and lucidly watches over himself—makes him all the more faithful to an unbearable dogmatism such that he becomes wary of his own effervescence. But the book that is being reviewed here shows that his constancy had firmer grounds, which were not merely sentimental ones.[1]

~

A philosopher, having adhered—in adhering to the Party—to a decision that signified the overcoming of philosophy and its culmination in the becoming of the world, sees very slowly, moreover, that official Marxism compromises his decision in two ways. On the one hand, the doctrine (dialectical materialism) continues to assert itself as a philosophy and imposes itself as dogmatism, a systematic conception, having an answer to everything and having become institutional while remaining ideological; but on the other hand, because philosophy has become one with the practice of the Party or the State, which gives itself as the immediate measure of truth, it is not the overcoming of thought to which philosophy is asked to consent, but rather to its silent abdication, to its unconditional surrender, to a death in the strict sense. To a certain extent, the philosopher in Lefebvre might be willing to accept the suicide of thought, were it to be understood—as Novalis had already wished it to be—as the final and highest act of philosophical freedom. But how to accept a form of suicide consisting in a survival so trite, that of a system in which everything that must be thought and everything that must be known is once again defined dogmatically: Hegel certainly overturned, but turned into platitude?

I can hear what the cheerful critics will say: So why did he stay? Why did he wait to be excluded? What can this demand for freedom be worth from a man who was not able to free himself in keeping with his secret thoughts? We are not admitted into the privacy of minds. I take the meaning of this history (which concerns us all) to be such that it was able, such as it must have struck him at his moments of greatest truth. To the extent that he appeared as the "representative" of Marxist thought because of his talent and his more active thought—an already unfortunate situation: how does one "represent"?—it was possible for him to maintain an interpretation of Marxist thought that he believed most open to the future, one that brought difficulties to the fore, that clarified questions and showed that truth was not yet settled (this is clear in several of his books). To this extent he had the right to judge that, in the very fact that he was expressing this thought while remaining under the discipline of official Marxism, he was making the latter responsible for it and thereby enriching it with this responsibility. A simple calculation, one might say. From the moment that the Party is the philosopher, the leadership of the Party is what possesses philosophical certainty; political hierarchy is doubled by a philosophical hierarchy, especially because the only thing remaining to be done is the task, as it were, of managing the truth; truth being acquired for the most part, it is only left to administer it in a suitable way. This is correct. However, according to another perspective, each person is also all of the party; possibilities remain; becoming is not arrested; an obscure struggle, in relation to the events, is pursued around concepts using men as expedients—a strange, often horrible struggle. The old philosopher feels that he belongs to this struggle, because the meaning of his initial decision, the one that brought him to action in the hopes of an overcoming, is also being put into question. Thus he must stay to guard over the meaning of this decision. What will become of it? Through what singular metamorphoses does it risk being modified? He is present before surprising turns; he undergoes the trials one imagines. The worst occurs when he must reorient his thought in order to adjust it to dogmas he does not accept. The liberal theoretician (and each of us in himself) will judge this reorientation to be scandalous. But we forget the affirmation that was at stake for the philosopher when he made the leap in adhering to "communism": that of the very end of philosophy.[2] Philosophy comes to an end; but in what form? In the glorious form of its fulfillment as world? In the more melancholic form of its liquidation pure and simple? As overcoming? As renunciation? An ambiguous question, always with a double meaning, apparently reserved for the specialist, and one that the latter, perhaps out of modesty, willingly makes more comic than tragic, more frivolous in its seriousness than grave, as if, by asking himself about the end of philosophy and still continuing to philosophize about this end and without end, he were only trying to save his philosophical livelihood until its final hour.

~

If Henri Lefebvre's book had this question for its center, this would be enough to make the book central. For, in spite of its appearance, this question is aimed not only at the professional thinker in a manner that is urgent, but also at every one of us in our everyday expectations. This is one of the features of the Marxist movement, as we know. Through it, with an obviousness that we cannot escape, the destiny of philosophy has become our destiny: not only, of course, when we hear one head of State admonishing another State in the name of the Marxist-Leninist doctrine from which the latter would have strayed, not only because philosophy has taken power and exerts it in its very name, but because philosophy has transformed the essence of power, which has become the whole of life and accomplishes itself as a whole. Even if Queen Christina had declared war on a whim in the name of Descartes, the war would not have been Cartesian; it would have evolved according to specific means of power that could only have fallen outside the sphere of the essential according to Descartes. There have been terrible theological wars; the sword was not held by an angel, and God did not fight, moreover, except on the side of large battalions. Today the decision is not philosophical because it translates a philosophy; it is philosophical, on the contrary, because philosophy has ceased to exist as a mode of questioning that is autonomous and theoretical, and because, in its place, in the *place* that was specific to it, the overcoming—demanded by the advent of a new power—of what is private and what is public, of thought and action, of society and nature, of discourse and life, of reason satisfied and without power, and of labor discontented and without thought, affirms itself or would like to affirm itself.

Every time that a true revolution is carried out, a void is produced in which there shines for an instant, with the brilliance of the absolute that belongs to it and the terror that is in this brilliance, something like the pure presence of philosophy in person. An admirable, formidable apparition. The French Revolution is this appearance itself, even the most distant witnesses of which are subject to an attraction so strong it becomes vertiginous, a revulsion that becomes horror. This is because one cannot look the philosophical sun in the face. At this moment, each person is a philosopher; philosophy is the cold and decisive reason that is affirmed in everyone by the possible negation of each person; its right is categorical; abstract, it has the clarity of a military decision; it is not carried out as State power but as armed force, incarnating finally the soul of the world in the master of war.

The October Revolution is thus no longer the epiphany of the philosophical logos, its apotheosis, or its apocalypse. It is the realization that destroys it, the universal discourse that painfully identifies itself with the active silence of the man of labor and need, the man of want who struggles to master nature and to reduce the pseudonature that society has become in the course of this struggle, as the result of a change that always begins again, because it is tied to the development of his mastery. I will not insist on this affirmation: it is our everyday reading. But I will insist precisely on the fact that we read it every day and that it belongs to our everyday world. Having become summary, pedantic, and popular, so be it; but it is always traversing our days and our nights with a philosophical exigency (even in the form of an overcoming of philosophy) and putting us before a rude challenge, on the inside of this exigency in which we participate as much with our refusal as with our consent.

This advancement of philosophy, which has become the all-powerful force in our world and the course of our destiny, can only coincide with its disappearance, announcing at the very least the beginning of its interment. To our philosophical time thus belongs the death of philosophy. It does not date back to 1917, or even to 1857, the year in which Marx, as if performing a carnival feat of strength, would have overturned the system. For a century and a half, in his name and under those of Hegel, Nietzsche, Heidegger,[3] it is philosophy itself that affirms or realizes its own end, whether it understands that end as the culmination of absolute knowledge, its theoretical suppression tied to its practical realization, the nihilistic movement in which all values are engulfed, or finally, by the end of metaphysics, precursor sign of a possibility that does not yet have a name. This is the twilight that must henceforth accompany every thinker, a strange funereal moment, which the philosophical spirit celebrates in an exaltation that is often joyous, moreover, leading its slow obsequies during which it expects, in one way or another, to obtain resurrection. And, of course, such an expectation, crisis and celebration of negativity, experience pushed to its term in order to know what resists, affects not only philosophy. All literature from surrealism onward has been subject to this trial, the trial of its end in which it also claims to discover itself and sometimes to recover itself. Henri Lefebvre, who has seen his way down all the paths of this critical time, is a witness to this disturbance who cannot be challenged.[4] He lives, intensely, as a truly philosophical man who can no longer simply be a philosopher, this enterprise of overcoming and of the end, learning, in the severe figure of the militant, how to write his certificate of death and to make himself his own testamentary executor.

∼

I would like, here, to ask myself whether the vitality—and, I would say, the philosophical exhilaration—that have allowed him to emerge apparently intact from the descent into hell, have not helped him evade that which was extreme in his resolution. The decision—I return to it because it contains the meaning of the entire movement—is the decision to be done with the philosophical mode of thinking by adhering to communist rigor. Such an abrupt break should not lead him to continue to philosophize while at the same time laying philosophy to rest, no more than it should lead him to outline a philosophy that would not be one, a philosophy thus of a nonphilosophical sort, like the philosophy that so many "philosophies of existence" have taught us to distrust. Something more radical is necessarily required by this decision or by this perilous leap of thought, with a view to its overcoming. What? This is what is at stake in this exigency and in this end. As a communist, Lefebvre remains a philosopher; he is a philosopher, he is a communist, not, certainly, in a clear separation that would make his life easy, but rather in a division that he tries to make dialectical but that cannot be dialectical, that is but an acute wrenching, a perpetual confrontation.

A communist because he is a philosopher, a communist who, however, cannot be a communist philosopher, because in the "practice" of communism, philosophy should precisely come to an end, and then what would he be? What could he do? Philosophical work on the inside of Marxism? Works of commentary, history, and erudition that would be of interest to Marxist thought, extending it, keeping it alive, and orienting it toward the "overcoming" it affirms? But is this not already too much? A philosopher's head is a hard head—indeed, unbreakable. When it knocks itself against the calm power of political control—clay against iron—when what is required of it, according to a given central concept, is an unconditional capitulation, Lefebvre can indeed consent to it and give it his signature. But the philosophical head does not give its consent to anything, it does not subscribe to the death sentence. A double game? It is something else, and if it is a double game, it is the official Marxism that encourages it by its visible contradiction if, on the one hand, the organization does away with philosophy, which disappears, making room for "practice," if it also does away with the philosopher, who can only be a militant; but if, on the other hand, it demands of him that he continue to philosophize in the frameworks of the system, in order to justify action, in the name of a philosophical authority that has been maintained, and ideologically crown its value. On this, Lefebvre's critique is the most interesting. I will cite this passage: "The official dia-mat[5] offers us this distressing and rather startling spectacle: killing off philosophy, materializing its demise, and resuscitating the living body in order to use it *'perinde ac cadaver'* in the service of the politics of the moment . . . Mephistopheles galloping on a dead horse that he has dug out of the charnel house." To which the old philosopher feels he has the right to respond in the end: Since such is the case, since you are resuscitating, addressing, and using the philosopher in me, I do thereby regain my life and my freedom as a philosopher; I cannot be dead and alive. A burst in which one must at least recognize the pathos.

However, one must continue to question oneself. It would be too easy, obviously, to understand the end of philosophy as a pure and simple end. What ends, continues. What completes itself, first completes itself by imposing itself with an all-powerful domination, while at the same time wasting away and degrading itself, finally—and always at the same time—by passing itself off illusorily, but perhaps also for real, as a "knowledge" that is already very other, praxis as the overcoming of thought and action. In other words, the philosophical suicide that belongs to the enterprise of overcoming and that is (if it can be said) one of its moments does not consist in a pure and simple refusal to think or a brutal, disciplinary training—Lawrence exhausting himself as a soldier, Rimbaud become a trafficker. It assumes something else, and it could be that the painful contradiction as it was represented by the dogmatism known as Stalinist (which was and remains, even in small doses, horror itself) belongs to this other thing: the state of living death, the scandal of critical thought, which, having arrived at the critical point, is brusquely fixed into a system that is bloody and functions as an allegedly scientific knowledge, as State practice. Dogmatism—a dogmatism that, while it uses dogmatic arrogance and power, naturally claims to fulfill itself as the destruction of all dogmatism—this is what would be, for the philosopher, liquidator of himself and philosophy, the truly fatal test, a killing that culminates in insignificance. One makes the leap, one risks more than one's life, one loses all possibility of speculative future, one leads— philosophically and humanly—the life of a dog, and finally later, much later, one sees that, far from elevating oneself with a beautiful movement of violence and rupture designed to be shattering, one has never ceased to lean firmly on the sufficiency, the horror, and the platitude of dogmatism. A derisory experience? But this is perhaps precisely what the perilous leap and the absolute risk required by the alleged overcoming are—and, one might say, its meaning.

∽

Yet how can one decide? We speak, and Lefebvre himself constantly speaks, of overcoming: philosophy comes to an end, but by overcoming itself; and Heidegger, of the overcoming of metaphysics; and Nietzsche, man is something that must be surpassed. Surpassed, overcome: I read this commentary attributed to Heidegger that has in part come from Hegel: "to make something one's own by entering more deeply into it and by transposing it to a higher level."[6] The truth is that we do not want to lose anything. We want to surpass, go beyond, and, all the same, remain. We want to dismiss and preserve, reject and recover, refuse and obtain everything in this refusal. When he leaves the Party, Lefebvre will say that he is not renouncing anything, that he abandons nothing. At another moment he says: "Thus it was that a philosopher saw his philosophical ambitions shrink unremittingly, uniting in his 'career' the themes of '*la peau de chagrin*' and '*illusions perdues.*' . . . He comes to think that the greatest hope that a man of thought can permit himself is to act on language, to modify a few terms. . . . It is possible that no one could throw himself into philosophy—the folly of wisdom—without placing measureless hopes in philosophy." But let us remark that it was precisely this hope and the measurelessness of this hope that made him accept, and decide for himself, through an initiative that engaged his existence, the very end of philosophy. There is no inconsistency here. It is clear that when philosophy lays claim to its end, it is to a measureless end that it lays claim and in order to reintroduce, through the measurelessness of the end, the exigency in it for a new measure beyond all measure. In this way, *measurelessness* would be the last word of a philosophy ready to be silent but still continuing to say to us: Measurelessness is the measure of all philosophical wisdom.[7]

§ 9 On One Approach to Communism

(needs, values)

In a book on communism, Dionys Mascolo has attempted to show that, to a certain extent, what is essential to the revolutionary movement is the movement of the satisfaction of needs. Nothing is certain except for this: nihilism is irrefutable, but an irrefutable nihilism does not suspend the play of needs for men as a whole. Men, deprived of truth, of values, of ends, continue to live and, in living, continue to search and to satisfy their needs, thus continuing to keep alive the search's movement in relation to this necessary satisfaction.[1]

Dionys Mascolo also says that communism is the process of the materialist search for communication. This can be expressed in a simple manner—too simple: the movement of the satisfaction of needs comes up against, and discovers that it comes up against, an obstacle that is the existence of an economic nature. This nature, which went unnoticed for a long time, is such that men have a market value for one another, are things and can be exchanged as such; thus, should men be hired, bought, employed by other men, they become instruments and tools. This toolness, this relation of use between men, gives men the value of things; this is as clear for the slave as it is for any man who hires out his work—his time—to another, but it is also clear for the master. The person who treats another as a thing—even without knowing it, and perhaps especially then—through the unseen detour of economic relations treats himself like a thing, accepts the fact that he belongs to a world in which men are things, gives himself the reality and figure of a thing, not only breaks off communication with one who is similar or dissimilar to him but breaks off communication with himself.

In our world, however, these relations to things are partially masked, partially blurred by the interference of values and value relations. Men employ other men, that is, in fact treat them as things but respect them (ideally). The result is a confusion, a hypocrisy, an absence of rigor that lead to our civilizations. In collective relations, the essence of Marxism would be to liberate man from things by taking the side of things, by giving power to things in some sense, that is, to what reduces man to being nothing but useful, active, productive—that is, by still excluding all moral alibi, all phantom of value. The essence of Marxism (at least according to a certain and *restrictive* understanding) is to give man mastery over nature, over what is nature in himself, by means of the thing:[2] any other means of liberation that has recourse to ideal hopes would only prolong his enslavement and, furthermore, deceives him, lets him remain in an illusory state where he soon loses his footing and forgets what is. From this perspective, the liberator would thus be the man who is already at this moment the most purely thing, the man-tool who is already reduced, without travesty, to his material condition, who is "nothing" except useful, the man of necessity, the necessitous, the man of need. Power must be given over to him, to this man: the man of labor, the productive man, that is, not immediately man (for he is "nothing," he is only lack, negation, need) but labor itself, anonymous and impersonal, and the things produced by labor, the works in their becoming in which man, subjected to violence and responding with violence, would come to himself, to his real freedom. But it goes without saying that any man, if he wants to "see" what he is (that is, nothing) through the unreality of values, is also this man of need.

The immensity of the effort that must be made, the necessity of again putting into question all of the values to which we are attached, of returning to a new barbarity in order to break with the polite and camouflaged barbarity that serves as our civilization, the unknown toward which we direct ourselves—for we absolutely do not know what man could be—the terrible violences that the inequality in the satisfaction of needs provokes, the enslavement to things, the governance by things, as well as the dialectic proper to technology, the inertia, finally, the fatigue: everything would contribute to putting off the realization of such a movement to the time of reckoning of a dream (or of blood), if the pressure of needs did not represent a force, a reserve of great duration. One could say that the speed of the movement's progression is surprising, but in any case, time is required for it; the essential, moreover, is not to arrive but to depart, the beginning of man would be the event par excellence, and we cannot say that we are at such a preliminary point—perhaps we perceive it, perhaps one must begin again and again, that is, one must never rely on the word *beginning*. In any case, no one doubts that Marx's statement—"the reign of freedom begins with the end of the reign of needs and external ends"—does not promise anything to his contemporaries but the search for the right direction and the determination of a possible future.

The result is that men today and also undoubtedly those of the future, if they do not want to run the risk of living with illusory relations, have apparently no other choice but to limit themselves to the form of the simplest needs: they need to convert all values into needs. This means that in collective relations we should have no other existence but the one that makes possible the movement by which the man of need is brought to power. This might also mean that we would not be able to have any existence save this collective impersonality and that any form of private, secret life would have to be proscribed and regarded as culpable, as happened in France during the Terror. But Mascolo precisely challenges this last consequence in the most inventive part of his work. We have two lives that we must try to live together, although they are irreconcilable. One life is the life of relations that are called private:[3] here, we have no need to wait nor are we able to wait. Here, it would seem that out of desire, passion, the exaltation of extreme states, and also through speech, *man can become the impossible friend of man, his relation to the latter being precisely with the impossible*: sufficiency is shattered, communication is no longer that of separated beings who promise each other a recognition in the infinitely distant future of a world without separation; it is not content with bringing together particular individuals in the intimacy of desire; communication alone affirms itself, it affirms itself not as a movement that affirms what it unites but denies it, the movement itself being without assurance, without certainty.

Can one live these two lives? Whether or not one can, one must. One life is tied to the future of "communication," when the relations between men will no longer, stealthily or violently, make things out of them; but for this it engages us, profoundly, dangerously, in the world of things, of "useful" relations, of "efficient" works, in which we always risk losing ourselves. The other greets communication outside the world, immediately, but on condition that this communication be a disruption of "the immediate," an opening, a wrenching violence, a fire that burns without pause, for communist generosity is also this, is first this, this inclemency, this impatience, the refusal of any detour, of any ruse, and of all delay: an infinitely hazardous freedom. Only the first life, of course, has a relation to a possible "truth," it alone moves—but by means of what vicissitudes and what pains?—toward a world. That it takes little account of the second life, one can easily see: the intimate "life"—because it does not belong to the day—is without justification; it cannot be recognized and could be only if it misrepresented itself as value. Who does not know that this results in tragic, perhaps unbearable, divisions? The tragedy of our age would lie here.

Thus we have two lives, and the second is without rights but not without decision. "Communication," such as it reveals itself in private human relations and such as it withdraws itself in the works that we still call works of art, perhaps does not indicate to us the horizon of a world free of deceptive relations but helps us to challenge the authority that founds these relations, forcing us to reach a position from which it would be possible to have no part in "values." Dionys Mascolo says that the writer must live both in the common world of needs and in the private world of values and ends. But perhaps on this point one must go further than he does in the direction of his statements. The poetic work, the artistic work, if it speaks to us of something, speaks to us of what is outside any value or what rejects all valuation, proclaims the exigency of the beginning (again) that loses and obscures itself as soon as it is satisfied in value. Nietzsche wanted to transmute all values, but this transvaluation (at least in the most visible and all too well-known part of his writings) seemed to leave the notion of value intact. It is undoubtedly the task of our age to move toward an affirmation that is entirely *other*. A difficult task, essentially risky. It is to this task that communism recalls us with a rigor that it itself often shirks, and it is also to this task that "artistic experience" recalls us in the realm that is proper to it. A remarkable coincidence.

§ 10 Marx's Three
Voices

In Marx, and always coming from Marx, we see three kinds of voices gathering force and taking form, all three of which are necessary, but separated and more than opposed, as if they were juxtaposed. The disparity that holds them together designates a plurality of demands, to which since Marx everyone who speaks or writes cannot fail to feel himself subjected, unless he is to feel himself failing in everything.

1. The first of these voices is direct, but lengthy. Speaking in it, Marx appears as a "writer of thought," in the traditional sense: it makes use of the philosophical logos, avails itself of terminology that may or may not be borrowed from Hegel (that's without importance), and works itself out in the element of reflection. Lengthy, in that the whole history of the logos is reaffirmed in it; but direct, in a double sense, since not only does it have something to say but what it says is a response. Inscribed in the form of responses, given as final and as if introduced by history, these formally decisive responses can take on the value of truth only at the moment of the arrest or rupture of history. In giving a response—alienation, the primacy of need, history as the process of material practice, the total man—it nonetheless leaves undetermined or undecided the questions to which it responds. This voice of Marx is interpreted sometimes as humanism, even historicism, sometimes as atheism, anti-humanism, even nihilism, depending

on whether past or present readers formulate differently what, according to them, should take place in such an absence of the question—thus filling a void that should rather and always be further voided.

2. The second voice is political: it is brief and direct, more than brief and more than direct, because it short-circuits every voice. It no longer carries a meaning but a call, a violence, a decision of rupture. It says nothing strictly speaking; it is the urgency of what it announces, bound to an impatient and always excessive demand, since excess is its only measure: thus calling to the struggle, and even (which is what we hasten to forget) postulating "revolutionary terror," recommending "permanent revolution" and always designating revolution not as a necessity whose time has come but as *imminence*, because it is the trait of revolution, if it opens and traverses time, to offer no delay, giving itself to be lived as ever-present demand.[1]

3. The third voice is the indirect one (thus the lengthiest), that of scientific discourse. On this account, Marx is honored and recognized by other representatives of knowledge. He is thus a man of science, responds to the ethics of the scholar, agrees to submit himself to any and all critical revision. This is the Marx who takes as his motto *de omnibus dubitandum* and declares: "I call 'vile' a man who seeks to accommodate science to interests that are foreign and exterior to it." Still, *Capital* is an essentially subversive work. It is so less because it would lead, by ways of scientific objectivity, to the necessary consequence of revolution than because it includes, without formulating it too much, a mode of theoretical thinking that overturns the very idea of science. Actually, neither science nor thought emerges from Marx's work intact. This must be taken in the strongest sense, insofar as science designates itself there as a radical transformation of itself, as a theory of a mutation always in play in practice, just as in this practice the mutation is always theoretical.

Let us not develop these remarks any further here. The example of Marx helps us to understand that the voice of writing, a voice of ceaseless contestation, must constantly develop itself and break itself into *multiple* forms. The communist voice is always *at once* tacit and violent, political and scholarly, direct, indirect, total and fragmentary, lengthy and almost instantaneous. Marx does not live comfortably with this plurality of languages, which always collide and disarticulate themselves in him. Even if these languages seem to converge toward the same end point, they could not be retranslated into each other, and their heterogeneity, the divergence or gap, the distance that decenters them, renders them noncontemporaneous. In producing an effect of irreducible distortion, they oblige those who have to sustain the reading (the practice) of them to submit themselves to ceaseless recasting.

~

The word *science* becomes a key word again. Let us admit it. But let us remember that if there are sciences, there is not yet science, because the scientificity of science still remains dependent on ideology, an ideology that is today irreducible by any particular science, even a human science; and on the other hand, let us remember that no writer, even Marxist, could return to writing as to a knowledge, for literature (the demand to write when it takes control of all the forces and forms of dissolution, of transformation) becomes science only by the same movement that leads science to become in its turn literature, inscribed discourse, which falls as always within "the senseless play of writing."

TRANSLATED BY TOM KEENAN

§ 11 The Apocalypse
Is Disappointing

A philosopher, or rather, as he himself said with modesty and pride, a professor of philosophy, decides to ask himself this question: Today there is the atomic bomb; humanity can destroy itself; this destruction would be radical; the possibility of a radical destruction of humanity by humanity inaugurates a beginning in history; whatever happens, whatever precautionary measures there may be, we cannot go backward. Science has made us masters of annihilation; this can no longer be taken from us.[1]

Let us proceed right to the outcome. Either man will disappear or he will transform himself. This transformation will not only be of an institutional or social order; rather, what is required in the change is the totality of existence. A profound conversion, in its depth, and such that philosophy alone—and not religion with its dogmas and its churches, nor the State with its plans and categories—can shed light on it and prepare it. An entirely individual conversion. The existence that must be reached by the upheaval can only be my existence. I must change my life. Without this transformation, I will not become a man able to respond to the radical possibility that I bear. I must become the person on whom one can rely, tied to the future by a loyalty without reserve, just as I am tied to men by a desire for communication without reticence. With this change, with the seriousness with which I will engage myself, in it alone and absolutely, I will also awaken others to the same exigency, because "if the transformation is not carried out by innumerable individuals, it will not be possible to save humanity."

From this conclusion one could briefly conclude that if what Jaspers says is true, then humanity is lost. But to answer so brusquely would not be to respond to the gravity of the question, even if I am struck by the way in which thinking here, under a pretext of seriousness, can mock itself with a sort of frivolity. Let us accept the premises that are entrusted to us. History has its twists and turns, and not at all secretly but manifestly and in broad daylight, since the most ignorant man knows this as well as the most learned man. We can characterize this turning point in the following way: up until these last few years, man had the power to give himself death individually and alone; now, it is humanity as a whole that has acquired, marvelously and appallingly, this power. It can do this. However, what it can do, it cannot master with certainty, so that it comes back to each of us to anxiously ask, Where do we stand? What is going to happen? Is there a solution? To which Jaspers answers twice: the first time, there is no solution; the second time, a solution will be possible if man achieves a radical conversion (this is the main point of the book).

~

The theme is thus that we must change. But right away we are surprised by something: in regard to Jaspers, in the very book that should be the consciousness, the summing up of the change and its commentary, nothing has changed—neither in the language, nor in the thinking, nor in the political formulations that are maintained and even drawn more tightly around the biases of a lifetime, some of them very noble, others very narrow-minded.[2] A striking contradiction. A prophet, perhaps, could say, *Let us change, let us change,* and remain the same. But a man of reflection: How could he have the authority to alert us to a threat so great that, as he says, it must shatter our existence utterly and, what is more, our thinking, while he persists, without contestation or modification, in the same speculative conception to which he was led well before becoming conscious of the unique event, the immanent possibility of universal catastrophe, the appalling innovation, the consciousness of which should alter us fundamentally, and on the basis of which another history should begin—or men themselves end?

It is not a question of hindering, in the way of the Sophists, with some ad hominem argument, the dialogue that is proposed to us. We simply ask ourselves, Why does a question so serious—since it holds the future of humanity in its sway—a question such that to answer it would suppose a radically new thinking, why does it not renew the language that conveys it, and why does it only give rise to remarks that are either biased and, in any case, partial when they are of a political order, or moving and urgent when they are of a spiritual order, but identical to those that we have heard in vain for two thousand years? One must therefore ask oneself, What are the difficulties that prevent us from broaching such a question? Is it because the question is too grave, to the point of indiscretion, and that thinking immediately turns away from it to call for help? Or else is it because, as significant as it is, it nonetheless contributes nothing new, limiting itself to making very visible and all too visible the dangerous truth that is, at every moment and at every level, the companion of the freedom of man? Or else because it is far from being as important as it seems to be (one would also have to ask oneself about this)? Or, finally, because the question only serves as an alibi or a means of pressure for bringing us to spiritual or political decisions that have already been formulated long ago and independently of it?

It is this last response that Jaspers's book initially suggests. What preoccupies him is the end of humanity, but more particularly the advent of communism. Thus he comes to this practical question: Should one say "no" to the bomb if this "no" runs the risk of weakening the defense of the "free world"? And the answer is clear: just as he blames the eighteen German physicists from Göttingen, guilty of voicing their opposition to the allocation of atomic power to Germany, so he sees in the thesis of coexistence a means of illusion, and in neutrality an invention of irresponsible intellectuals ("the idea that one could come to a profitable polarization with Bolshevism makes political morality worth very little"). In the end, after

proposing this dilemma to us—to save oneself from total exter-
mination, to save oneself from total domination (and persuading
us that these two tasks are linked)—he invites us to choose by considering the circumstances in which the supreme sacrifice might
coincide with the exigency and, one might say, the hope of reason.

Such a choice is perhaps inevitable. It is the oldest of thoughts.
Life should not be preferred to the reasons for living. The bomb is a
fact. Freedom is the value and foundation of all values. Each person
invited to choose can, when the time comes, prefer death to
oppression. However, where the liberal philosopher—and with
him a good number of men—speaks of totalitarianism without
examination or critique, others—and with them a large number of
men—speak of liberation and the achievement of the human community as a whole. Once again the dialogue is stopped. The event,
the pivot of history, does not change the options or the fundamental oppositions in the least. Whence the suspicion that each person
can nurse against the other: reflection on the atomic terror is but a
pretense; what one is looking for is not a new way of thinking but a
way to consolidate old predicaments; from the moment one declares, "Opposite the atomic bomb, deemed to be the problem of
the existence of humanity, there is only one other problem that has
the *same value*, the danger of totalitarian domination," one has
already ruined the thesis of a decisive turning point, and it becomes
clear that humanity will continue to turn around old values, be it
for all eternity.

But perhaps one should express oneself very differently. If thinking falls back into its traditional affirmations, it is because it wants
to risk nothing of itself in the presence of an ambiguous event
about which it is not able to decide what it means, with its horrible
face, with its appearance as absolute—an event of enormous size
but enormously empty, about which it can say nothing save this
banality: that it would be better to prevent it. On the one hand,
what happens is not to be attributed to our disgrace; men want to
know; their knowledge should not accept any limit; he who refuses
the final consequences of technology must also refuse its first signs,
and then it is man himself, in his freedom, in his becoming, in his
risky relation to himself, that he will end up refusing. Nietzsche has

expressed this with incomparable force. Knowledge is dangerous. The will to truth is a will that can lead to death. The scientist who deplores catastrophe is a hypocrite, for it is one of the possible outcomes of science. "We are experimenting on truth. Perhaps humanity itself will perish from it. So be it!" To understand the world is to give oneself the possibility of destroying it³—and in the same way, to lead man from his fetters is to make him conscious and possessor of his infinite incompleteness, which is first an infinite power of negation. The risk is thus immense. However, and here I repeat Jaspers's powerful expression, if we want to be ourselves, we must also want this greatest risk to be run: "If we cannot endure the trial, man will have shown that he is not worthy of survival."

~

What does the problematic event teach us? This: that insofar as it puts into question the human species in its totality, it is also because of this event that the idea of totality arises visibly and for the first time on our horizon—a sun, though we know not whether it is rising or setting; also, that this totality is in our possession, but as a negative power. This singularly confirms the preface to the *Phenomenology of Spirit*: the power of understanding is an absolute power of negation; understanding knows only through the force of separation, that is, of destruction—analysis, fission—and at the same time knows only the destructible and is certain only of what could be destroyed. Through understanding, we know very precisely what must be done in order for the final annihilation to occur, but we do not know which resources to solicit to prevent it from occurring. What understanding gives us is the knowledge of catastrophe, and what it predicts, foresees, and grasps, by means of decisive anticipation, is the possibility of the end. Thus man is held to the whole first of all by the force of understanding, and understanding is held to the whole by negation. Whence the insecurity of all knowledge—of a knowledge that bears on the whole.

But let us reflect a little further. The problematic event about which we should rejoice because it confirms us in our relations to totality—it is true, only in a negative way—and also in our power over the whole—a power, it is true, only of destruction—why does it disappoint us? It is indeed a power, but one in relation to which we remain at a loss. A power that is not in our power, that only points to a possibility without mastery, a probability—which is, let us say, probable-improbable—that would be our power, a power in us and power over us, only if we dominated it with certainty. But for the moment we are just as incapable of mastering it as we are of wanting it, and for an obvious reason: we are not in control of ourselves because this humanity, capable of being totally destroyed, does not yet exist as a whole. On the one hand, a power that cannot be, and on the other, an existence—the human community—that can be wiped out but not affirmed, or that could be affirmed, in some sense, only after its disappearance and by the void, impossible to grasp, of this disappearance; consequently something that cannot even be destroyed, because it does not exist. It is very probable that humanity would have no fear of this power of the end if it could recognize in it a decision that belonged exclusively to it, on condition thus of being truly the subject and not simply the object of it, and without having to trust to the hazardous initiative of some head of State who is just as foreign to humanity today as formerly the turtle that fell from the sky and crushed his head was to the unfortunate Aeschylus. One is constantly speaking to us about suicide; we are told, You have finally become the masters and rulers of yourselves, you possess not only your own death but, in you, the death of everyone. A strange discourse that childishly represents thousands of human beings divided according to the model of a single individual, the supreme hero of the negative, deliberating, as the final Hamlet, on the reasons for giving himself death, and dying at his own hand in order to preserve the power of dying until the very end. Supposing this image of common suicide made any sense whatsoever, it would do so only if men could be shown all that they are lacking in order to reach the decision of a death said to be voluntary, whose subject would be the world.

~

Let us summarize what we have said. The apocalypse is disappointing. The power to destroy, with which science has invested us, is still very weak. We could perhaps annihilate life on earth, but we can do nothing to the universe. This inability should make us patient. And it is not even true that the radical destruction of humanity is possible; for it to be possible, one would need the conditions of possibility to be united: real freedom, the achievement of the human community, reason as principle of unity, in other words, a totality that must be called—in the full sense—communist.

However, understanding has confirmed the force that is specific to it. Understanding has placed us beside a mortal horizon, which is that of comprehension, and in so doing, it helps us to imagine what we are exposed to: not, that is, to die universally but to elude the knowledge of this universal death and to end up in the platitude of an end devoid of importance. Understanding lets us choose. Either to accept, henceforth, this end for what it will be when it will have taken place: a simple fact about which there is nothing to say, except that it is insignificance itself—something that deserves neither exaltation nor despair nor even attention. Or else to work to elevate the fact to concept and empty negation to negativity. It is in this sense that understanding addresses—it is true, in an indirect manner, for the choice does not belong to it and understanding is in fact indifferent to it—a call to reason. Reason is totality itself at work, but because it is achieved not through the effect of some quiet goodwill but through antagonism, struggle, and violence, it risks provoking, as it realizes itself, the unreasonable event against which and also, in some ways, with the help of which it raises itself. Hence the turmoil that this perspective introduces into old ways of thinking: one still does not know what to say about it. If, for example, Jaspers gives himself the task of reflecting on the atomic peril and at the same time never stops reflecting on the communist "peril," it is because he senses that, with the approach of this destructive totality, humanity risks being awakened to the idea of the whole and pressed, as it were, to become conscious of it by giving the whole form, that is, by organizing and uniting itself. Therefore, to better divert us from this, he concludes that the atomic bomb and what he calls explosive totalitarianism are one and the same thing: "they are," he says, "the two final forms of annihilation." But, on the other hand, how can one not be struck by the confusion of "Marxist reflection" in the face of this avatar of totality, which it approaches only through a painful lack of thought, at times exposing itself to the accusation of reformism by appearing to go so far as to question the necessity of violence, which is suspected of carrying within it the beginnings of disaster (just as others would be prepared to condemn science, guilty of putting us in such great peril), at other times pushing the abstract shadow of this apocalypse away, as if it were an importunate fly, and obstinately continuing in the custom of a tradition and a language in which one sees nothing to change?

What takes place, finally, is both disappointing and instructive. Reason, in anticipation of itself and immobilized by this anticipation, seems only to want to win time, and, in order to win time, passes off to the understanding the task that it is not yet able to master. (In such a way that the caption that would best illustrate the blackboard of our time might be this one: The anticipation of reason humbling itself before understanding.) Understanding is cold and without fear. It does not mistake the importance of the atomic threat, but it analyzes it, subjects it to its measures, and, in examining the new problems that, because of its paradoxes, this threat poses for war strategy, it searches for the conditions in which the atomic threat might be reconciled to a viable existence in our divided world. This work is useful, even for thought. It demystifies the apocalypse. It shows that the alternative of all or nothing, which turns the atomic weapon into a quasi-mystical force, is far from being the only truth of our situation. It shows that a few bombs do not give power and that only naive and weak heads of State may, nostalgic for the strength they are missing, hope to summon this magical compensation, as in the Middle Ages the small princes who had very limited resources called on alchemists who, under the pretext of making them gold, succeeded in finally ruining them. Yes, this lesson of understanding is sound. Only, it is almost too sound, because it exposes us to a loss of fear, the fear that misleads but also warns.[4]

§ 12 War and Literature

I would like to answer briefly.[1] The change undergone by the concept of literature—which those attempts marked by the names "the new novel," "new criticism," "structuralism" have helped to render spectacular in France—is not in immediate relation to the "Second World War," having been in the process of becoming long before; however, it found the accelerated confirmation of the fundamental crisis in the war, the change of an era that we do not yet know how to measure for lack of a language. Which amounts to saying, In the crisis that keeps getting deeper and that literature also conveys according to its mode, war is always present and, in some ways, pursued. Which also amounts to saying, The war (the Second World War) was not only a war, a historical event like any other, circumscribed and limited with its causes, its turns, and its results. It was an *absolute*. This absolute is named when one utters the names of Auschwitz, Warsaw (the ghetto and the struggle for liberation of the city), Treblinka, Dachau, Büchenwald, Neuengamme, Oranienburg, Belsen, Mauthausen, Ravensbrück, and so many others. What happened there—the holocaust of the Jews, the genocide against Poland, and the formation of a concentration camp universe—is, whether one speaks of it or whether one does not speak of it, the depths of memory in the privacy of which, henceforth, each one of us, the youngest as well as the most mature, learns to remember and to forget. When, in France, in the course of a spontaneous demonstration during the uprising that was May 1968—a unique and always brilliant moment—thousands of young revolutionaries let forth the cry "We are all German Jews," this was to signify the relation of solidarity and fraternity with the victims of the totalitarian omnipotence, of the political and racist inhumanity represented by Nazism—a relation thus with the absolute. This is also why the books stemming from the experience of which the camps were the place forever without place, have kept their dark radiance: not read and consumed in the same way as other books, important though they may be, but present as nocturnal signals, as silent warnings. I will cite only one, which for me is the simplest, the purest, and the closest to this absolute that it makes us remember: Robert Antelme's *L'Espèce humaine.*

§ 13 Refusal

At a certain moment, in the face of public events, we know that we must refuse. The refusal is absolute, categorical. It does not argue, nor does it voice its reasons. This is why it is silent and solitary, even when it asserts itself, as it must, in broad daylight. Men who refuse and who are tied by the force of refusal know that they are not yet together. The time of joint affirmation is precisely that of which they have been deprived. What they are left with is the irreducible refusal, the friendship of this certain, unshakable, rigorous No that keeps them unified and bound by solidarity.

The movement of refusal is rare and difficult, though equal and the same for each of us, when we have grasped it. Why difficult? Because one must refuse not only the worst but also what seems reasonable, a solution one could call felicitous. In 1940, refusal did not have to be exercised against the invading force (not accepting it was a given), but rather against the opportunity that the old man of the armistice thought he could represent, not without good faith and justifications. Eighteen years later, the exigency of refusal did not arise with regard to the events of May 13 (which could be refused in and of themselves) but against the power that claimed to reconcile us honorably with the events, by the sole authority of a name.

What we refuse is not without value or without importance. Indeed, this is why refusal is necessary. There is a reason that we will no longer accept, there is an appearance of good sense that disgusts us, there is an offer of agreement and conciliation that we will not hear of. A break has occurred. We have been brought back to a candor that no longer tolerates complicity.

When we refuse, we refuse with a movement that is without contempt, without exaltation, and anonymous, as far as possible, for the power to refuse cannot come from us, nor in our name alone, but from a very poor beginning that belongs first to those who cannot speak. One will say that it is easy to refuse today, that the exercise of this power does not involve much risk. This is no doubt true for most of us. However, I believe that to refuse is never easy, and that we must learn to refuse, and, with a rigor of thought and modesty of expression, to maintain intact the power of refusal, which henceforth each of our assertions should confirm.[1]

§ 14 Destroy

❧ *Destroy*: It was a book (is it a "book"? a "film"? the interval between the two?) that gave us this word as an unknown word, put forward by an altogether other language of which it would be the promise, a language that may have only this one word to say.[1] But to hear it is difficult for us who still belong to the old world. And when we hear it, we are still hearing ourselves, with our need for security, our possessive certainties, our little dislikes, our lasting resentments. *Destroy* is then, at best, the consolation of a despair, a word of *order* come only to appease in us the threats of time.

How can we hear it, and without using the vocabularies that a knowledge—a legitimate one, moreover—puts at our disposal? Let us say it calmly: one must love in order to destroy, and the person who could destroy in a pure movement of loving, would not wound, would not destroy, would only give, giving the empty immensity in which *destroy* becomes a word that is not privative, not positive, the neuter speech that conveys a neuter desire. *Destroy*. It is only a murmur. Not a singular term, glorified in its unity, but a word that multiplies itself in a rarefied space, and that she who utters it, utters anonymously, a young figure come from a place without horizon, youth without age, whose youth makes her ancient or too young to appear simply young. Thus in every adolescent girl the Greeks hailed the hope of an oracular speech.

∾ *Destroy.* How this rings: softly, tenderly; absolutely. A word—infinitive marked by the infinite—without subject; a work—destruction—that is achieved by the word itself: nothing that our knowledge can recover, especially if it expects from it possibilities of action. It is like a light in one's heart: a sudden secret. It is entrusted to us, so that, when it destroys itself, it destroys us for a future that is forever separated from any present.

∾ Characters? Yes, they are in the position of characters—men, women, shadows—and yet they are *points of singularity*, immobile, although a movement's path in a rarefied space—in the sense that almost nothing can take place in it—can be traced from one to the other, a multiple path, through which, fixed, they constantly exchange themselves and, identical, they constantly change. A rarefied space that the effect of rarity tends to make infinite as far as the limit that does not restrict it.

∾ Certainly, what happens there, happens in a place we can name: a hotel, a park, and beyond it, the forest. Let us not interpret. It is a place of the world, of our world: we have all dwelled there. However, although it is opened on all sides by nature, it is strictly delimited and even closed: sacred in the ancient sense, separated. It is there, it seems, before the action of the book begins, the questioning of the film, that death—a certain way of dying—has done its work, issuing in a fatal inaction. Everything is empty in it, at a loss in relation to the things of our society, at a loss in relation to the events that seem to occur in it: meals, games, feelings, words, books that are not written, are not read, and even the nights that belong, in their intensity, to a passion already defunct. Nothing is comfortable in it, for nothing can be altogether real, nor altogether unreal, in it: it is as if the writing were staging semblances of phrases, the remains of language, imitations of thought, simulations of being against a fascinating background of absence. A presence that is not sustained by any presence, be it one to come or one that is past; a forgetting that does not assume anything forgotten and is detached from all memory: without certainties, ever. A word, a single word, ultimate or first, intervenes here with the full discreet radiance of a speech borne by the gods: *destroy*. And here we are able to grasp the second exigency of this new word, for if one must love in order to destroy, one must also, before destroying, have freed oneself from everything—from oneself, from living possibilities, and also from things dead and mortal—by way of death itself. To die, to love: only then can we approach capital destruction, that destruction which the unfamiliar truth intends for us (as neuter as it is desirable, as violent as it is remote from all powers of aggression).

∾ Where do they come from? Who are they? No doubt, beings like us: there are no others in this world. But, in fact, beings already radically destroyed (whence the allusion to Judaism); nonetheless, such that, far from leaving unhappy scars, this erosion, this devastation, or this infinite movement of death, which is in them as the only memory of themselves (it is in one of them with the flash of an absence revealed at long last; in another it is through the slow progression, still incomplete, of a duration; and, in the young girl, it is through her youth, for she is purely destroyed by her absolute relation to youth), has freed them for gentleness, for care of the other, love that is not possessive, not particularized, not limited: free for all this and for the singular word they both carry, having received it from the youngest, the nocturnal adolescent girl, the only one who can "say" it in perfect truth: *destroy, she said.*

At times, they mysteriously evoke what the gods were for the ancient Greeks, the gods who were always there among them, as familiar as they were unfamiliar, as close as they were distant: new gods, free of all divinity, always and still to come, though born of the most ancient past—men, thus, only abstracted from human weight, from human truth, but not from desire, nor from madness, which are not human traits. Gods, perhaps, in their multiple singularity, their nonvisible split, this relation to themselves by way of the night, the forgetting, the shared simplicity of Eros and Thanatos: death and desire finally within our reach. Yes, the gods, but according to the unelucidated enigma of Dionysos, the mad gods; and it is a kind of divine exchange that, before the final laugh, in the absolute innocence they allow us to reach, leads them to designate their young companion as the one who is *mad* in essence, mad beyond all knowledge of madness (the same figure, perhaps, whom Nietzsche, from the depths of his own distress, called by the name of Ariadne).

∾ Leucate, Leucade: the brilliance of the word *destroy*, this word that shines but does not illuminate, even under an empty sky always ravaged by the absence of gods. And let us not think that such a word, now that it has been uttered for us, could belong to us or be received by us. If *the forest* is nothing more, without mystery or symbol; if it is nothing other than the *limit*, which is impossible to transgress, yet always breached as what is unbreachable, then it is from here—the place without place, the outside—that the truth of the unfamiliar word arises, in the din of silence (such was Dionysos, the most tumultuous, the most silent), apart from any possible signification. It comes to us from the furthest reaches, through the immense rumbling of a music destroyed, coming, perhaps deceptively, as also the beginning of all music. Something, sovereignty itself, disappears here, appears here, without our being able to decide between apparition and disappearance, or to decide between fear and hope, desire and death, the end and the beginning of time, between the truth of the return and the madness of the return. It is not only music (beauty) that reveals itself as destroyed and yet reborn: it is, more mysteriously, *destruction as music*, to which we are present and in which we take part. More mysteriously and more dangerously. The danger is immense, the sorrow will be immense. What will become of this word that destroys and self-destroys? We do not know. We only know that it is up to each of us to bear it, the innocent young companion henceforth with us at our side, she who gives and receives death, as it were, eternally.

§ 15 Idle Speech

I will not engage here in a "work of criticism." I would even have
given up—in a move for which I do not have to explain myself—all
speech that might seem to be that of commentary, were it not that I
remembered a few words that were said to me, shortly before his
death, by Georges Bataille concerning *Le Bavard*. For him, this
narrative was one of the most overwhelming narratives ever written; he felt it close to him, in the way a truth, which slides and
carries you along in its slippage, is close. This was perhaps one of
the last things he read; but because he himself had almost no desire
left to write, he asked me, knowing how much the narrative had
touched me as well, if I would not speak about it some day. I kept
the silence. It is to this silence, common to us today, but that I
alone remember, that I must try to respond by giving, as it were, a
continuation to this conversation.

~

Le Bavard is a bewitching narrative, yet one without magic.[1] Let
me first say that for us, for people of an era without naïveté, it is the
equivalent of a ghost story. Something spectral inhabits it, a movement that plays itself out in it, from which all the apparitions arise.
However, this must be understood in the strict sense: a pure ghost
narrative where even the ghost is absent, such that the person who
reads it cannot remain at a distance from the absence, and is called

on either to sustain the absence or to dissipate it, or to sustain it by dissipating himself in it through a game of attraction and repulsion from which he does not depart intact. For what comes to haunt us is not this or that unreal figure (thus prolonging beyond life the simulacrum of life), it is the unreality of all the figures, an unreality so extensive that it touches the narrator as well as the reader, and finally even the author in his relation to all of those to whom he might speak from this narrative. It seems to me that in entering this space in which every event is doubled by its absence and where the void itself is not assured, we are only given to hear a light, sarcastic laugh whose echo—a tender echo—cannot be distinguished from some plaintive sigh, itself barely distinct from an insignificant sound or from an insignificant absence of sound. However, when everything has disappeared following a bitter dismissal, there remains a book, the trace that cannot be erased, the reward and punishment of the man who wanted to speak in vain.

The narrative is entitled "The Chatterer," which could be the title of one of La Bruyère's pieces, but *Le Bavard* is not the portrait of the chatterer. Nor are we in the presence of one of Dostoyevsky's characters, inveterate talkers who in their desire for provocative confidences constantly reveal themselves for what they are in order to better conceal it, although the exhausting force of *Notes from the Underground* often emerges here as well. We would be more tempted, in looking for a point of reference, to evoke that movement that runs through the work of Michel Leiris and in particular the page in *L'Âge d'homme* where the writer finds no other reason for his inclination to confess himself but the refusal to say nothing, showing that the most irrepressible speech, the speech that knows neither boundary nor end, has for its origin its own impossibility. Here, the narrator, when he very tendentiously invites us to find out who he is, describes to us those individuals who experience the need to express themselves and yet have nothing to say, and perhaps because of this say a thousand things without being concerned about the approval of the interlocutor whom they cannot, however, do without. Where is the difference between the two texts? The

Bavard says "I," and Michel Leiris also says "I." The Bavard is the narrator. The narrator is, at first glance, the author. But who is the author? What is the status of this "I" who writes, and who writes in the name of an "I" who speaks? What do they have in common, given that, during the entire course of the narrative, the relation of one to the other and the signification of the one and the other do not change? It seems the "I" of Michel Leiris is more resistant. The impression remains that we could interrogate it and that we could even ask it to account for itself; someone is there who is answerable for what he puts forward; there is a promise and a kind of oath to speak the truth, from which we draw faith and certainty for ourselves. Even when the autobiographer plays the most dangerous game with words and when he sinks—at the risk of losing himself—into the thick of the linguistic space in his indefinite task of truth, even when none of himself emerges in a light that is at all personal, still the pact remains—reinforced, on the contrary, by the difficulty of the task and its unlimited movement. In this sense, Michel Leiris gives us the gift, to us as readers, of the security of which he deprives himself. This is his generosity: we find our comfort—our ground—where he exposes himself and where he will perhaps lose his footing.

I suspect a book like *Le Bavard* of an almost infinite nihilism, a nihilism such that it enters into even the suspicion with which one would like to delimit it. This is because it is the nihilism of fiction reduced to its essence, maintained as close as possible to its void and to the ambiguity of this void, inciting us, thus, not to immobilize ourselves in the certainty of nothingness (this would be too easy a repose) but to tie ourselves to non-truth in our passion for the true, this fire without light, that part of the fire that burns life without illuminating it. The respect for fiction, the consideration for the force that is in it, a force that is neither serious nor frivolous, the indefinite power of expansion, of development, the indefinite power of restriction and of reserve that belongs to fiction, its ability to contaminate everything and to purify everything, to leave nothing intact, not even the void in which one would like to revel:

this is what speaks in such a book, and this is what makes it a deceptive and traitorous book; not because it plays an underhanded trick on us, but on the contrary because it constantly gives itself away in its ruses and its treachery, demanding of us, because of the rigor that we see in it, a complicity without limit—which, at the end, once we have compromised ourselves, it revokes by dismissing us.

Hence, and I now return to it, the spectral nature of the story, and no doubt any story that seeks to rejoin itself at its center: a narrative of the narrative. There are several levels or aspects to this ambiguity—the ghostly presence. I will point them out without method, as I find them in my memory. Everything begins with the fraud introduced by the mode of narration in the first person. Nothing is more certain than the certainty of the "I." To live in the first person, as we all naively do, is to live under the guarantee of the *ego* whose intimate transcendence nothing seems able to attack. But if the "I" of the Bavard attracts us insidiously, it is in what it lacks that it attracts us. We know neither to whom it belongs nor to whom it testifies. An I that recounts, it crumbles, just as a world of solid materials begins to constitute itself around it. The more it convinces us of its reality (and of the reality of the pathetic experiences it shares with us), the more unreal it becomes; the more unreal it becomes, the more it purifies itself and thus affirms itself in the mode of authenticity that is specific to it; finally, the more it mystifies us, the more it returns us to ourselves in this mystification and gives itself to us who are without authority to pass a judgment of value or of existence on what is taking place. And, let it be noted, it is not because it is a maker of fantasies, inventing I don't know what stories to nourish its passion for chatter, that the I of the Bavard undoes itself and defrauds us; it is because this I-Myself is already a fable for itself that it must tell us stories, in an attempt to recover itself in them and no doubt to keep us with them, obscurely maintaining a relation to the true by the uncertainty of its own lie. When candor becomes an act of falsity, when a player cheats in all obviousness in order to denounce himself as a cheater, but also perhaps in order to make a trick of what is obvious, one must think of the evil genius under the suspicion of which there is nothing of us that does not fall, a thought that this very suspicion prohibits us from truly thinking.

~

It is that the ambiguity can be found at work at another level. The Bavard is a man alone, more alone than if he were confined to the solitude of a silence. He is a mute who gives expression to his muteness, wearing it away in words and wearing away speech in pretenses. But his "I" is so porous that it cannot be kept to itself; it makes silence on all sides, a silence that chatters on in order to better dissimulate itself or to better mock itself. However, this solitude needs to find someone to speak to. It needs someone to hear, obliging and tacit, able, through his attention, to orient the flow of words toward a given point, words that otherwise would not pour out. A very equivocal exchange. First of all, there is no exchange. The auditor is not being asked to take part in the conversation—on the contrary, he is only being asked to turn toward . . . to be interested in . . . yet not even that: rather, to feign interest, a politely measured interest; the person who listens excessively upsets the man, who only wants to chatter, that is, to speak in excess, with a superfluity about which he does not delude himself and does not seek to delude. The Bavard does not fail to say that he is nothing but a chatterbox, and really says nothing else, either in order to anticipate and divert the grievance, or else because of a need to identify himself with a speech without identity, as if he desired to nullify his relation to others at the moment he makes this relation exist, by saying (implicitly) that if he confides, it is through an inessential confidence, addressed to an inessential man, by means of a language that is without responsibility and refuses all answer. Whence the discomfort of the "interlocutor" who also feels himself to be in excess, indiscreet, at fault, deprived of being, and deprived of all power to regain himself by moving away, for this is well known: one does not leave a chatterer; this is in fact one of the rare experiences of eternity, reserved for the man of everyday.

In this infinite conversation, the other beside the indefatigable

talker is not really an other, he is a double; he is not a presence, he is
a shadow, a vague power of hearing, interchangeable, anonymous,
the associate with whom there is no company. Yet, by pressure of
the prattling narration, the double who plays this role is double on
two accounts: he is not only an auditor but a reader, the reader of a
story in which he already finds himself represented as a pseudo-
presence, a presence falsified and finally false, the reflection of a
reflection in a mirror of speech. So (one will say) is any reader. For
the author, the reader of any book is the unhappy companion who
is only asked not to speak, but to be there, at a distance and keeping
his distance, a pure gaze, that is, a pure ear without history and
without personality. To read *Le Bavard*—for we are this reader
doubling a double and splitting him into writing by an act of
repetition that, vaguely, seeks someone who could in turn repeat it
and who could in turn go in search of a perhaps definitive someone
to repeat—it often seems that the boundless monologue, raging
and controlled, in which everything is done in order to irritate and
seduce, to disappoint and fascinate, and then to fascinate by a
disappointing admission, the alternation between a meaning that
gives itself and a meaning that takes itself back until the final erasure, itself not very erasable—this monologue from which Camus's
narrative (*La Chute*) seems to have borrowed—gives us the greatest
sense of the ambiguous relations between reader and author. Perverse relations that are perverse right from the start, if everything
suggests that the man who speaks (and on the sly writes) has no
other counterpart but himself. "I often look at myself in the
mirror." These first words are very revealing: they reveal both that
the man who is speaking to us is only speaking to himself, and that
the man who here speaks to himself in the way that one looks at
oneself, a speech barely divided and because of this without hope of
unity, is in search of his difference, a difference that only makes
him different from himself, against a background of indifference
where everything risks being lost.

∼

   I think this must be made clear: there is hardly another work
that, by means of the detours of a subtle technique, succeeds better

in introducing the reader of these narratives into the narratives themselves as a character; a trap is laid in which the reader catches himself, whether or not he falls into it. I am thinking in particular of the text entitled "Dans un Miroir."[2] Just as what we know of reality is only what we are given to know by the child-adolescent in the fictitious version he composes for the benefit of his (adult) cousin who plays a major role in it, and who cannot fail to recognize herself in it while at the same time refusing it, so she, a reader of the fiction, reverses the respective positions of the characters at a certain point and reveals that the young writer, an apparently irreverent but objective spectator, has in fact staged himself in an imaginary role under the name of one of the principal actors of the story (in order, through this indirect communication, to make his secret desires better known without avowing them). And so the reader of the whole cannot keep himself at a distance, if only because he must determine the meaning of what he sees "in the mirror," and what he sees is what he desires; what he is repelled to see in it, his inclination in the refusal itself.

Nonetheless, if so malicious a move does not strike us as merely a clever stratagem, and if we feel ourselves caught in a game that is not only refined but harrowing, it is because the relations formed by the author with the reader, relations I will qualify as relations of strangulation—where each party holds the other by the throat without seeming to do so and with cold politeness—are first and foremost relations of the author with himself, a way for him to see himself as he would see himself if, instead of writing, he were to read and, in reading, to read himself. But this cannot be. In the end, once the work is finished, the one who has finished it finds himself expelled from it, thrown outside it, and thereafter incapable of finding access to it—no longer having, moreover, any desire to accede to it. It is only during the task of realization, when the power of reading is still completely internal to the work in progress, that the author—who still does not exist—can split himself off from himself into a reader yet to come, and can seek to confirm, through the indirect means of this hidden witness, what the movement of the words would be if grasped by another, who would still only be himself—that is, neither one nor the other, but only the truth of the splitting. This is why in the course of these narratives, which are not in fact very long, there is a constant reversal of perspectives, which extends the narratives indefinitely and yet in a way that is unreal, as if everything were seen—heard—by a virtual existence about whose identity one can make no determinations, because it is almost without identity and because it escapes, in any case, the very one, the narrator, who would like to recover himself in it.

This is also why there is a distance—particularly in *Une mémoire démentielle*—a distance that constantly increases and at the same time disappears, between what was, the attempt to remember it, the decision to fix it in writing, and then, at each of these levels, the splitting of the manifold acts into another reality, a second reality, that one could call purely negative, yet decisive. (What was, perhaps was not, perhaps was only dreamed, but, as such, took place all the same; what memory has lost is not only forgotten, but finds in the impossible memory and the impossible forgetting the very measure of the immemorable, as if forgetting here was the only correct way of remembering that which perhaps was not; finally the presumption of the writer, when at a certain moment he sacrifices the infinite search for the true—the evocation of the originary event—to the completion of a work that can be lasting, that way of pridefully extending in the form of a book that lasts, a non-memory that has disappeared forever and is, moreover, destined to remain secret and silent [the very act of keeping the silence], is also a way of remaining faithful to what was perpetual in the original fear, and consequently of reproducing it, unless the presumption constitutes the disavowal or justification of this fear.)

The antagonism, which in *Le Bavard* opposes narrator and auditor, is not only an opposition of incompatible though inseparable functions; this apparent antagonism has its origin more deeply in the double game of speech, and it is here, it seems to me, that we approach one of the centers of the narrative. Chattering is the disgrace of language. To chatter is not to speak. Prattle destroys silence while preventing speech. When one chatters, one says nothing true, even if one says nothing false, for one is not truly speaking. This speech that does not speak, entertaining speech that is always going from here to there, with which one passes from one subject to the next without knowing what is at issue, speaking equally of everything—of things serious, of things insignificant, with as much interest, precisely because it is understood that one is speaking of nothing: such a way of speaking, an escape before silence or an escape before the fear of expressing oneself, is the object of our constant reprobation. In truth, everyone chatters, but everyone condemns chatter. The adult says it to the child, you are just a chatterbox, just as the masculine says it to the feminine, the philosopher to the plain man, the politician to the philosopher: chatter. This reproach stops everything. I have always been struck by the willing and eager approbation that has been universally given Heidegger when he condemns inauthentic speech under the pretext of analysis and with the sobering vigor that is characteristic of him. Speech scorned, which is never that of the resolute "I," laconic and heroic, but the non-speech of the irresponsible "One." One speaks. This means no one speaks. This means we live in a world where there is speech without a subject who speaks it, a civilization of speakers without speech, aphasic chatterboxes, reporters who relate and give no opinions, technicians without name and without power of decision. This discredited speech brings the discredit with which it is fraught upon the judgment that is made about it. The person who calls the other a chatterbox causes himself to be suspected of a chattering that is worse still, pretentious and authoritarian. The reference to seriousness, which requires that one speak only advisedly, in accordance with solemnity, or else that one not speak, but that one only begin to speak, soon seems an attempt to close language; words are to be stopped under the pretext of restoring them their dignity; one imposes silence because, alone, one has the right to speak; one denounces idle speech and for it one substitutes a peremptory speech that does not speak but instead commands.

~

We are fascinated, disturbed by *Le Bavard.* This is not because it represents the chattering nullity, which is characteristic of our world, as a symbolic figure, but rather because it gives us the sense that once it is engaged in this movement, the decision to get out of it, the claim to being out of it, already belong to it, and that the immense erosion that is prior, the empty interior, the contamination of words by muteness and of silence by words, perhaps designate the truth of any language, and particularly of literary language—the one that we would encounter had we the strength to go all the way, resolved to abandon ourselves, rigorously, methodically, freely to a vertiginous disorder. *Le Bavard* is this attempt. Whence the oscillating reading that it imposes on us. Certainly, to chatter is not to write. The chatterer is neither Dante nor Joyce. But perhaps this is because the chatterer is never enough of a chatterer, just as the writer is always diverted from writing by the being that makes him a writer. To chatter is not yet to write. And yet, it could be that both experiences, infinitely separate, are such that the closer they come to themselves—that is, to their center, that is, to the absence of center—the more they become indiscernible, though always infinitely different. To speak with neither beginning nor end, to give speech to this neuter movement which is, as it were, all of speech: Is this to make a work of chatter, is this to make a work of literature?

This infinitely speaking possibility that the inexhaustible murmur would open to us, according to André Breton; the infinite recurrence, which, once attained, no longer allows one to stop, as if speech were mysteriously losing speech, no longer saying anything, speaking without saying anything, and always beginning again: What is it that authorizes us to exalt the former under the name of inspiration and to denounce the latter as alienated speech? Or is it perhaps the same speech, which is at times a marvel of authenticity, at other times a hoax or pretense, now the plenitude of the enchantment of being, now the void of the fascination of nothingness? One is the other. But one is not the other. Ambiguity is the last word of this third language that one must necessarily invent if one wants to judge or simply speak of these two possibilities, both of which are such that they occupy all space and they occupy all time, universe and anti-universe that coincide to such a degree that we never know when we are passing from one to the other, which one we are living in, which one dying in, all the while knowing, however, that the only way for us to decide is to maintain the undecidability and to accept the ambiguous exigency that prohibits one from deciding once and for all between the "good" and the "bad" infinity. It could be that there is an authentic speech and an inauthentic speech, but then authenticity would be neither in the one nor in the other; it would be in the ambiguity of the one and the other, ambiguity itself infinitely ambiguous. This is why the speech that gives itself as manifestly authentic, serious speech in which the spirit of solemnity is speaking, is the first to arouse our suspicion even if, with this suspicion, we lose the power to break with the unhappiness of everyday equivocation, an unhappiness that, at least, we share with everyone.

~

I will go no further in the reading of *Le Bavard*. Each of us should be able to pursue it on his own account by relating it to the essential that is specific to him. Even less will I attempt to clarify it through a reading of the other stories collected in *La Chambre des enfants*, even though all of these texts, separate and as if singular, form a closely bound unit in which the theme of childhood is present, that is, the impossibility of speaking. One feature, however, strikes me, and I will mention it because it seems crucial to me: How is it that so many words obstinate in being only words, a discourse that exhausts its resources against itself, how is it that this verbal expanse all of a sudden gives way to something that no longer speaks but that one sees: a place, a face, the anticipation of evidence, the scene that is still empty of an action that will be nothing more than the emptiness made manifest? Yes, nothing is more startling: here, the cliff in the late afternoon brightness, the smoke-filled cabaret, the young woman, the garden under the snow, the little seminarians who invisibly sing behind the walls from a distant past—confined spaces, circumscribed and not in the least out of the ordinary, but such that only an immense vision could encompass them. Something infinite has been opened, forever immobile and silent. It is as if the emptiness of the empty words, having in some way become visible, gave rise to the emptiness of an empty space and produced a bright interval. A wondrous moment without wonders, the spectral equivalent of silence, and perhaps death, death being but the pure visibility of what escapes all grasp; and thus all sight, silence, speech, and death for an instant reconciled (compromised) in song. Following which, following this gaze of Orpheus, no less than a hecatomb of words is needed, what the Bavard calls his crisis, imaginary crisis and narrative crisis, to perpetuate the moment and straightaway to nullify the moment by reducing it to the memory of a derisory incident—a memory that, in order to better destroy itself, passes itself off as something invented, sustained and ruined by invention.

I will add one last remark in order to mark—distinguishing it from the other narratives—what is particular to *Le Bavard*: the movement that carries it along, a kind of mocking violence, a fury, a power to ravage and rage, the effort to carry out the breach. It is with this movement that Georges Bataille indicated the novelistic works over which he would have liked to linger. I quote what he himself has written: "The narrative that reveals the possibilities of life is not necessarily an appeal, but it calls forth a moment of *rage* without which its author would remain blind to these *excessive* possibilities. I do believe this: only a suffocating, impossible ordeal can give an author the means of achieving that distant vision that a reader wearied by the narrow limits set by convention is waiting for. How can we linger over books to which the author was not obviously *compelled*?" The power of revelation in the work of Louis René des Forêts is tied to this *compulsion* that the author had suffered in order to write it, where something impossible came to him, and which we, in turn, receive at times as an exigent and constraining call, but also, at other times (this is the mystery and the scandal of the written), as the approach of a joy, the affirmation of a happiness—desolate and ravishing.[3]

§ 16 Battle with the Angel

Michel Leiris's effort to put what he is in relation to the truth of what he is, by means of a literary work of which he is the only subject, is an attempt that is perhaps mad, perhaps exemplary. From the sole point of view of the history of genres, it is remarkable that after so many books devoted to autobiography, and after writers for some centuries seem only to have been occupied with speaking of themselves and telling the story of themselves, a new possibility should have arisen. How can one speak of oneself? From Saint Augustine to Montaigne, from Rousseau to Gide, from Jean-Paul to Goethe, from Stendhal to Léautaud, from Chateaubriand to Jouhandeau, we find ourselves before essays that surprise us, seduce us, convince us of their perfect success, but not at all of their truth, and about which, moreover, we are not concerned. Yet we also are concerned. We are not disinterested in this desire that has led so many important men to write down what they are, to recapture themselves in writing by making the effort to be true.

How to speak of oneself truthfully? The result is important, but the intention, the rigor with which it is pursued, the persistent, cunning, methodical, inspired struggle to establish between self and self a relation of truth, a struggle without end and without hope, count far more. This is why Rousseau continues to touch us. He was ill suited to obtain a correct view of himself and an accurate account of his not very accurate life. He lived within himself in an environment so agitated, so tainted, in such anxious contact with so many enemy shadows, and, finally, with madness so close, that one must be surprised not about what was distorted, but about how little was distorted in this enterprise of defense against himself and against others, where everything is misrepresented from the beginning, except the obscure will to be true or, more precisely, to open oneself entirely to a kind of truth. *Les Confessions* remained unfinished. There occurred a moment at which Jean-Jacques, lost in himself, in the surprise of unhappiness, in the doubt of suffering, could no longer find in truth the just measure that he had hoped to apply to his life: truth no longer suffices him, and he himself no longer suffices truth; what is unknown in him asks to remain unknown. Thus he is silent. Silence henceforth is present in everything he still writes as the great power that his cries were unable to break. Jean Guéhenno, the faithful companion of this mistreated man (and always treated as a liar by those least concerned with truth), indeed says: "It is one of the beauties of the *Confessions* that they could not be finished." "Suddenly, when it came to looking at himself as he had become in London, in February 1766, he could no longer speak, he could no longer write and abandoned his work there. Perhaps there is no greater sign of his will to be true. The critics and biographers that we are may well say everything, fix everything. It does not cost them anything. He, however, was rendered speechless."

Would the proof that a book of autobiography respects the center of truth around which it is composed then be that such a center draws it toward silence? The one who goes to the end of his book is the one who has not gone to the end of himself. Otherwise he would have been "rendered speechless." However, the drama—and the force—in all "true" confessions is that one only begins to speak in view of this moment at which one will no longer be able to continue: there is something to say that one cannot say; it is not necessarily scandalous; it is, perhaps, more than banal, a gap, a void, a region that cannot bear light because its nature is its

inability to be illuminated—a secret without secret whose broken
seal is muteness itself.

~

It is perhaps one of Michel Leiris's strengths to have firmly seized
in himself the moment at which the inclination to speak of himself
and the refusal to speak came together in a troubling and profound
way. He speaks precisely because he has been rendered speechless,
and he speaks of himself from a feeling of isolation that, while
cutting him off from others, finds in the anxiety of separation the
strength to make itself be heard: "All of my friends know it: I am a
specialist, a maniac of confession; yet what pushes me to confidences—especially with women—is timidity. When I am alone
with a person whose sex is enough to make her so different from
me, my feeling of isolation and misery becomes such that, despairing to find anything to say to my interlocutor that might be the
basis of a conversation, incapable also of courting her if it so
happens that I desire her, I begin, for lack of another subject, to
speak of myself; as my sentences flow, the tension rises, and I am
able to establish between my partner and myself a surprising,
dramatic current."[1] This is, as it were, the point of departure: an
empty need to speak, made of this void and in order to fill it at all
costs, and the void is himself having become this need and this
desire that still treads only emptiness. A pure force of sorts, of
melting snow, of drunken rupture, and often obtained under the
cover of drunkenness, where the being who speaks finds nothing to
say but the flimsy affirmation of himself: a Me, Me, Me not vain,
not glorious, but broken, unhappy, barely breathing, although
appealing in the force of its weakness.

Such a movement should have resulted in one of those "Dostoevsky-like confessions" where everything is said with a passionate
incoherence that, in the end, says nothing but this turmoil and this
disorder (and this is already a lot). But if he arrives at an altogether
different result, if he seeks to express himself, in a work ruled by a
firm consciousness, a work that is constantly controlled and mas-

tered in view of rules that, it is true, are only hinted at, it is first because Michel Leiris greatly distrusts this drunken speech, without rigor and without form, in which what is expressed is what he is most ready to push away from himself: the relaxation of being, the dangerous need to abandon oneself, a weakness that is not even a "true" weakness, for it only looks to be comforted. Hence in the third volume, the slightly perfunctory condemnation of former confidences: "these Dostoevsky-like confessions after drinking, which were my custom but which today I detest like everything in me that is the reaction of a sentimental drunk." The speech of pure effusion, the attempt at irruption in order to break through the dams—but which also at times benefits from the easy rupture that drunkenness permits—is thus impugned. Superficial speech, which is perhaps only faked and which is only speech, whereas Michel Leiris intends to write and expects from a written text—a true "literary" work—the very thing that is obscurely in play in this whole affair: less to reveal himself than to grasp himself in a manner that does not do violence to what he is, and does not betray that which he seeks confusedly to be.

To reconstruct himself by disclosing himself. A formula that is undoubtedly too simple to give an account of the intention, poorly illuminated and reticent, that imposed itself on him, in the hopes that he would know it better at the time he would carry it out, for after *L'Age d'homme* he undertook a new work entitled *La règle du jeu*, two volumes of which have been published in the last fifteen years and are to be followed by another two volumes.[2]

∼

To give a sequel to *L'Age d'homme* was a dangerous temptation. When it seems that one has accomplished perfectly that which one set out to do, and when, in addition, the success involved speaking of oneself "with the greatest lucidity and sincerity," it is very dangerous not to stop. On the one hand, it is tempting for the author: the "self" is inexhaustible, less because of its richness than its insatiable poverty. But for the reader, who is satisfied with a book, the great literary merits of which he has admired, recalling the rare balance that is maintained between the violence of the things to be said—what the I says of itself, the nakedness that speaks in it, is always violence—and a form capable of giving a cohesion to what does not tolerate cohesion, there is this anxiety and this unease: Why does he continue to speak of himself? Has he not already said everything? Does what was courage not become complacency? In the beginning, the author spoke, impelled by the irrepressible force—but a force contained and held back—that appears when a being wants to speak from the point at which it *can* say nothing; however, now, does he not simply speak of himself because he has nothing to say? And, certainly, it is understood that an autobiography can be extended for as long as the story has not come to an end. But *L'Age d'homme*, far from being a story, formed a portrait in depth, a search for the sensitive points of a being, a web rigorously elaborated upon which the threads of memories and events, outside of any chronological simplicity, made out, in the end, a figure with marked boundaries and a great appearance of truth. Before us was a being who rose up from his history without being distinct from it but was, as it were, pushed outside of this history by the forces at work behind the temporal surface: being without "character" and yet very characterized, almost mythical, and in search, moreover (in order to project itself in it), of a certain mythological sky, of which the names of Lucretia and Judith formed the principle constellations. And to this being, it is true, we were attached, as we were to the book with which we liked to confuse him.

The most malevolent reader is convinced of the imperious reasons that forced Michel Leiris to go beyond himself and beyond the image of himself with which we were so satisfied as to want it to be unique. But it is perhaps for this reason that he could not hold himself to it: it was not possible for him to be, as we were, happy with himself. He often says that one of the ends he pursues in writing is the erection of a statue of himself to oppose the destructive work of time: a desire for fixity to which the rigor of a classical form corresponds. But then, why did he risk damaging his first effigy, so satisfying to us and more capable of enduring than he?

Instead of writing another book, why not use all of his efforts to conform to the book he had written and to disappear in it, as Ducasse one day disappeared into Lautréamont? It is because he is afflicted by a need for truth that does not allow him to be happy with his permanence, if the latter distorts what he believes he is. He would like—he says this—to be able to throw people off and put forward a heroic, admirable, and likable Ego, but he would also have to manage to deceive himself and to persuade himself that he is the being of marble that he is not. What good is enduring eternally in a form that will eternalize someone other than himself? It is he himself, as he lives and as he sees himself; it is in the strict truth of his life that he desires to become image, figure, and book, a true book but one that is also literarily valid, capable of being read and exalted in others. Was *L'Âge d'homme* then not a faithful portrait, not true to life? Necessarily unfaithful, because lifelike, at a distance from him: this very effigy whose fixed truth could only betray the constant inaccuracy of the living being.

How to speak of oneself truthfully, if this truth must be not only behind but also ahead, no longer that of a past history but of a future that presents itself not as a simple temporal future but as an ideal and an unknown ideal, free and always revocable? For Michel Leiris, who is hardly satisfied with this almost faithful image that a true book offers him, would be no more satisfied with the impersonal statue that duty would substitute for what he is: he does not want to be the writer, the militant or ideal ethnographer, any more than he wants to be the perfect spouse or the perfect libertine (which he very well knows he is not). Furthermore, if all perfection attracts him because it offers him the possibility of jumping outside of time, all fulfillment repels him: to fulfill oneself is to be dead, and death is the Angel whose enemy intimacy drives Michel Leiris to write while giving him over to the very thing that he flees, and does so with the effort he makes to flee it.

Between *L'Âge d'homme* and *La règle du jeu* there is perhaps this first difference: that the former was written in order to satisfy a present (and quasi-eternal) truth, whereas the new work is written under the close light of a truth always to come, toward which the author turns with caution, desire, and doubt, in order to learn from it the rules of the game he is playing by living and writing, with the weak hope that he will know, in time, why it is he writes and in what name he must live. A project that cannot be completed except by remaining a project, and one that, at each of the stages at which it affirms itself, makes a mysterious sound, a sound that is sometimes cracked and seemingly strangled through the meanderings of an infinite search, at other times grave and with a fullness in which, however, we cannot desire that all should end.

∿

Thus Michel Leiris writes *Biffures* in an appeal to the slippery truth that will not be a simple acknowledgment, or the immobile decision of an absolute future, or the narrowness of a present that can be lived but not written up as a story: a truth that is perhaps, then, no more than that of a slippage. And this is precisely what his book first tried to be: the experience of a slippage. It is no less anchored in the past than is *L'Age d'homme*, perhaps even more steeped in distant childhood, but it is engaged in the past by its search for the turntables formed by certain privileged words and for the enigmatic series according to which these words arrange themselves (a serial movement), by its discovery of the sudden changes of itinerary—the bifurcations—that these words provoke, of the holes they form that are filled by the influx of memories and still more by the evocations of a directed and oriented reverie. "A strange discrepancy that takes place on the occasion of words," "a slippage of thought on the occasion of a crack," awakening and listening to himself as he hears himself move and start, when he touches on certain points whose hardened contact—a small pebble, cold and inert—unleashes, with the approach of provocative words, a current of life where, for an instant, the real and the imaginary, the present and the past, and, finally, the whole of being in motion are brought forward and outlined.

The first feature of such an experience is that the greatest concern for truth forces him to make much greater allowances for the imaginary: before himself, lending an ear to the echo to which he gives rise, the author no longer knows if he is remembering or if he is inventing. But this confusion that he rigorously watches over is necessary to the new dimension of truth: it is no longer the real being in himself that he seeks, nor is he doing his own psycho-analysis; he has for some time been in possession of the important themes around which what he knows of himself forms, adjusts, and readjusts itself. So what does he want? First, to keep in motion this sphere, which the need to affirm it in books risks dangerously immobilizing.[3] But also to recover, not this or that hidden event or the great veiled features of his destiny, but that which, while putting him in precarious balance with himself, at those moments at which his being loses its footing, might also put the essence of the shock at his disposal: no longer simply what he is and has been, not the openness or the latitude, but the secret of becoming, the joy and speechlessness, the jolt and flash in which freedom is set ablaze, in the light of a consciousness that, for an instant, discovers it.

Experiences with which it seems his childhood was favored, and which, because of this, he incessantly questions, in the perhaps deceptive hope of rediscovery, experiences of a *gap*, which poetic activity could recover for a short time and which he searches for, now that he judges himself deprived of such resources—he no longer dreams, he writes almost no poems or imaginary narra-tives—not in order to delude himself with them, but in order to give his existence the comfortable freedom of a great movement, and to give his book the plenitude of those brief moments of harmony in which life shines forth as a whole and the whole as a deployment of life.

In this effort to liberate and master the unpredictable in him-self—the unpredictable that he fears as much as he searches for it— one might think that Michel Leiris was returning to the caprice of spontaneous speech that drunkenness, timidity, and surrealism each revealed to him in turn. But chance alone does not lead him. The originality and difficulty of *Biffures* are that it involves an experience in which discovery is more important than what there is to discover: the author who deceives himself far too little and is far too little disposed to abandon himself to a lack of reflection and, what is more, is accustomed to certain scientific methods, gives to this word *experience* the meaning of a search in which a deliberate work of preparation, a spirit of rigorous control, and a certain giving way to language, understood as a magical power "of detection and exaltation," would cooperate. Thus he works on index cards, and these archives of himself in which the fragments of his history are deposited, mute dust as long as nothing disturbs it, give him the raw material of thoughts and facts that writing will have as its object to animate and to attract, in the manner of a magnet, in order that they group themselves, and in grouping themselves, form some new figure, true and exalting, in which, perhaps, a more exact knowledge of the conduct of life will also be affirmed.

For such work, a number of very different talents must, it seems, come together: a little method, a lot of patient rigor, and, under the greatest suspicion, a receptivity to this free speech that has remained intact, in relation to the marvel that makes possible the commerce of beings and things. I think, moreover, that one would be mistaken if one made the author of *Biffures* into a man too knowledgeable about himself, an archivist and accountant who classifies himself and puts himself on file before putting himself together according to the flamboyant instinct of words. The notes in which he fixes himself are the products of distress more than science, written when he does not feel himself "equal to a literary work," and can live only on the order of small projects and with a very small margin of hope. In *Biffures*, where the anecdotes are reduced to a minimum and the memories are fragmented, atomized by the movement of thought that incessantly agitates them in order to return to them their power as seed and their active force, the experience rests almost entirely on the life of reflection, the surveillance it exercises, the extreme effort and tension of a consciousness that is on the alert all the more because it not only has to verify facts but also must weigh the imaginary. Even the language has been transformed from *L'Âge d'homme*. The sentences are longer, heavier, always weighed down by scruples, precautions, nuances, detours; by the refusal to go straight to the fact, because the "fact" risks being betrayed and then, once it has been communicated, risks giving way only to void. And precisely before this void the author withdraws, yet cannot withdraw, for he sees too clearly into himself to be able to consent to this flight that is but a feint. A torment that takes form in writing and that is its exigency, its very life.

∼

It is easy to say that the result is a book that is tethered, contorted, and without joy (I think it is an extraordinary book for the spirit of truth that incessantly comes to light in it). But one would also have to add that in the volume that followed and was published under the name *Fourbis*—a reversal and ironic weakening of the word *Biffures*—the author and the reader receive the reward for this difficult struggle. It is as if, by dint of disturbing what he is, by dint of shaking his days and nights with the obstinate movement of an invisible riddle, he had made himself so lithe as to be able to model himself on two or three great images around which are reconciled the torment of being true, the hope of remaining free, and the desire to make himself readable and visible to himself and to others. The episode of Khadidja, the streetwalker of Beni-Ounif, which actually ends the work, is also its apotheosis. A figure whom the author does not in the least seek to idealize by making her baser—more infernal—or more superb than she is. Michel Leiris is not Marcel Jouhandeau, who imposes on those beings, with the industry of a perhaps divinatory imagination, the truth of the legend he ascribes to them. Relations with Khadidja are described to us such as they undoubtedly were, and with a concern for exactitude, for rectitude, that strangely unifies candor and restraint—a delicacy in the formulation of so-called obscene details, not because the latter are artfully eluded but, on the contrary, because they are faithfully transcribed without respect for anything but the true feelings of which they were the occasion. Where, then, does the mythical grandeur of the episode come from? The Angel's dignity that he confers on "Khadidja the tramp," "a unique combination of hardness and gentleness," the Angel whose obscure, silent discourse finally leads the author to abandon his reserve?

Perhaps from the ability to bring together, around two or three gestures, the gravity of his relations with other beings and the ungraspable truth whose overwhelming presence they have, with a word, an attitude, made perceptible to him for an instant. Such is the case of the young woman, referred to by the name of Laure, several of whose pages—unforgettable in their violence and outraged purity—those who did not know her were able to read. This young woman is spoken of only from afar, from the distance from which she rises up as from death itself with the silent force of two or three images, but these images are enough to make her, more even than Khadidja, the Angel, the dark power whose great adversarial approach is what forces Michel Leiris to write, and to write in accordance with the truth, of which she promises him, however, only the ruin.[4]

§ 17 Dreaming, Writing

I remember the limited, slender series entitled "L'Age d'or" in which, alongside French and foreign works (those of Georges Bataille, René Char, Maast, Limbour, Léonora Carrington, or those of Grabbe and Brentano, among others), the first *Nuits* of Michel Leiris appeared. Now that we can read these dreams, the companions of forty years, in their dated sequence, precisely as they were transcribed, we are tempted to see them as a complement to life, or better yet as a supplement to the project of self-description and self-understanding through writing that Michel Leiris has pursued without respite.[1] This is perhaps how I first read them, and I remember the impressive dream that seemed to carry into the night itself the watchfulness, the search that the author of *L'Age d'homme* has placed at the center of his concern as a writer: "Awakening (with a cry that Z. prevents me from uttering), having dreamed the following: I put my head, as if to see something, through an orifice very much like an œil-de-bœuf that is overlooking an enclosed and dark area, similar to the cylindrical pisé granaries that I saw in Africa. . . . My anguish comes from the fact that when I lean over this enclosure, which I surprise in its inner darkness, it is into myself that I am looking."

One sees, however, that the dreamer here in no way carries out the project of introspection to which he seems so attached during the day. It is a matter of translation, a transcription of this project into a nocturnal language rather than its implementation; and the anguish is not provoked by the discovery of the strange realities contained in one's inner depths, but by the movement of looking into oneself, where there is nothing to see but the constriction of a closed space without light. Three years later, a new dream reconsiders this movement by taking itself directly as theme: it is the dream of a dream that comes to an end, but instead of ascending to an awakening in an effort to rise and to emerge, this dream surreptitiously invites the dreamer to find an exit from below, that is, to enter into the depths of another sleep that will no doubt never end. What these two dreams have in common, what is grasped and lived as image by both of them, is the very movement of turning back: in the first dream, a turning back upon oneself such that simple imagery might attribute it to introspection; in the second, a turning back of the dream as if it were turning back to surprise or watch over itself, identifying thus, with an inverse vigilance, a state of wakefulness of the second degree in search of its own limit.

A detour that is characteristic. The one who dreams turns away from the one who sleeps; the dreamer is not the sleeper: sometimes dreaming that he is not dreaming and therefore that he is not sleeping; at other times dreaming that he is dreaming and thus, through this flight into a more inner dream, persuading himself that the first dream is not a dream, or else knowing that he is dreaming and then awakening into a very similar dream that is nothing other than an endless flight outside the dream, a flight that is an eternal fall in a similar dream (and so it is through other twists and turns). This perversion (whose disturbing consequences for the state of wakefulness Roger Caillois has described in a precious book),[2] seems to me to be tied to a question that surfaces naively, perfidiously in each of our nights: In the dream, who is dreaming? Who is the "I" of the dream? Who is the person to whom one attributes this "I," admitting that there is one? Between the one who sleeps and the one who is the subject of the dream's plot, there is a fissure, the hint of an interval and a difference of structure; of course it is not truly another, another person, but what is it? And if, upon awakening, we hastily and greedily take possession of the night's adventures, as if they belonged to us, is it not with a certain feeling of usurpation (of gratitude as well)? Do we not preserve the memory of an irreducible distance, a distance of a peculiar sort, the distance between me and myself, but also the distance between each of the characters and the identities—even certain—that we lend them, a distance without distance, illuminating and fascinating, which is like the proximity of the remote or contact with the faraway? An intrigue and a questioning that refer us to an experience often described of late: the experience of the writer when, in a narrative, poetic, or dramatic work, he writes "I," not knowing who says it or what relation he maintains with himself.

In this sense, the dream is perhaps close to literature, at least to its enigmas, its glamour, and its illusions.

But let me return to Michel Leiris. For a man who is so deeply concerned with himself and so intent on explaining himself, I find the reserve he shows in relation to his dreams remarkable. He notes them down, or more precisely, he writes them. He does not question them. This is not out of prudence; we know there is no one more intrepid than he when it comes to self-inspection, an inspection into which he draws us by his daring candor. He is familiar, on the other hand, with psychoanalysis; he is familiar with its mythology, its ruses, its interminable curiosity; he could unravel his dreams and read them as documents better than anyone else. This is precisely what he forbids himself to do, and if he publishes his dreams, it is not so that we might then have the pleasure of deciphering them, but rather so that we might show the same discretion, receiving them as they are, in their own light, and learning to grasp in them the traces of a literary affirmation that is not psychoanalytic or autobiographical. They were dreams; they are signs of poetry.

Naturally we must admit that there is an exactness of relation between the dreamed state and the written state. It is not a matter of making a literary work out of nocturnal elements that have been transformed, embellished, perverted, or mimed by poetic resources. Precision is one of the rules of the game. Writing takes hold of the dream in its exteriority; the present of the dream coincides with the non-presence of writing. At least, this is the postulate of the enterprise that one could formulate in this way: I dream, therefore it is written.

~

Let us in turn dream about the supposed kinship between dreaming and writing—I will not say speech. Certainly, the one who awakens experiences a curious desire to talk about himself; he is immediately in search of a morning auditor whom he would like to have participate in the wonders he has lived through and is sometimes a little surprised that this auditor is not filled with wonder as he is. There are dark exceptions—there are fatal dreams—but for the most part we are happy with our dreams, we are proud of them; we have a naive pride befitting authors, certain as we are that we have created original works in our dreams, even if we refuse to claim any part in them. One must nonetheless ask oneself if such a work truly seeks to become public, if every dream seeks to be told, even while veiling itself. In Sumerian antiquity, one was advised to recount, to recite one's dreams. This was in order to release their magical power as quickly as possible. Recounting one's dreams was the best way to escape their bad consequences; or one might decide to inscribe their characteristic signs on a slab of clay, which one then threw into the water: the slab of clay prefigured the book; the water, the public. The wisdom of Islam nonetheless seems more reliable, which advises the dreamer to choose carefully the one in whom he will confide, and even to keep his secret rather than give it away at the wrong moment: "The dream," it is said, "belongs to the first interpreter; you should tell it only in secret, just as it was given to you. . . . And tell no one your bad dream."[3]

We recount our dreams out of an obscure need: to make them more real by living with someone else the singularity that belongs to them and that would seem to address them to one person alone; and further still, to appropriate them, establishing ourselves, through a common speech, not only as master of the dream but also as its principal actor and thus decisively taking hold of this similar, though eccentric, being that was us during the night.

~

Where does this eccentricity come from, this eccentricity that marks the simplest dream, makes of it a present, a unique presence to which we would like to make others besides ourselves the witnesses? The answer is perhaps first given by this word itself. Deprived of center or, better yet, slightly exterior to the center around which it is organized (or around which we reorganize it), and thus at an inappreciable—insensible—distance from us, is the deep dream from which we can nonetheless not say we are absent because, on the contrary, it brings with it an invincible certainty of presence. But to whom does it bring this? It is like a presence that would disregard or forget our capacity to be present in it. Do we not often have the impression that we are taking part in a spectacle that was not intended for us or that we have come upon some truth as from behind someone's shoulder, some image not yet grasped? This is because we are not truly there to grasp it; because what shows itself, shows itself to someone who is not there in person and does not have the status of a subject who is present. The fact that we are in the position of strangers in the dream, this is what first makes it strange; and we are strangers because the I of the dreamer does not have the meaning of a real I. One could even say that there is no one in the dream and therefore, in some sense, no one to dream it; whence the suspicion that when we are dreaming, it is just as easily someone else who is dreaming and who dreams us, someone who in turn, in dreaming us, is being dreamed by someone else, a premonition of the dream without dreamer, which would be the dream of the night itself. (An idea that from Plato to Nietzsche, from Lao-tzu to Borges, is found at the four cardinal points of dream thought.)

However, in this space that is, as it were, filled with an impersonal light whose source would escape us (we almost never succeed, even after the fact, in determining the lighting of a dream: as if it retained—diffuse, scattered, latent—its clarity in the absence of a

precise center of light and vision), there are figures that we can
identify and there is the figure that figures us. In Michel Leiris's
Nuits, not only do we find him in the different periods of his life,
we find his friends, who keep their names, perhaps their faces and
their usual singularity. Of course. Far from being absent, resemblances abound in dreams, for each person tends to be extremely,
marvelously resemblant: this is even his sole identity; he resembles,
he belongs to that region in which pure resemblance shines forth: a
resemblance that is sometimes certain and fixed; at other times,
always certain but unstable and wandering, though fascinating and
enthralling every time. Let us remember the bewitching power
with which any passerby seems to us endowed if, for an instant, he
becomes the bearer of some resemblance; how his face attracts us,
haunts us, familiar and remote, yet also frightens us a little; we are
in a hurry to identify it, that is, to erase it by redirecting it to the
circle of things in which living men are so bound up with themselves that they are without resemblance. A being who suddenly
begins to "resemble" moves away from real life, passes into another
world, enters into the inaccessible proximity of the image, is present nonetheless, with a presence that is not his own or that of
another, an apparition that transforms all other presents into appearances. And this resemblance, during the time—the infinite
time—that it asserts itself, is not an undecided relation to some
individuality or other; it is resemblance pure and simple and, as it
were, neuter. Whom does the resembler resemble? Neither this one
nor that one; he resembles no one or an ungraspable Someone—
as indeed one sees in deathly resemblance, when the one who
has just died begins to resemble himself, solemnly rejoining himself through resemblance, rejoining this impersonal, strange, beautiful being who is like his double slowly resurfacing from the
depths.

Such is the case in the dream: the dream is the place of similitude, an environment saturated with resemblances where a neutral
power of resembling, which exists prior to any particular designation, is ceaselessly in search of some figure that it elicits, if need be,
in order to settle on it. It is Faust's mirror, and what Faust sees is

neither the young girl nor something resembling her face, but resemblance itself, the indefinite power to resemble, the innumerable scintillations of reflection.[4] And let us note that the dream is often traversed by the premonition of this game of resemblance that is played out in it. How many times do we awaken to ask ourselves: But who is this being? And immediately, in the same instant, we find one person, or another, or yet another to answer for this being until the moment when the resemblance ceases to move furtively from figure to figure and allows itself to be reincorporated into a definitive form, in keeping with the waking self that alone has the power to interrupt the movement.

I will not develop these reflections further. We will not readily admit that the dreamer has only a relation of resemblance with himself, that he, too, is the Similar—the non-identical—and that, under this similitude, he is ready to become anyone or anything else. However, this self as image, which is but an image of Myself that is without any power to withdraw into itself, and thus to put itself in doubt, is, in its inflexible certainty, indeed a strange self, no more subject than object and rather the shadow of itself, a sparkling shadow that frees itself of us like a truer copy because it is at once more resemblant and less familiar. In the depths of the dream— admitting that it has a depth, a depth that is all surface—is an allusion to a possibility of being that is anonymous, such that to dream would be to accept this invitation to exist almost anonymously, outside of oneself, under the spell of this outside and with the enigmatic assurance of semblance: a self without self, incapable of recognizing itself as such because it cannot be the subject of itself. Who would dare transfer to the dreamer—be it at the invitation of the evil genius—the privilege of the *Cogito* and allow him to utter with full confidence: "I dream, therefore I am"? At most one might propose for him to say, "Where I dream, there it is awake," a vigilance that is the surprise of the dream and where there lies awake in effect, in a present without duration, a presence without person, the non-presence in which no being ever arises and whose grammatical formula would be the "He" that designates neither this one nor that one: this monumental "He" that Michel Leiris anxiously sees himself becoming when he looks at himself in the empty, lightless depth of his silo.

~

The dream is a temptation for writing perhaps because writing also has to do with this neutral vigilance that the night of sleep tries to extinguish, but that the night of dream awakens and ceaselessly maintains, while it perpetuates being in a semblance of existence. One must therefore specify that in borrowing from night the neutrality and uncertainty that belong to it, in imitating this power to imitate and to resemble that is without origin, writing not only refuses all the ways of sleep, the opportunities of unconsciousness, and the joys of drowsiness, but it also turns to the dream because the dream, in its refusal to sleep at the heart of sleep, is a further vigilance at the heart of the gathered night, a lucidity that is always present, moving, captive no doubt, and for this reason captivating. It is tempting to think that the impossibility of sleeping that sleep becomes in the dream brings us closer, through allusion and illusion, to the wakeful night that the Ancients called sacred, a night laden with and deprived of night, the long night of insomnia to which the unmastered movement of inspiration, in its undying appeal, corresponds every time that anteriority speaks to us: speaking, not speaking, indefinite, seeming to say everything to us before saying anything and perhaps saying everything to us, but only in a semblance of speech. "Were it not for the terrible nights of insomnia," said Kafka, "I would not write." And René Char, in a less anecdotal manner: "Poetry lives on perpetual insomnia." It lives on it, it passes through this night without night, as Michel Leiris has called it, a night that is doubly nocturnal in the absence and removal of itself, this night from which we, too, are removed and concealed; we are changed into that which stays awake and which, even when we sleep, does not let us sleep: suspended between being and non-being. As Hölderlin reminds us in such precise terms: "In the state between being and non-being, everywhere the possible becomes real, the real ideal, and in art's free imitation the dream is a terrible one, terrible but divine."

By means of a violent division, Mallarmé separated language into two forms almost without relation: the one, raw language, the other, essential language. This is perhaps true bilingualism. The writer is en route to a speech that is never already given: speaking, waiting to speak. He makes his way by always drawing closer to the language that is historically intended for him, a proximity, however, that challenges, sometimes gravely, his belonging to any native tongue.

Does one think in several languages? One would like to think, each time, in a single language, which would be the language of thought. But finally one speaks as one dreams, and one often dreams in a foreign tongue: it is the dream itself, this ruse, that makes us speak in an unknown speech, diverse, multiple, obscure in its transparency, as Jean Paulhan shows us with *Le Pont traversé*.

§ 18 The Ease
   of Dying

I think the first letter I received from Jean Paulhan is dated May
10, 1940: "We will remember these days," he said to me. Then,
eighteen years later there occurred a certain May 13 that, because of
its consequences, left us in disagreement—then another ten years,
and what happened prevented me from learning that Jean Paulhan
was beginning to move away, at a moment when, with the return of
the spring, it had been planned that we would see each other again.
I would first like to recall this gravity of history: not in order to use
it, by trying to evoke through it all that was grave, it seems to me, in
relations without anecdote. However, because only the unseen is
important in the end, the fact remains that great historical changes
are also destined, through all of the visibility that they carry with
them and by preventing anything but themselves from being seen,
to liberate more effectively the possibility of agreeing or of disagree-
ing intimately and as if by a mutual understanding, the private
keeping quiet in order for the public to speak, and thus finding
expression. Communism is this as well: the incommensurable
communication where everything that is public—and then everything is public—ties us to the other (others) through what is closest
to us.

∾ I often remarked that his narratives—which touched me in a
way that I can now better remember—almost all are written against

a background of war or by means of war even when the latter is not their subject. (Sometimes, brief allusions—*Progrès en amour assez lents*—sometimes nothing but a date—*Le Pont traversé.*) Too easily did I tell myself that we need the great void where war displaces us, depriving us of ourselves and according us only private happiness and unhappiness as privation, so that it should be possible for us then to speak of it, that is, really not to speak of it. I thought, moreover, that it was during wartime that Jean Paulhan most readily published his books—why? Perhaps in order to leave them in the margins of time; but perhaps also because we all have a need for this immense emptiness that frees us from the usual literary society, in such a way that the very act of publishing even under our own name, in a time outside of time, leaves us anonymous still or allows us, without too much immodesty, to hope to become anonymous.

∾ I am ready to think that Jean Paulhan only wrote narratives or always in the form of narrative. Whence the gravity that he would like, out of discretion, to make light for us, a search that does not end and is not interrupted except to take up again in a continuous movement (the movement of telling), even though this continuity can only hide the gaps that cannot be seen, and yet might let a light either pass through or lose itself, as it happens with the phenomenon of transparency. Whence also the feeling of a revelation, as in the dream where everything is manifest save the failing that allows the dream, ensures it, functions in it, and, as soon as one claims to have discovered it, dispels it in changing reflections. If everything is narrative, then everything would be dream in Jean Paulhan, up until the moment of awakening by darkness, just as writing is a dream, a dream so precise, so prompt to reveal itself, to say the word of the enigma, that it continues to reintroduce the enigma into the dream and, from there, to *reveal* itself as enigmatic. Let us remember the first paragraph of *Le Pont traversé*: "Scarcely had I made the decision to search for you than I answered myself with an abundance of dreams. This was already the next night; a dream does not have a beginning, but these dreams stopped when they were about to resolve themselves in a pure feeling and were so satisfying that there was no longer a need for images."

∿ It is perhaps through the movement of the narrative (the discontinuity of the continuous narrative) that we best know Jean Paulhan, who distances himself from the movement, but who also does not fail to confide himself insofar as he discovers—this is one of the first discoveries of the writer—that it suffices to say things for them not to be believed, to point to them for one no longer to see anything but the finger pointing (this is again Poe's "purloined letter," of which Jacques Lacan has made such good use). There is neither ruse nor perversity here, save that detour that is specific to writing-reading, this double game which he will henceforth try to account for by telling it, not only in order to make further use of it but to grasp, in this duplicity, the trace of a single Truth or the discovery of the secret *as* secret, thus identical to itself yet separate, secret in that it discloses itself. I would like to say, with a solemnity that, as certain letters of his show, was indistinguishable from modesty, that few philosophers today have been as impassioned as he with the One, the distracted certainty that the revelation, always deferred, always thwarted so that it might remain faithful to his patience, would not fail him even in the final failing. But what sort of Unity?

∿ "I do not doubt that I will one day discover the thought that will provide me at almost every moment with rapture, the absence of boredom. I have more than one reason to think that this discovery is close."

∿ I return to the idea of a narrative that goes from book to book, in which he who writes recounts himself in order to search for himself, then to search for the movement of the search, that is, how it is possible to recount, thus to write. But first it should be remarked that the search is rendered both more difficult and easier, insofar as happiness always precedes it, or at least an obvious joy— though it is but poorly felt—the joy of having already found and of constantly finding. The search begins here. This is why it takes the (fallacious) form of a narrative: as if, the thing having taken place, there remained only to tell how it took place and thus to search for it, less in memory than in order to be worthy of it and to respond to the always future promise that it represents. Otherwise, it might well be that it did not take place, and how would one know, were one not always able to find it again—anew? "Now that I see these adventures behind me, which have merged together, I am surprised that they are so simple. Their greatest quality is, no doubt, that they happened to me; this is also the most difficult to explain." And this, which is even more to the point: "Everything happens to me as if I had found a life that were *already* too far advanced. I would indeed bring myself up to date on things that are considered complicated, but I know it is the simplest things that I am missing; I do not want to cheat. Really the simplest."

It is that this simplicity is always already given and consequently lost. How does one find it again at the end and, Hegel would say, as result, thus produced and reproduced by this "cheating," the ruse of reason that I think never satisfied Jean Paulhan, for his under-standing of opposites put him at a distance, in a significant way, from the so-called dialectical process. (This is one of the most important features of his search.) Simplicity, the simplicity that is simple only in the duplicity of writing, must repeat itself in order to designate itself. It is thus only when it is split that it simplifies itself. And what must then be done for the first time to be the second time already (several times, *all* times—or the infinite)? In other words: in order to avoid the temptation of death, whose mediation offers itself to us in a manner that frightens us only in order to keep us from making use of it too easily.

∾ This relation to death—let us call it sickness—plays a role in narrative that should not be underestimated. As if being sick taught us all that is strange in the normal use of life that we receive from "recovery." ("Severe Recovery," "Imaginary Pains," "Letter to the Doctor," in which I reread the following, which disturbs us: "I sometimes think I feel several drops of blood lose their way in me, stray and form a sort of lake. I recognize the place by the confusion that occurs there. I hear, with my inner ear, an anxiety rise up in that place. . . . As if my body were trying to give me a signal that I could not manage to hear. . . . It is in a dream, usually, that I first see myself alerted. I wake up immediately. It seems to me that, by attending to it quickly enough, I will understand the warning.") Thus I do not have to dwell on it; it is with a modesty of vocabulary that is, moreover, the effect of the same movement (effacement), that the term *sickness* is proposed, protected by its lack of serious-ness (avowing nothing irreversible) instead of the word that would be capable—in what is it capable?—of ending all words. The narrator speaks readily of his indifference, either because he sees in it the reason for his passions (because one must make great efforts of feeling to move from such a lack of sensitivity), or because he responds to this indifference with a tireless curiosity that car-ries him toward so many things and people and that would seem to be more a proof of disinclination to be affected by himself and others—with this reservation, that he thus frees himself from kind-ness, a kindness that often embarrasses him (and masks his confu-sion), all the while protecting, through such dispersal, the only movement for which he feels an attraction: an obstinate relation to unity—unity of a single great design whose aim is also the divided relation to the One. But *indifference*: this is not a character trait. So, what is it? Nothing more than the ease of dying that we are awkwardly forbidden, however, by the very ease that leads us to suspend it; or, to speak more metaphysically, nothing less than the indetermination, the reserve of difference, that also always leaves indeterminate—for a lifetime—the question of knowing whether we are in the initial or the final indetermination.

∾ "Do I have the same sort of indifference for her that I dread having for myself?" "I was often surprised by my indifference. . . . I assumed that the failing was a common one. And the most com-monly expressed emotions in others easily seemed to me to be deliberate and of an artificial nature." "It has twice happened that I have made great discoveries—of those discoveries that change one's life. The first time, I was about ten years old, and it was not a happy discovery, no. It was this: that I was dumb. Dumb, or more exactly empty: thought did not come to me." "It is that I do not take my own side enough, out of a sort of indifference." "And certainly, it is true enough that few things touch me profoundly—but then again I also think that few things *should* touch us today." (This last quotation is excerpted from a letter to Marcel Arland.)

∾ The narrative reveals, but, in revealing it, hides a secret: more exactly, it conveys it. This secret is the visible-invisible attraction of any narrative, just as its effect is to transform texts that do not seem to belong to narrative practice into pure narrative. The secret: simply something to find, which gives some narratives a false air of being documents "à clef"; at the end we have the key, a way of opening up the story, of rewarding the anticipation, of producing the meaning by orienting it—the only difficulty being (which we are not always aware of) that this key itself has no key and that the way of explaining, which explains everything, remains without explanation; or else, on the contrary (and this is what makes the most beautiful, also the most resistant narratives), is nothing other than all of the narrative obscurity gathered, concentrated in a *single* point, the simplicity of which, in its literal sense, transports us, because we are taken back and forth, in the same moment, from beginning to end, from end to beginning, given everything in a single "detail," in the unity, in some sense, of a word. But this word sheds light only because it *reunites* the obscure dispersal of the parts, their dis-course: it is from here that this word gloriously refers us back to the great whole upon which it shines, until the moment when it is itself that seems to us not only secret but forbidden, excluded from the law that it proclaims. Furthermore, we sense that the narrative also has as its secret its very possibility, and along with it, the possibility of all narrative. Which leads to these questions: How does one make the continuous out of the discontinuous when raising both to the absolute, when maintaining both together, when ensuring their passage? And why this passage that confuses the exigency of a void with the affirmation of a plenitude, the hiatus that separates with the relation that unifies, the means with the obstacle? Why "the bridge crossed"?

∾ But let us search more patiently. If there is a secret, the secret that makes possible the flow of the narrative, then the narrative must possess it in advance but does not say so (at least directly), conveyed by what conveys it, and does not say so because to say it would be to withdraw it or to *reverse* it. But this secret, is it not precisely the mysterious "fact" of the reversal, reversal of the pro to the con about which Pascal, before Hegel, tells us and which he was, in a certain manner, wrong to tell us, if it is true that such an operation can work only on the condition that it not be proposed as a formulation that could preserve it only by nullifying it? This secret is thus the most common (and because it is too well known, fortunately unknown): it is something that belongs to everyone, the common ground by which, divided, we communicate without knowing it. That Jean Paulhan should have identified it in language, and even with language, to such an extent that he appears to have made language his sole study, and seems to see in this secret only the secret of languages, and not an implementation of the secret in languages—this we can understand; we could even say that it is of no importance to speak of the one in view of the others or conversely, because here, too, the law of reversal is in play. Thus, as soon as one has affirmed that language contains the secret (and would thus be beyond it), one must add that the secret is beyond language if it is not only that of which language always speaks without speaking of it, but that which gives it speech, on condition that it be itself left outside discourse.

∾ Pascal: from Pascal to Jean Paulhan, I would say that the procedure is the same, and sometimes the exigency. Nothing is more striking—more enlightening—than this kinship of minds so apparently dissimilar. The procedure: for the one, one must begin with diversion—equivocation or indecisive ambiguity—for the other, with an indifference in which everything is given without discernment. From this ambiguous or indifferent indecision, one must proceed to the distinction among differences, then to their being put in relation according to an opposition term by term, a juxtaposition so precisely structured that, in language, we always come up against something that gives itself as verbal *and* as nonverbal, then as meaning *and* non-meaning, then—always in discourse but already outside of it—as pure language *and* pure thought, then, in thought, as mind *and* world, then, outside of thought and thus always in it, as world *and* God, light *and* darkness, this both without end and necessarily (but perhaps this is what is surprising) not without end, if, in an experience that is momentarily ultimate or provisionally definitive, we succeed in covering in a single stroke and retaining in an irreducible term the mystery of this contrasted alternation, whose rigor is thus such and whose darkness so violent, so incompatible with the ego that is subject to it, that the ego, escaping as if by surprise or sinking into the void of a *passivity beyond all passivity*, gives way to an event at which it is not present but in which it participates (taking part, as it were, without knowing it), a naked event, whose absolute darkness is also absolute clarity: that which makes the whole clear. From which, henceforth, this exigency: to search for the anomaly in order to find in it the norm, to explain by means of the inexplicable, to think against thought, that is, *"according to mystery"*; exigency, it is true, that loses its necessity as soon as necessity is organized into a system, thus forcing the obscure part to be just an anticipated manner of seeing, or else appealing to incoherence only in order to bring out, in its deficiency, the coherence that has always in advance nullified (assimilated) it and can thus be reduced to itself.

∾ I question myself about the movement that, by juxtaposition, leads to a hidden God (certain as uncertain) and this other movement that makes illumination and night, law and its transgression, coincide in an experience both unique and banal. From one to the other, there is a difference that should not surprise us: the experience singled out by Jean Paulhan is a mystical experience, whereas Pascal's thought prohibits itself from being mystical. It is mystical because it recognizes itself in illustrious experiences of this sort ("one must also return to the mystics, the only ones, among all the philosophers, who openly test and in the end *realize* their philosophy"), but especially because it is no longer a matter, in this movement, of *knowing* but of *being*: "obscurity having become the reason of light, the problem having become the solution"—"but on condition that it *be* itself the realm of night and metamorphosis." Elsewhere, Paulhan speaks of ecstasy or transport, even if it must be added, in a gesture of modesty that is an effect of rigor, that the ecstasy is weak and the transport repeatable. Language itself (but perhaps we are, then, in relation to the mystical tradition, in a position of singularity because, according to this tradition, whether it be religious or not, the experience can have no relation to the act of saying, of writing, whereas here it is the saying that would be its first consequence and in some sense its "center") is also the place of this ecstasy, insofar as there could be no speech that did not make the irreconcilable compatible and did not maintain between the physical part and the idea part, between the "signifier" and the "signified," a distance, an interval, and a void of sorts; a small, impassable abyss that is nonetheless, at every moment and out of distraction, passed over (but never abolished) every time that language functions and that we accomplish this mystery through which we know what it means to speak. It is this void—minute, infinite—in which the conversion and the reversal take place, whether one calls it passage from signifier to signified, from subject to object, from thought to world, from visible to invisible—or, more precisely, it is in this void that the juxtaposition of terms, opposed two by two, is both experienced as radical difference, because discontinuity prevents these terms (or these moments) from following upon one another, and is consumed as unity if, through the conversion or the reversal that is realized in it, one regains the certainty that where there are two, it is nonetheless the One that governs: the Unique that would possess the relation of indifference of all differents. Thus, if indeed we want to listen for it, the exigency or the constraint is such that we must affirm—experience—the discontinuity, the division, or the split, in order to experience—to affirm—the Unity to which we not only belong but

"*in which we are merged*"—and every time (it is I who specify it,
perhaps in an exaggerated way), discontinuity, division, unity require that they be thought and carried to the absolute.

ɷ Therefore one must not be fooled by the modesty of expression: it is a formidable experience, to which we are called to testify,
one that is always at a loss in relation to itself and to whoever makes
claims in its name. Only at rare moments did Jean Paulhan agree to
come out of his reserve, sometimes in public texts: experience or
thoughts "that one reaches in a flash and that one cannot sustain,
but from which, once they have appeared, the visible world un-
winds ad infinitum with its brilliance and its night," sometimes in
letters (to M.A.): "In the course of a life each person inevitably
suffers an experience that is almost intolerable, for which a place
must henceforth be made if he wants to live and live sound of
mind." To which he adds, in order to mark his distance from
religious experience: "It goes without saying that religious faith is a
way of coming to terms with this terrible experience and, *by
extending it to all of life*, of removing its venom from it: if you like, a
way of attenuating the poison." "This gives rise to many events,
which are not necessarily joyful. How I pulled through, I don't
know. . . . As long as all of this leaves no traces! This is what I fear
sometimes in what I write."
    But I would like to mark another difference between the re-
ligious way of proceeding, be it a mystical one, and the way that
Jean Paulhan proposes to himself or proposes to us: and this is that
the former way agrees to succeed (rapture and ecstatic union being
the gift and the sign of success), whereas the latter way implies, if
not its failure, at least its breakdown: the fault, failing, or lack
through which it allows itself to be seized or seizes us and, in seizing
us, releases us or slips away. This is why "there is no rest." For the
very failing that would belong to the ultimate experience and
would be its proof (just as, earlier, it is the lack of coherence or the
want of meaning with which reason endeavored to see itself completed and, hence, justified, recognizing in it *something other* than
itself), such a failing, from this point on, as it becomes the promise

or the condition of experience, reestablishes itself as its necessary part, and thus invests and affirms itself in experience and immediately fails its failing, "like an argument that is less convincing the more convincing it is." This is why, of course, we cannot be satisfied with anything. This is also why the process is itself marked by the juxtaposition that it seeks obscurely to bring to light, a patient, obstinate, modest procedure and one that is always clearly and calmly articulated, as the procedure of a scientist must be, a procedure that is nonetheless "mystical" if it tends toward the inexplicable with a view to explaining; and if it engages us, through the transports of narrative, in an experience in which it is given not to know but to be and, more precisely, to feel the suspension of being, in the place where a certain interruption, introducing its play, furthers the reversal and the metamorphosis. Or else, let us say that this method or this procedure is itself also, being both a procedure of science and a procedure of non-knowledge, the disjunction of the two and the hesitation of the mind between the former and the latter, that is to say, in turn, their mutual suspension before the jump, this leap that alone would allow one to accomplish the forbidden passage from one to the other.

∾ "The secret that we are pursuing could well enough be told: none of the differences in the world to which you attach such great importance exist. Everything is one."

∾ Perhaps one should add that the work of science prepares the leap, not only by making it easier (for example, by bringing out this general structure of juxtaposition that reflection, out of either indifferent simplicity or ambiguous indecision, understands and itself puts into practice) but also by making it difficult, because it succeeds, through interrogative analysis, in making the emptiness that interrupts these terms appear between them, and in *fixing* attention on the necessity of the impossible passage and thus, by arresting the leap as it accomplishes itself, in making it almost fatal. Thus it is as if the test—through which the meaning of this transport is revealed, or rather than its meaning, its reality as event—implied its nonaccomplishment, or as if we were aware of the leap only when, through our illicit discovery, we prevented it from realizing itself, and thus aggravating it, we gave it its proper scope, which would be to coincide with the eventuality of a death.

If it is certain that anyone at all can accomplish the leap with the help of distraction, which would allow him to cross the abyss with great strides and continuously, and if it is certain that such a leap passes by way of what would have to be called (and how otherwise?) death itself, we could conclude that it is the "ease of dying" that, in any life, shields us from death or makes us neglect, forget to die. How discreet, therefore, one must remain in not using words that are too categorical, and here I find one of the reasons that guards Jean Paulhan against all language that is intentionally moving or strong or dark: the casualness that he allows himself to be suspected of at times is indeed at the same time a defense against the spirit of weightiness that hinders the reversal—the volte-face—an invitation nonetheless to leap, and also an insistence on levity that seems by contrast to warn us, and that turns us back toward gravity, but to an uncertain gravity that is lacking the guarantee of the serious.

Indeed, I see that Jean Paulhan does not readily consent, in terms so direct, to mention the exigency to die, which is, perhaps, constantly in play in experience except, that is, in letters (always addressed to Marcel Arland): "I mean: this emptiness that can hardly *be felt*, from and to ourselves, except as a sort of death." And this avowal: "It seems to me that what I feared for a long time was much less death than the longing to die (a longing I felt myself capable of having, from one moment to the next). It can hardly be told." An avowal, no doubt, but one that touches experience in its secret. For as soon as the suggestion of a decisive absence has been made to us or as soon as thought is invited to open itself to its own discontinuity in order to complete itself as thought, it is almost the ease of the movement, the temptation of being able to give in to the movement immediately (without having had "the time" even to complete it), that risks interposing itself and taking away the possibility of the movement. *The ease of dying*: such would be the danger watching over us.

~ Let us take this from another angle: the only means of being reasonable is not to claim to be free from all unreason, nor yet (supposing this could be) to remove ourselves from it in effect, but rather to make unreason so close to us, so accessible, so familiar that we constantly pass through it, lightly, without lingering or dwelling on it. Reasonable out of a negligent practice of unreason such that unreason would make itself invisible: that is, saved by the speed of the shipwreck.

Still there must be a shipwreck, madness, and this rapid death capable of shielding us from itself by turning us away from its "longing." That it should be so easy to die to the point of feeling its attraction and, subject to this attraction, of dying as if inadvertently: this is the danger, a double danger, for either we die, as it were inattentive, or else the inattentiveness permits us to live because in this inattentiveness we are not able to perceive that the distraction is the very touch of death. But it is also a danger that *keeps watch*: this vigilance is the "subject" of the experience, that which undergoes it, leads it, precipitates it, and holds it back in order to delay it at its moment of imminence, if this experience consists first in suppressing itself or in making itself possible through its suppression, because the Unity, which is its end, does not give itself as such until the moment at which all the differences that designate it are erased by erasing it. Just as, through language and "in spite of their appearance, thing, word or thought amount to the same and are but one," which implies that each of these terms renounces the identity that distinguishes it and, in renouncing it, destroys this concept of the "same" that seems to found the understanding of the "One," so the "*All-One*" that scorns differences (according to Jean Paulhan) nonetheless receives from these differences the condition that functions only by obstructing them.

Whence this essential trait: it is never full-face but rather at an angle that this "single world in which we are merged" presents itself (thus outside presence)—it is through a deflection that the simple surprises us, through indirection that the straight surprises us, and through indifference, the reserve of differences, that we are surprised by the indifference in which these differences, having become opposed, refer back to the One in which they obliterate each other (fold back into pure simplicity).

෨ I would like to mark again and more distinctly the intentions, characteristics, and conditions of such a movement in that which discloses it.

 1. It is not a matter of personal experience. Jean Paulhan does not claim to discover anything that is specific to him. His task, on the contrary, is, on the one hand, to show why and how the knowledge, which anyone at all has fully at his disposal, is lost or split—in opposing theses—as soon as attention is drawn to it; on the other hand, as a result of the attention directed in some sense against attention or as the result of a new procedure, to return to the whole of knowledge (the initial non-difference), enriched, however, by the knowledge of the illusions that had destroyed it and the recognition of this void—this death—a moment tragically fixed and through which one had to pass in order to return. Procedure thus, I would emphasize, of the scientist and the non-scientist, at the intersection of the two and permitting perhaps, if not their reconciliation, at least a better understanding of the necessity of their opposition. That such a procedure should satisfy no one, neither linguists (for example) nor philosophers, is understandable. Literature, which welcomes everything, is, alone, prepared to welcome it, either academically, by taking advantage of the benevolence made perceptible by a concern for the conciliation of opposites and in order to better deprive a work qualified as perfectly literary of its most savage part, or esoterically, in the name of the secret that reveals itself as secret in the work and that literature animates without exposing.

 2. Unity. Again I ask the question: What sort of unity? The answer could itself only be ambiguous, diverted from any one possibility. The formulation that Jean Paulhan uses most readily indeed remains—it seems to me—the one I have just recalled: this "single world in which we are merged" or, to quote more fully: "It is

a society whose members—all of us, just about—know how, in any language, to recognize or at least suspect the sacred presence of a single world in which we are merged. Or if one prefers of a God that our divisions, our study, our sciences tear apart." This "single world," divine in its unity, is nonetheless a world. It is not the One that, as such, would transcend Being, as Plato invited us to think it in the Good. (Jean Paulhan speaks in some places, however, of a "transcendent event," terminology that is quite rare in his work, which uses very few scholastic terms.) This single world in which we are merged is coextensive with us and thus exceeds us from all quarters, and furthermore is radically alien to us, being the absolute exteriority of thought that is integrally united with it. Thus the experience that seems the most important to Jean Paulhan is the one that would verify "the reality of the external world," an experience that does not, except in appearance, correspond to the traditional problem, for what comes to affirm itself here is the shattering surprise of the outside itself, shattering because it enters as if by chance into our own coherence, in order to draw us from it, draw us from ourselves, and, in this withdrawal, deprive us of an "I who am All," transporting us—pure transport or trance or *trans*—into the One. "All-One": formula of supreme duality and of ultimate unity, or of the irreducible duplicity of the One.

3. Still, Jean Paulhan cannot be satisfied with a simple affirmation that would restore "the sacred presence of a single world" by making "our sciences, our study, and our divisions" responsible for what tears it apart. For this again would be to regard as inessential not only this study and these sciences, but also (beyond knowledge) the exigency of discontinuity that possesses, through the gap and non-coincidence of which thought learns in completing itself, the possibility of the One, which is postulated and discovered only in the fleeting perspective of infinite difference. For it is not simply, in the metaphor of the Möbius strip, a matter of showing that there is a displacement thanks to which infinity would be met when inside and outside, up and down are erased: it must be further shown that restored continuity depends on this displacement or reversal, on

this twisting or recasting that the continuous is unable to account for (and is even less able to make possible).

This is to recall, I think, two (inevitable) difficulties:

a) When one moves from the indecisive indifference and returns to a recognized non-difference, following the passion of the One, it is necessary not only to pass through the work of differences, but to decide that the structure of these differences is what is called binary, and can be reduced to a rigorous opposition of terms to terms that are always disjointed two by two. (Whence this *and* that is so often made visible by italics in the statements proposed to us: sound *and* meaning, language *and* thought, thought *and* world, time *and* space, the *and* splitting itself into an *and/or*, that is, an alternative of opposition that would, in the end, coincide with a nonsimultaneous simultaneity.) To posit in advance all plurality, including dispersion, as reducible to alternate duality—because the latter, as Heraclitus had already formalized it, would enter into an ordering: "disperses itself-assembles itself"—is to submit beforehand to the unitary procedure that one rediscovers because one has always postulated it.

b) The same opposition discontinuity-continuity (which, moreover, paradoxically, is presupposed if between discontinuous and continuous there must already be a prior discontinuity) forces us to ask ourselves whether the void, which the *and* covers over and points to, is the *same* every time in every relation of juxtaposition of terms. Let us assume this continuous chain of discontinuities: sound/meaning, language/thought, thought/world; what would lead us to regard the hiatus between the terms or figures or positions as identical every time? Why would there be an identity among disparities? And why would the discontinuous, even without escaping a ruled usage, not be such that it would assume a function that is *other* every time and, with this function, specify itself as difference always different? In other words, are we not already thinking this rupture or division unitarily and according to the principle of the Same, a rupture or division that might attempt to distract us temporarily from this principle in order to keep hold of the continuous thread in this play of closeness and remoteness—the true clew of

Ariadne—because of which we always succeed, lost but not irremediably so, in finding our way out of the labyrinth of dispersion?

Unless this void is implicitly thought or carried to the absolute and the absolute, as such, necessarily escapes all distinction (all plurality). But is infinity not—save if an exigency intervenes that would then have to be called purely religious, indeed ethical—indifferent to the One as well as to the Not-One? In the same way that the division (this division sound/meaning, language/thought, discourse/writing) is perhaps so decisive only because it is minute and therefore such that it can also be considered functionally null and even a supplementary mark of unity, and yet (like any infinitesimal) unidentifiable, thus alien to identification as well as all unification. In such a way that the infinitely small division—disjunction—would possess the radical non-relation to which the One could not apply, be it as lack, if it is a matter of indifference whether the One governs or does not govern this non-relation. In such a way also that, in the presence of the reunited God, unity would finally be made to fail only by the division that does not divide—the split that leaves (God) undivided and, in this indivision, always already divided, with no relation of presence and/or absence.

∾ "As if our world existed alongside some other world, invisible ordinarily, but whose intervention, at decisive periods, were alone able to save it from collapse."

"But how does one succeed in seeing at first glance things for the second time?"

". . . and I, I let myself go to the pleasures of a death that my body was the first to suspect."

"This life of anticipation and assent."

"Who shows me to be wrong attracts me. Who shows me to be right, I imagine that he has not truly understood me; I do not readily take my own side. As if, to be satisfied, I were waiting to be both others and myself."

"Here begins my despair as a writer."

∾ The narrative alone gives space, by withdrawing it, to the experience that impedes itself, at all of its moments and on all of its levels, including in this the appeal of the One to which experience is subject and which it obstinately designates as the obsession that turns it against itself, to such an extent that it cannot be a question of experience—as something that takes place or could take place— but rather of non-experience and, as it were, of a call to make itself manifest by suspending (deferring) manifestation. These are the stakes of the narrative, the ceaselessness that the narrative carries with it and that, while preventing the narrative from realizing itself, leads it to the formal perfection that is, in Jean Paulhan, its painful denial, in order to respond better to the exigency of incompletion. An easy death thus remains, in the very clear expression that contains this subversive proposition, the evidence of the secret by which we are always questioned, because we do not know that at every moment of writing-reading we constitute the answer to it. The easy death from which we believe we protect ourselves, al- though it is always already out of the question to escape it, is thus the manner in which transgression—this step beyond and belong- ing to the outside—proposes itself to the failing of the Law, exceed- ing the latter as that which cannot be exceeded, or more enigmat- ically producing the Law only by infraction, as if the limit—a limit *impossible* to transgress—could be marked only by the decision that had already broken it in its "may-be." This is what writing an- nounces to us, writing tied to the appeal without desire of "an easy death": that there is no "law" save by transgression, and certainly no transgression save in the eyes of the "law," but with no reciproc- ity whatsoever, no relation of symmetry between the two; for just as in the law all transgression not only refers to it but confirms it, so, in the step that trans-gresses, that is, accomplishes its beyond (thus designating the unknown), the prohibition finds a space in which to legislate only through the adventure and the future of the unknown that has always "made fun" of the interdiction.

Transgression designates the limit in its beyond; the law designates the limit from within; between the two, in the interval of irregularity, this alleged limit rules—the same yet never the same— a caesura all the more decisive in that it may be nothing or infinite (concerning neither affirmation nor negation), because, according to the perspective of the law, the limit is absolute delimitation (impassable even if it is passed over) and, according to the absence of perspective of a transgression, the limit is only the "as if" (a turn whose power of transport Jean Paulhan has precisely reinvented) that serves to measure, by rendering it incommensurable, the complete through the violence of incompletion. Line thus of demarcation that marks, by means of a mere nothing, the distance taken from one indetermination to the other, that is, a nothing, or the indeterminable, separating nothing from nothing (and yet nothing that is null if the law, as if in advance, always establishes itself in this nothing to demarcate itself from it). "It is impossible," says the Law in effect. "Impossible," says the transgression—every impossible, every time, first declaring itself. The radical difference, in the absolute identity of the two terms, the one tending to mark the extreme of the possible, the other, the indeterminate space of non-power, this difference of the identical or this non-identity of the same (invisible fissure of unity) belongs to a writing that conveys death, "an easy death."

∾ "And my first awkwardness at defending myself against the ease it takes to die."

∾ An easy death. Let us remember one last time the constraints of this double word, simplicity itself. (1) Death: the prohibition erased or suspended by the ease of dying. (2) But the ease, far from erasing it, heightens what is most scandalous in the scandal par excellence that is mortal violence. Dying—the impossibility—is easy. (3) Death forbidden and indiscreet, the death conveyed by and conveying writing, is restored to the secret of discretion by a reading, an innocent, happy, *easy* reading. (4) "The ease it *takes* to die": ease, power to do, pure power to produce that comes to us— through a violent *seizure*, however—from the disposition given in what must be suffered absolutely, the passivity of the most passive; but also the singularity of writing, which is a unique "doing" that only reading, in its repetition, can render such that it does and undoes itself; and because repetition is the mode of mortal absence, reading, in its ease, holds in turn, reversed, the power of death that writing, as unique violence, has spirited away at the detour of this death.

Thus it is through the duplicity of an easy death that the reversal is accomplished, reversal whose possibility Jean Paulhan maintained and mastered for a moment, at the cost of his life's patience, the possibility as once and always again it had been revealed to him, like an inexhaustible secret, by *reading-writing*, the play of the necessity of an indifferent difference.

§ 19 The Laughter
of the Gods

I do not know whether it is owing to his narrative, *Le Baphomet,*
and to the reedition of the big *Roberte*[1] trilogy that the importance
and singularity of Pierre Klossowski as writer, man of thought, and
creator of a world of images will finally appear under a light that is
suitable—a light that will preserve the obscurity and preserve itself
from too dazzling an appearance. It would be easy, by making it
appealing or picturesque, to make this work exaggeratedly visible,
be it by means of a few biographical details smugly attributed to its
author; the distant memory of Rilke, the more present memory of
Gide, a few images escaped from the surrealist hearth, then the
turns and detours of a strange vocation that receives many names,
demands many forms, and, from theology to marriage, complicates
itself without ever renouncing any of its acquisitions until it finds
its center of gravity in the essential complications of writing. From
all this, one could find detail enough to compose a public figure,
after the fashion of Jouhandeau. But this is something that need
not be feared. Whatever the recognition may be, discretion will
remain its center. Discretion is here the guardian power, guardian
of a thought that is not content with a simple truth nor even
perhaps with the too simple name of truth, guardian also of a work
plastically rich and no less abstractly tenebrous.

Thus I will content myself with several comments intended

to prepare a reading by situating the reading rather than contribute
to it.

1. Here is a work that is principally literary, even if its richness
and its strangeness give one the right to see in it the suggestion of a
new gnosis. As a literary work, it brings to literature what, since
Lautréamont and perhaps always, it has lacked: I will call it the
hilarity of the serious, a humor that goes much further than the
promises of this word, a force that is not only parodic or a force of
derision, but calls forth a burst of laughter and points to laughter
as the goal or ultimate meaning of a theology (later we will see how,
if we get this far). *Roberte ce soir* is in this regard a marvelous
book. How can one not be grateful to the person who has written
it? And how can one not be surprised that there ever could be, in
some author, through I do not know what privileged coincidence,
so much innocence and so much perversity, so much severity and
so much impropriety, an imagination so ingenuous and a mind so
learned, to give rise to this mix of erotic austerity and theological
debauchery, from which a sovereign movement of ridicule and
levity is born? A laughter without sadness and without sarcasm that
asks for no spiteful or pedantic participation, but on the contrary
asks for the giving up of personal limits, because it comes from far
away and, traversing us, disperses us in the distance (a laughter in
which the emptiness of a space resounds from the limitlessness of
the void). I think that in order to understand the most important
moments in Klossowski's work well, one must know how to laugh
about them, laugh with this laughter they give us, which echoes
their intensity.

2. Of this work, centered around a laugh that, at times, is
bursting forth, at others dissimulated and seemingly stifled by its
burst, I would like to point out another feature that makes it, in
spite of everything that sets it apart, very close to the modern
characteristics of literature: by this I mean the use of the indirect.
The first narrative, *La Vocation suspendue*, gives us the simplest
example of this, insofar as it is a novel that is the exegesis of another

novel. Unnecessary complication or convenient expedient? I see another exigency in it. Let us first call it discretion. But discretion is not simply politeness, social behavior, a psychological ruse, the adroitness of the one who would like to speak intimately of himself without revealing himself. Discretion—reserve—is the place of literature. The shortest path from one point to another is in literature the diagonal or the asymptote. He who speaks directly does not speak or speaks deceptively, thus consequently, without any direction save the loss of all straightforwardness. The correct relation to the world is the detour, and this detour is right only if it maintains itself, in the deviation and the distance, as the pure movement of its turning away. Without being overly concerned with external verisimilitude, Pierre Klossowski has recourse to multiple procedures: newspaper, exposition, dialogue, comedy, historical staging, description of gestures, commentary of myths. Strange imaginary tableaux or, failing this, scenes, as if arrested in their visible immobility, constitute the essential moments of a plot that obeys a necessary play of multiplication. And these tableaux or these scenes, intended to be seen (sometimes even translated into large-scale illustrations) and thus to satisfy both the one who looks and the one who likes to be seen—scenes subtly laid out by provocative spirits and certainly provocative, but finally, above all, provoking in us the divine part, laughter—essentially deceive sight in reality, for, described minutely and giving rise to an infinite exegesis, these scenes are carried forward by speech that, by dint of revealing, re-veils, and by dint of describing, does not show, but hides what it shows under the multiplicity of a description that is purely (impurely) spoken.

We have here a particularly beautiful and perfidious usage of the indirect. A tableau, in general, appeals to this sense of straightforwardness that is sight. No doubt, what we see in the world and, all the more so by means of plastic art, we see only at a distance, through distance and on condition that we do not touch it: the intact—the inaccessible—alone is visible.[2] However, in compensation, what I see, be it far off, be it the distant star, I see immediately; the light that assumes an emptiness between the eye and the object

and illumines only by means of this emptiness, being this emptiness itself illumined, also obliterates it, instantaneously (instan-
taneity that Descartes was right, philosophically, to raise to the
status of physical law). Only what is, though at a distance, in a
relation that is direct and without mediation lets itself be seen. Yet,
the imaginary tableaux and scenes, which are no less imaginary,
play, in Klossowski's narratives, the role of the unimaginable and,
in the mode of a language rigorously reflexive, see themselves (this
is, in effect, almost visible) withdrawn from the immediate, which
is their place, in order to be introduced into the place of a reflection
in which everything at first suspends itself and stops itself, as if at
the very threshold of vision, and then reflects itself—that is, splits
itself off, dissolves itself, even goes so far as to withdraw itself into
pure abstract invisibility (thus attaining its greatest power of evocation). Nothing more impressive and more telling than such a
detour by which sight sees itself deceived—rewarded also—turned
away to the benefit of I do not know what turbid spirit of obscurity.

3. Pierre Klossowski's books are narratives, even when they com-
ment on myths, as in the profound book entitled *Le Bain de
Diane*.[3] As narratives, they recount, describe, state, intrigue. Some
will say that they are theological; others, that they are erotic; others,
that they are psychoanalytic. I think that we should not take great
account of such qualifiers. Rather, I am struck by a trait of originality that manifests itself in the invention of a new form, in truth
destined to remain unique. Let us read, unfamiliar and knowing
nothing of their author, these singular works. We will not fail to be
drawn in by the feeling that something grave is at play in them and
that this gravity, which can be revealed in laughter, evidently
touches the fate of the one who writes before it comes to touch the
one who is called upon to read (to complete the closed cycle of
writing). But what is at issue here? We are well aware that what is
happening here, even if it relates to an intense reality, has a relation
to this reality that is not only not direct but excludes the unfortunate indirectness that is allegory, symbol, or parable. I would not
even call it a literature of experience. Certainly, an experience is

pursued, but as if imposed by a *sign* that remains outside of any practice. This sign, the strangest one, signifies only itself. A sign that one could call arbitrary, mysterious, secret (without secret), like a living point that would express and affirm the energetic life of thought reduced to the unity of this point. A sort of intense coherence, in relation to which everyday life, the one that is content with the everyday system of signs, becomes, both within and without, the place of an intolerable incoherence. And the sign is itself without guarantee (there is no God behind it, nor any sovereign Reason).[4] Perhaps even to see in it the trace of a thought at its unique point of coherence and intensity is already too much. Thus, it happens that someone is invested by such a sign to the point of being reduced to the unique exigency of this intense sign whose pure intensity constantly returns to itself, without beginning or end. In a postface to the reedition of *Roberte*, Klossowski explains this in the most dramatic pages abstract writing has to offer us today. But it seems to me that every writer, in his way, also knows this experience, which is that of a man enclosed in a circle drawn around him—a circle, or rather an absence of circle, the breaking of this vast circumference from which days and nights come forth to us.

Yet, this unique sign in which thought designates itself and which thought arbitrarily designates as its perfect coherence, demands its disclosure: first, because one cannot live without madness in the unique relation with a unique sign, but also at the same time because this sign, arbitrary to the highest degree, without guarantee and refusing all guarantee, causes any life that does not submit to its supreme coherence to shatter as incoherent and mad. Thus, madness threatens from both sides: the madness that comes to thought through thought, when the latter is called on to reduce itself to its unique coherence, and the madness that comes to us from everyday incoherence, if we resist—to the point of eluding it—the madness of a unique coherence and its intense constraint. Disclosure is therefore necessary. It is already given in advance in the empty sovereignty of the sign, this movement of intensity that always returns to itself, like the circle—the absence of circle—

drawn by writing. But how can this disclosure occur? How can the unique coherence of the sign find anything to satisfy it in the incoherent diversity in which the ego that lives and the lived world achieve their everyday happiness and unhappiness? How can one avoid the delirium, the false glare that the disclosure of the sign would not fail to take on, insofar as, even without compromise, this sign would have to compromise itself with other external signs? Delirium is no doubt inevitable, just as compromise is inevitable, that is, a certain imposture. The sign, whose intense and empty sovereignty has seemingly devastated and pillaged memory, denounces itself, one day, in the simplicity of a name—the name Roberte, for example. This is, as it were, admissible. The name itself is also unique; it is silent; it does not give away anything but itself; it is the sign denouncing itself in the pure silence of its coherence. However, the movement is already malicious. The malice consists in this: that henceforth, as name, the sign will also correspond to a physiognomy—even if it means eliciting it—that will be external to it: a physiognomy, silent in its turn, a great figure that will say nothing, and even when it lets itself be seen in the most provocative manner, will continue to belong to the sovereign invisibility of the sign. A name without incident, a great mute figure, always given in the oblivion of words and stories with which it seems nonetheless to agree when, in turn, it becomes a portrait accompanied by other figures, a narrative peopled by events and intended to teach us a lesson of sorts, a lesson that in turn affirms itself in the institution of a custom: for example, *Les Lois de l'hospitalité*. One can therefore say that, step by step, the sign, in the inevitable compromise that the madness to be avoided demands, thus finds its equivalent in the strange situation that this strange custom seeks to represent. But the word *equivalent* is deceptive, unless it is taken in a new sense: it "stands for," but not in the way in which, in symbol or in allegory, the sign stands for some transcendent or immanent meaning. For here it is the meaning that stands for the sign, and the equivalence is never given in an equality, even an infinite one, but rather in a pure inequality. For example (this is only a superficial example): the complexity of the intrigue, a complexity that seems to be the secret law of Klossowski's narratives, goes, as it were, against the simplicity of the sign that cannot even be called simple, but rather pure intensity, an intensity that demands to be expressed only in a reversed manner (by the vicissitudes of the detour), pillaging memory, certainly, but in order to devastate it; devastating it, but in order to make an emptiness in it, and bringing complexity to it, because it destroys all identity, all unity, but perhaps under the constraint exerted by an always unidentifiable unity.[5]

4. How can we approach the unique sign as it is deployed in the inequivalence of narratives, in themselves without equivalents, which affirm the influence of the sign only by moving away from it? I will, for my part, remain discreetly on the side, seeking only to designate certain means of access through which the space of these narratives might open itself to us. One sometimes has the impression that Pierre Klossowski is standing courageously at the center of a shattered region that is besieged and fought over by the violence of three foreign discourses: the sadistic discourse, the Nietzschean discourse, and, most perverse of all, the theoretical discourse. Foreign to one another, what do they have in common? Might one not first venture to say of Sade that he is a major theologian, the only theologian, in the very impossibility of his being Sade? Yes, how can one be Sade? How can one be the absolute negator of God, the fundamental atheist, without also being, by virtue of a reversal, the affirmer of an absolute that is more venerable still? How can one derive pleasure and truth from such a negation, if this negation does not give itself, as a limit to be violated, precisely that which it always denies in its very non-limitation? The falsity of all direct discourse already leads one to pose such a question, but from the opposite direction. To speak directly of pure things (assuming that there are any), to speak of pity, of saintliness, and of virtue, as if such possibilities were already given in ordinary language, that is, as if they were possibilities of this language, is to speak the most vicious and impious language. This is why all moralizing language is not only ineffectual (which would be almost laudable) but

corrupting. And so it is said, in *La Vocation suspendue*, that the task of the Christian novelist is much more to thwart the unpredictable ways of the Lord than to imagine them—though it must not be any easier to thwart the unpredictable, even by exposing it *a contrario*; it would be better to give oneself over to chance, to true, mysterious chance, and here we would be approaching surrealism: the only god is chance. It is therefore tempting, when one reverses the discourse, to ask the violence of a provocative language for the resources or powers of anguish capable of silencing what speaks vainly in us: Is it not always the sacrilege that attests to the sacred? And is the transgression not the most true relation, the relation of passion and life, to the prohibition that transgression does not cease to pose and to presuppose in a contact in which flesh is dangerously made spirit? On condition, it is true, of turning the discourse around again and of saying that if transgression requires an interdiction, the sacred requires sacrilege, such that the sacred, which is attested to purely only by the impure speech of blasphemy, will not cease to be indissociably linked to a power always capable of transgression.

Where does this power come from, this power that is in one sense the most mysterious, the least speakable? Is it second? Is it first? Though nonidentical, is it not the same as the Sovereign Power? And if the Other has always been what represents evil, its place or its spirit, will we not perceive, through a discovery that will shatter us, that the Other is other only insofar as it is the Same, though nonidentical; insofar, therefore, as the Other, being the same, denounces in this way the non-identity of the Same? The consequences are infinite, not only for the exposition of "last questions" and what one calls the spiritual domain, but even as far as our logic is concerned, in which the calm principle of identity suddenly finds itself demolished, without, however, ceding its place to the no less calm principle of opposition that is invoked by the dialectic. For the negative (let us call it the "spiritual power of malice") no longer consists in what is opposed to the same, but in pure similitude, in the minute distance and the insensible gap, not even in the deception of imitation (which always pays homage to the portrait), but in this strange principle: that in the place where there are likenesses, there are an infinity of likenesses, and where infinity glitters in the plurality of distinct indiscernibles, the image must cease to be second in relation to an alleged first object and must lay claim to a certain primacy, just as the original and finally the origin will lose their privileges as initial powers.

Of course, I am simplifying; I am only trying to indicate an order of questions. Where is the sacred, where is the sacrilege, if they are not only indissociable but indifferent, even in respect to the intensity of their difference? Should we, like Sade, exhaust language linearly, should we say everything, nullifying the interdiction, in order to resuscitate it in this inter-diction—the rupture of inter-ruption—to which only he who never stops speaking has access? Or else must we understand that transgression—the exceeding of the unexceedable limit—is not only a possibility that is more difficult than others, but points to that which, being radically outside our reach, is open to man only when the personal power or control that is in him (be it raised to the highest degree) ceases to be the ultimate dimension? The interdiction, in this case, is no longer the positivity that transgression—as would happen in Hegelian logic—would need in order to further negativity, which would then be content with restoring it at a higher level until some definitive absolute was reached; the interdiction marks the point at which *power* ceases (and, at this point, the primacy of the *ego* as well as the logic of identity), whereas transgression is the experience of what escapes power, the *impossible* itself.[6]

5. Let us stop here. I have said enough to show how and why the incessant mutations that reverse, inflect, and grip Klossowski's narratives as well as his syntax are different from dialectical reversal. Fascinating reversals. The "laws of hospitality," which provide at present the general title for the trilogy, are not in the least susceptible of a simple, even singular meaning. If, after almost becoming a priest, the strange theologian who is married wants to give Roberte to the host each time, it is because the saintliness of the sacrament of marriage demands the gift; the wife is the sacred itself, the

unique, the inexchangeable singularity. To give one's wife to the other is the gift par excellence, the renewed act of the consecrator who has received the power to share the undivided "real presence." High power in which the temptation of a malefic spiritual pride is reflected—but is it still a power? In the same way, is the husband who gives away his wife, pushing the guest to some adultery, not content to give in to the temptation to do evil without doing it, by having it performed more comfortably by others? But it is more profoundly that one must search for the meaning of an act that appears so unreasonable. The stranger to whom the gift without return should be made is, according to the ancient mode of thought, the unknown and, as such, the very presence of the god (as if the sacred, through an act of repetition, could be given only to the sacred, which confirms that the gift is the sacred twice over); the unknown to whom the wife is consecrated without reserve is therefore what must reveal the unknowable in her, her secret, the part that familiarity, intimacy, and the usual knowledge of memory dissimulate, this divine part that belongs to *oblivion* and that Octave, the perverse theologian, can know only indirectly through the gift without reciprocity, from which he himself is excluded, yet participating in it fully if he is its initiator. But is he the initiator or the puppet or at most a mediocre, clever director? And this incommunicable identity that communication must render visible, revealing to us what Roberte's true face is and what her naked being is—her large and beautiful ungloved hands, her austere, unsheathed body—is communication's effect not to multiply her, that is, to multiply the identical, to repeat Roberte, to such a degree that we must live, like Theodore, henceforth in the realm of a plot that divides and proliferates, in which every event is nonetheless tied to the center—a center always decentered—by a rigorous relation? All the more so that Roberte, for her part, in substituting, out of a healthy atheism and temperament, the principle of an economy of exchange for the exigency of the gift—the institution of the Hôtel de Longchamp, borrowed directly from Sade, teaches us how this economy might arrive at the profane sharing of men and women—constantly disrupts the theological experiment, and she disrupts it not by opposing it but precisely by doubling it with another that simulates it, dissimulates it, and is completely equivalent to it in all things, although nonidentical.

Let us nonetheless remember—must one insist on it?—that it is not a question in these narratives of psychological motivations, nor of bizarre characters, moreover believable—a perverse theologian, a wife who is liberated and even a radical socialist—but rather of the affirmation of a new logic, such that when it is applied to everyday reality, theological reflection can bring it close to us through uneasiness and disturbance. I have cited the mystery of "real presence" and the act of the consecrator as origin of the custom of the gift. It should also be recalled how, in the perspective of the dogma of the Trinity, the communication of the incommunicable offers itself to us in a completely new way, just as, moreover, in pagan theology, we are placed before the problem of the Twelve Great Gods, identical in essence but distinct in person, a single divinity in twelve presences having no other role but to give themselves as spectacle to themselves and, in their multiplicitous theophanies, to reflect their inexhaustible simplicity in the complex imagination of men. To which one will remark that theology goes mad and drives one mad as soon as it is applied, as a knowledge of the absolute, to a domain that is not its own. A madness, perhaps, but one that is capable of conveying another reason. And let us not forget that the experience that these surprising books give an account of is not a pure game of the mind, but entertains a relation with the coherence of the *unique sign*, the silent constraint of which must always be grasped behind the name Roberte and her mad stories.

6. Let us pursue a little further, if it is possible, the movement that has been marked out. Existence simulates, it dissimulates, and it dissimulates the fact that even when it is dissimulating and playing a role, it continues to be authentic existence, and thus with an almost inextricable malice, binds the simulacrum to true authenticity. A challenge to the principle of identity and the identical I, as soon as the belief in God, guarantor of personal identity, falls away (profane atheism) or else when, with "an impiety of divine

inspiration," the thought of a single divinity is replaced by the feeling that even in God or in the pleroma of the divine space the simulacrum lives, the Other is still present, this other who is only the distance from the Same to itself, a distance that, in its difference, makes it the same as the Same, though nonidentical. Such a splitting, which sets before every being, and at odds in every being, an infinity of likenesses, without our having the right to identify the original or the image, the unique sign and the equivalents in which it discloses itself, is translated—existentially, by a renunciation of personal primacy (others will say by madness, the fragmentation of personality); theologically, by divinity conceived in some manner as plural; metaphysically, by the idea of the eternal beginning again.

Here, we catch a glimpse of the new intercessor, Nietzsche. I will say only one word, referring to the essay "Nietzsche, le polythéisme et la parodie," one of the most important writings on Nietzsche in French.[7] We should not think, however, that like Sade, Nietzsche was simply destined to impose himself on Klossowski because like Sade, an atheist, and even the Antichrist (something that Sade was never concerned with being), he would fall under the banal malediction of atheism, incapable of expatiating upon the absence of God without making God present by this very absence. There is (happily) more in Nietzsche and in the idea that Klossowski proposes to us of Nietzsche. The strange thought that everything returns, begins again, is the strongest affirmation of modern atheism. Why? Because it replaces infinite unity with infinite plurality and replaces linear time, the time of salvation and progress, with the time of spherical space, a malediction that reverses itself as joy because it challenges the identity of being and the unique character of the *hic et nunc*, and thus of the *ego*, of the soul, and of One God. And perhaps more: because this thought decidedly places us in a universe in which the image ceases to be second in relation to the model, where imposture lays claim to truth, where finally there is no longer an original, but an eternal scintillation in which the absence of origin, in the blaze of the detour and return, disperses itself. A thought that certainly has its traps, but a thought that is powerful in its impossibility, preventing us from falling back—as every atheism threatens to do—within human limits and, far from delivering us complacently to the insurrection of dark forces, images, and tenebrous phantasms, instead invites us to call on the inexhaustible capacity of metamorphoses in which to appear and to disappear testify equally to the favor and disfavor of being.

In the beginning was the return: such is the new gospel that, thinking of Nietzsche and accepting all of its consequences, one might readily substitute for the old, without, moreover, losing sight of the fact that the old already affirmed it (how otherwise?) insofar as speech, be it that of the origin, is the force of repetition, that which never says "once and for all" but, rather, "yet again," "this has already taken place once and will take place once again, and always anew, anew." Whence the great burst of laughter that is the shudder of the universe, the opening of space in its seriousness and the divine humor par excellence. For the eternal return indeed must, even into the oblivion in which its revelation as law culminates—this eternal return in which the infinite absence of the gods is affirmed and in some sense proved—also come to desire the return of the gods, that is, the gods as return. What Pierre Klossowski expounds in a superb development that I would like to cite partially here, because it gives account not only of Nietzsche but, it seems to me, also of Klossowski: "And thus it appears that the doctrine of eternal return is conceived yet again as a *simulacrum of doctrine* whose very parodic character gives account of *hilarity* as an attribute of existence sufficient unto itself, when laughter rings out from the depths of truth itself, either because truth bursts forth in the laughter of the gods, or because the gods themselves die laughing uncontrollably: when a god wanted to be the only God, all of the other gods were seized with uncontrollable laughter, until they laughed to *death*." A phrase that will precisely constitute one of the leitmotivs of *Le Baphomet* and that holds in its simplicity the endless movement of truth in the error of its return. Why, in fact, this laugh? Because of the divine, yes: "What is the divine if not the fact that there are many gods and not God alone?" But in laughter, the gods die, hence confirming the laughable pretension of One

God (who does not laugh); however, laughing to death, they make laughter divinity itself, "the supreme manifestation of the divine," where, if they disappear, it is to be reabsorbed, waiting to be reborn from it. But everything has still not been said definitively; for if the gods die laughing, it is no doubt because laughter is the movement of the divine, but also because it is the very space of dying—dying and laughing, laughing divinely and laughing mortally, laughter as bacchic movement of the true and laughter as mockery of the infinite error passing incessantly into one another. And thus everything returns to the absolute ambiguity of the unique sign that, wanting to divulge itself, looks for its equivalences and, in finding them, loses itself in them, and in losing itself believes it finds itself.[8]

§ 20 A Note on
Transgression

Earth: Chaos

If the Greek gods teach us that incest is not forbidden, they seem responsible for fixing the line of separation elsewhere, that is, between Earth and Chaos: a line of separation that one cannot cross without producing monsters. The difficulty of thinking about what separates these two terms is that one of them not only represents itself but, already in the constriction of its opening, an insurmountable distance. How, through disunion, does one unite with non-unity? How would "limit" be joined to the "without limit" according to the disjunction proper to the absence of limit? Chaos, in this non-relation of the two terms, is figured twice, in conformity with the excess that marks it: to unite with chaos is to support oneself on the abyss in order to rejoin the abyss by turning away from it. Is there a desire that could do this? All the less likely because Eros has perhaps not been engendered yet. Thus there would be unions alien to unity and lacking the unifying relation, be it perverted, of desire. But is it a question of union? Chaos, far from figuring the beautiful void, immutably at rest, multiplies according to the fury of a wild rage without beginning or end: it is the proliferation of a repetitive vacancy, the proliferating subtraction, the plurality outside unity. In what manner does the archaic narrative recount to us the event through which passes what (for us) would symbolize the major interdiction? Furious hatred pushes the Earth (power of the firm limit) to a conjunction with Chaos; but this fury—the abysmal, wild rage—is already the monstrous trait marking what belongs to Chaos. It would therefore be—for all that a consequence has its place here—the chaotic animosity or *repulsion* (pulsion that repeats itself the wrong way) with which limitlessness would have seduced (diverted) the limit in order to bring it to lose itself in the disorder without origin. The repulsion, backward repetition, that extends far beyond any principle of aggressivity is, however, not first in relation to Eros. It belongs to a lineage from which nothing stems, even though it does not cease to produce, in the bottomlessness, what does not have the right to the name *existence*. Re-pulsion precedes all pulsion without being primordial, or having any relation to life, love, destruction, and death, as we like to call the latter. Re-pulsion: double word, split, in which we would be wrong to see a first figure of "conflict," for repulsion divides only as an effect of repetition, which begets while begetting nothing: generation without begetting.

∼

Earth: Chaos. The archaic Narrative—with these powerful names that do not let themselves be mastered and, in the manner of old grievances, fall prey to uncertain excesses, remote from our meanings—recites in a rhapsodic manner, with adjustments or juxtapositions of pieces, the Narrative immemorial. These names, which are not, strictly speaking, terms of power, but sudden decisions, name nothing, perhaps: our translations appease them, less by translating them than by reusing them. What does the Narrative bring with it? An obscure right to be recited, as well as the transgression that this right without right, in spite of the rituals that delimit it, transmits or conveys, without one being certain about what is allowed and what is not. The Narrative begets itself, and it recounts begettings: rhapsodic, never saying a first time, but always reiterating according to the recitative that repeats the very thing that has not been said; it goes from lacunae to lacunae, from fragments to fragments, which it articulates differently without having, finally, any authority save the power of its reiteration and the wearied vigilance of repetition. The rhapsodic narrative, of which we are all tributary, is constituted by repeating itself around strange names—formidable, enigmatic, external to the language of the community—one does not know what they name, nor is it proper to stop them, rather, one should enclose them in the space of the narrative. Repetition and strange names (or simply names, the unnamable of the name), such would be the two possibilities at work in the narrative.

But the names in turn put into play a duality that excludes all common measure and produces on both sides a series or lineage according to the double meaning of repetition. However, these names name that which, immediately, we translate even when we keep it in the language of origin. Earth, Gaia, the power to beget and be begotten, but all the same the earth with which what forms is already formed, firm and worked by living coherence. The Earth is not a first principle, even less so when its name is referred to by the always younger names Rhea, Demeter, and Kora; when one names Demeter—the mother region—one also names Gaia, only on a level at which narratives salute things that are close, whose manifestations are developed and narratable in many episodes; with Gaia we do not lose our footing; even the mystery of a faceless begetting, associated with terrible things, remains because of the matter—the rich silt—in which it takes form, in a relation to the already manifest divine. Such is not the case with Chasma. One could not call him originary, since nothing about him originates. Time, named by the first Chronos, does not have time to call itself a contemporary of the old Chaos, for Time is first, and Chaos, without anteriority in time or in power in relation to Time, escapes primacy as well as perpetuity.

So how is it, then, with Earth and Chaos in the Narrative? Earth, an essentially generating power, begets; Chaos begins again. Earth begets according to desire, and out of desire produces the beautiful unions that are always permitted, even if illicit. Chaos, without desire, without love, not open in the least but always tightly drawn around its opening, reproduces itself incessantly in a proliferation that moves from Same to Same, destroying it.

~

But again the question is posed: Earth, sinking into Chaos or Erebus, under the power of repulsion, loses its right to beget (the similar by the similar) and enters into a dire genealogy where the dissimilar (the Other) forms a chain with the dissimilar (the Other), a feature of multiple separation. Between the monsters born of this unhappy union and what are referred to as the children or derivatives of Chaos there is the same difference as between living beings, monstrously alive, and a lineage of powers, outside being and non-being, which cannot be said to be prohibited, even if they are names of exclusion that escape all law: Chaos, Erebus, Tartarus, Night (itself in a double and triple position: night that loses itself in the night, night that proclaims the day, and the midnight of the two). When we receive these names from the Narrative—names that, though they do not come out of one another by means of a filiation, nonetheless progress toward us, toward a possible experience—we notice that they name what could not appear and that, without belonging to the divine cosmos, they have a relation to space (to all appearance, the Greek *chaos* and the Greek *space* are words that are dangerously close). It is time that begets. Space has no part in the genealogy, giving rise but to the Other, whether the accent is on obscurity (that which does not reveal itself, *Erebus*) or on the resounding discordance (*Tartarus*, *barbarous*, stuttering murmur without end, words that are not words).

The Narrative, however, makes them heard. Ancient language, echo of more ancient languages still, languages institutionally placed, no doubt, under the authority of the guardians of speech, different depending on the sanctuaries and the gods. Vainly do we interpret it, in part because other languages, close and separate, have served them as relays and because, for example, Anaximander, by citing the "without-limit," provides us, in the place of Chasma, with a term that is not only semantically rich, etymologically vertiginous, but one that can be used according to new rules that allow for other transformations and herald other kinds of users toward whom, or so we think, it will be easier for us to work our way. When, evoking the union of Earth with Chaos or with its derivative Erebus, we speak of the greatest transgression, we can obviously do this (the interpretation is there, within our reach), just as we may remark that prohibition here (a word no less out of place) does not reach the relation of kin with kin (as in incest) but marks the non-relation of the One with the Other or, as I have abusively suggested it, of Time and Space.

There remains the Narrative itself. It carries the enigma it utters. It says terrible things because it reiterates them: a reiteration that, according to the double game of repetition, happily escapes the peril of the origin but falls prey to the danger of repulsion, this beat without measure that beats neither according to desire nor according to life. A narrative thus always perhaps outside of the genealogy that is nonetheless its vocation to recount. A narrative in which Chaos has its place, which is very strange, which exposes it to a risk, not of becoming itself chaotic but of including the exclusion that comes with Chaos. Transgression passes and is erased by way of the Narrative; it is always incomplete and always allows itself to be thwarted further still because incompletion is its only mode of affirmation. Thus only the narrative passes by way of the Narrative, a mark of a past that never belonged to Time and (could one say?) a summons to this "step beyond" toward which, by repulsion, the intransgressable and yet namable Outside draws us.[1]

§ 21 The Detour Toward
Simplicity

I am thinking of the letter written to Tolstoy by Turgenev on his deathbed: "I am writing you to tell you how happy I was to be your contemporary." It seems to me that, with the death that has struck Camus—and I must add now, sadly, Elio Vittorini, Georges Bataille—this death that has made us, in a profound part of ourselves, death ridden already, we have felt how happy we were to be their contemporaries and the traitorous way in which this happiness was both revealed and obscured. And what is more, it is as if the power of being contemporaneous with ourselves, in that time to which we belonged with them, suddenly found itself gravely altered.

We cannot put aside the feelings of friendship or the sadness. And to speak coolly of the works of friends, ignoring the shadow that has withdrawn into them and that they throw on us, would be a movement without truth, and moreover beyond our power. That these works should suddenly desert us, we must indeed be convinced of this, even if they are there, around us, with all of the strength that belongs to them. This desertion does not take them away from us; it is the manner in which they are close to us, the pain that this proximity introduces in our thought every time that, in turning toward them, we come up against the presence of resistance that is proper to a work already closing itself up, and we cannot help it to close itself up (or to undo itself) by valuing it or by putting it in the service of an intellectual strategy.

Camus: he often experienced a feeling of discomfort, at times impatience, to see himself immobilized by his books; not only because of their resounding success, but by the finished quality he worked to give them and against which he turned, as soon as, in the name of this perfection, one wanted to judge him prematurely accomplished. Then, on the day of his death, the abrupt, decisive immobility: it ceased then to threaten him. It risks overtaking each of us, forcing us to stop beside a work henceforth too calm, which we nevertheless feel called upon to preserve, in order that the secret meaning that is specific to it not become frozen in the obvious. For it is a secret work.

∼

Secret is what the work of Camus seems to be in relation to himself. Each of his books hides him and points to him, speaking of him but of another besides himself. Literary and philosophical essays, narratives, short stories, writings for the theater: they have as their center, in situations chosen exemplarily, a state of his sensibility, a movement of his existence, finally an experience that was his own, that was specific to him, but specific to him to the extent that, far from experiencing it as singular, he holds it to be characteristic of a common condition: ungraspable when it is in common, however, and always poorly illuminated in the perfect light he directs upon it.

His great narratives owe their form to this reserve in which he slips away in order to reveal something essential that cannot be affirmed directly. *L'Etranger* is not Camus—it would be great simplicity to believe this—no more than is the lawyer in *La Chute* or Doctor Rieux in *La Peste*: everything rejects this identification. However, we recognize, and the feeling is very certain, that these characters, drawn with such decisiveness, are only characters, that is, masks: the figured surface behind which a certain voice speaks and, through this voice, a presence that could not reveal itself. Masked, what advances behind the mask—must I make this clear?—is not the man who is natural, and simple, and often direct, who is Albert Camus. In fact this is where the secret begins. Descartes, Nietzsche, when they evoke illustrious masked figures, participate even as far as their existence in this indirect way of being that is required by the proper affirmation of their thought, and no doubt, still more, Kierkegaard. With Camus, it is only when he begins to write that this simple communication with life refuses itself or slips away and perhaps is altered and no longer affirms itself except by a detour, and to affirm the new truth that is this detour. And yet what does Camus want when he writes? To rediscover this simplicity that belongs to him, this immediate communication with happiness and unhappiness, perhaps also something more (or less), another simplicity, another presence.

∼

Because he expresses himself with clarity, one wants to enclose Camus in the visible affirmation at which he arrives. Because he is without equivocation, one attributes to him a truth without ambiguity. Because he says what he says extremely, one stops him, one immobilizes him in this extremity, but when he speaks in favor of the clear limit, one reduces him to this limited speech without shadow, this man who, "born for a clear day," immediately grasped the breach that is light, the secret opening through which light pushes away all present (even the present of light) in its presence thus obscure.

The misunderstanding begins with the word *absurd*. One makes it a concept, and Camus himself, when he wants to extricate himself from the immobility of this "term," critiques it as concept. But it is not a philosopher's word: decisive, definite, hard, very removed in its outburst from the deadening it contains, it is there, in our language, as something naked; it does not give its reasons, a marker refusing to belong to what it marks off; an intransigent word that takes and gives leave.

It is almost an oath; it affirms, it defies. A word that is nonetheless neuter, curiously deprived of irrational resonances and, in truth, as firm as the word *reason,* for which it stands in. We know its origins. It does not come from Kafka, nor from German philosophy (must one make an exception for Stirner's *The Unique?*): it has nothing to do with phenomenology or with Heidegger, both of them oriented toward very different horizons. It is instead Dostoyevsky and Chestov who prepare the way for its arrival. The one who goes straight down his path, says Chestov, looking only in front of him, creates logic and lives in the assurance of his reason, but the one who turns and looks back sees terrible things that petrify him; having seen them prevents him from seeing anything else; everything flies to pieces—principles, morality, science. The absurd is what one sees when one turns back, but more precisely it is the movement of turning back: the look back, the gaze of Orpheus, of Lot's wife, the turning back that violates the prohibition and thus touches on the impossible, for this turning back is not a power. We *cannot* turn back. And yet turning back is the passion of thought, the decisive exigency.

Camus speaks of Chestov's "admirable monotony." And Chestov himself: "I irritate people because I always repeat the same thing." This is because repetition is the dimension of this world that is revealed in the turning back. It is not another world, it is the same become estranged from all order and, as it were, the outside of all world: the same, but not identical (without the guarantee of the principle of identity, which we lose by looking back); the nonidentical same, always dispersed and always collecting itself by dispersion, the fascinating mark of the multiplicity of reflections.

In *Le Mythe de Sysiphe,* we find the principal movements of experience: man with stone, the stone in its dry obstinacy that is to go back and down, man in his narrow-minded steadfastness, which is to go straight ahead and up, the indissoluble contradiction of the direction of these movements, and finally the sudden *turning back* of both, from which is revealed the necessity of absurd *repetition.*

The absurd that in Chestov leads man to faith, leads Sisyphus to joy. At least this is the interpretation that we are ready to accept, simplifying, on this basis, the hidden affirmation that Camus's clear statements allow discreetly to show through. For happiness is not drawn from the absurd through some sort of moral deduction, an austere happiness provided by fidelity to a truth without hope. To the person who turns back—who cannot turn back—a more difficult secret is revealed: the absurd as happiness, that is, the mysterious relation between these two movements, the unity of their difference, the enigma of the simplicity that gives us happiness in the presence of the absurd and the absurd in the possession of happiness, but also takes from us one by means of the other, dooming us to the endless passion of the impossible present.

~

I would like to indicate briefly why this experience of Camus's is complex and easy to betray. What was revealed to him in exceptional moments, the memory of which the prose writings of his youth have given form—it was always as though he had to develop it for himself, in two directions that correspond to two cultures: the Russian experience, the tragic Greek wisdom, the absurd according to Kirilov, necessity according to Anaximander. Of course, the word *culture* is not here to make us believe that what is at issue can be found in a book. Camus is respectful of books and he is not a smasher of statues, but if the art he loves passes through great and glorious names, what nourishes his art is in life and in his immediate life.

This immediacy is the simplicity that is grasped as always double and also in two traditions: one expresses the silence of the suffering world, the other the beauty of the silent world; one discovers the impossible, which is the unjust misery and the unjust unhappiness of men, the other unveils the impossible in a "nature without men," the arid immobility of the landscape, the present of light that deprives us of all project and all hope. On both sides, a mute indifference, a passion on the order of indifference, a speech on the level of muteness. And every time there is refusal, there is assent: refusal of what refuses us, the stone, the naked wind, the desert of suffering, refusal that *reverses* itself in affirmation as soon as man takes what repudiates him upon himself and takes it at its word:

empty light of day, inflexible lucidity of man; volt of the stone, revolt of Sisyphus.

This reversal is hard to decipher. It keeps the secret and the ambiguous truth to itself, but also the contradictions of meaning whose opposing constraints tend to disjoint experience, and that certainly darkened Camus's intellectual existence. Everything leads us to hear it in a dialectical way: our appropriative spirit wants it, the development of history (in one of its forms) makes it manifest. It is a matter of turning the impossible into power; one must, from unjustifiable suffering, incomprehensible death, from the negation that is essential to men and to a certain class of men, draw another kind of understanding and a mastery that is finally total, and just, if it is equal to everything.

Camus vigorously critiqued such a movement. His critique did not always seem convincing, and it seemed to mark the abandonment of this choice in favor of justice, which he had represented, at an important time, with so much honor.

It is because Camus's critique, as grounded as it might be, is grounded less in the reasons that it gives than in the scope and complexity of his experience, a source to which he was always as ready to return as he was to his origin in order to find in it the measure of all his words. An experience that—one indeed feels it— was put off balance by the responsibilities of political and social action and harnessed by the great simplifying forces of time. The word *absurd* made the misunderstanding complete. (If I am not mistaken, this word is almost absent from the first works: "Men and their absurdity," says *L'Envers et l'endroit*; and in *Noces*, in a more significant way: "Everything that exalts life increases its absurdity at the same time." But one would have to specify here that the absurd is not absurdity; there is a great distance between these two words; absurdity is of a conceptual nature, indicating the meaning of that which has none, whereas the absurd is neuter, it is neither subject nor object, it belongs neither to the one nor to the other, it is *That* which slips away from the grasp of meaning, like the divine.)

Camus's struggle to rejoin himself, in spite of the forces of the day and the dictates of one part of himself, is moving. It hardened and constrained him. It is a sadness today to think of the strange solitude to which he felt himself condemned, even in the discomfort of fame that seemed destined to isolate him and to age him prematurely.

~

"*I feel my heart is Greek.*" If he says this in Eleusis, it is in an undertone and in memory of another life in which he was in a relation of simplicity, subsequently almost unbelievable to him, with the great presences that he did not call "gods" at the time: the sky and the sea, the stone and the wind, night and day, and always again the sun, light. It is the heart that is Greek; it is not an acquisition of the spirit, a discovery of the museum: on the contrary, he will protest first against the recourse to the poverty of myths, this intervention of Dionysus and Demeter where he can directly appropriate their words and say, as if coming from himself: "Happy is the mortal on earth who has seen these things." (But already he knows their names; they are there, immobile, silent, absent.) The life of a civilized writer, witness to time, begins with poverty on the level of things without history: in face of their naked presence. What is particular to this relation, I would like to mark in this way: one speaks, and it seems with good reason, of his pagan manner of being with the world, which (for him, in his language) always designates the only natural powers: the absolute of sky, of earth, of sea. But to say *pagan* is to speak of an ancient attachment to a land on which one is immemorially established and that one works: there is, then, possession, entrenchment in the depth of certainties that one preserves and that shelter one. Completely other is the poverty of modern conglomerations, urban poverty, uprooted, without place and without ties. In the big city of Algiers where he spends his youth, no doubt "nature" is there, in abrupt proximity, but not in an ancestral vicinity; he does not inhabit it, strictly speaking; he does not live with it in a traditional way, protected by it and protecting it, cultivating it. A poor existence without roots, nature naked without dwelling place: it is on the basis of this double simplicity that relations reduced to bareness and to the plenitude of the essential are constituted; in this, irreducible.

It is like an immediate relation, without past, without future. The body, here in its certain reality, is the only truth of this presence where nothing is promised but where everything is given, affirmed in a tie that does not bind. And, on the level of the body— which has this special quality that it cannot cheat, that it knows refusal but not renunciation, that it knows pleasure, suffering, fear, but not hope, regret, or resignation—a sober truth will take form, with the rectitude that is specific to it, alien to the deceptions of feeling, "a mix of asceticism and intense pleasure," "an exercise of passion to the detriment of emotion." "Yes, I am present. And what strikes me at this moment is that I cannot go any further." One of the most illuminating sentences of the meditations of his youth.

It makes us feel that there is something else in this first experi- ence besides the limited certainties of an art of living, the authority for which one would have no trouble finding in the prosaic honesty of a certain antiquity.[1] What Hölderlin calls the fire of the sky, the affirmation of the earth, but not the earth of which one makes a dwelling place; that day, on the contrary, in which one does not sojourn, which must be borne face to face and which is such that he who recalls it in the detail of its various gifts, misses it miserably, but such also that to greet it in its power is to accept a tragic happiness: this presence without present certainly corresponds to one of the oldest discoveries that Camus will always find in himself, obscurely, veiled and hardly perceptible, moreover in a unique form that our equivalences betray when they seek to determine it. Camus, we will not forget, said, "Poverty was never an unhappiness for me: light spread its riches over it." Light illuminates poverty, but poverty opens light; it gives light as the truth of bareness and also as this naked appearance that is the characteristic of truth. "Poverty was never an unhappiness for me." Here, with all of the reserve of which he gives us an example and which he learned from this event itself, we remember how he evoked what was the central event of his beginning life, and we think with him of "the child who lived in a poor neighborhood," of the mother of this child, of the "exhausting work" from which she returned in the evening, not saying anything, not hearing, having no thoughts on the order of the common world: "muteness of an irremediable desolation," "strange indifference," which did not signify an indifference of the heart but the strangeness of existence reduced to its truth alone, without anything to misrepresent or denounce it, only present and equal, in its solitude, to "the immense solitude of the world." "She is not thinking about anything. Outside the light, the noises; here the silence in the night. The child will grow up, he will learn. He is being raised and will be asked for gratitude, as if one were preventing him pain. His mother will always have these silences. He will grow up in pain." Such a moment would be changed were one to see in it a first perspective on life that was only unhappy. On the contrary, what is revealed to the child in this moment is something more fundamental; he learns that happiness and unhappiness can be exchanged, as can plenitude and dispossession, just as man and the world are silently united in the solitude that is common to them: a moment analogous to the moment of "turning back," a knowledge already of this *kingdom* that is *exile*.

~

"Time suspended," he says. In the interim, at the very heart of separation, men separated and things separated communicate: there, the intimacy deprived of everything and the massive whole of the empty outside, the lack that becomes brightness in the light where everything presents itself, that becomes refusal in an existence where everything withdraws itself. And, each time, the immense certitude that everything here below is given. Grave and exalting gift, mysterious simplicity, the same that is affirmed in *L'Etranger*, a work close to the sources that entertains with the text of *L'Envers et l'endroit* a very moving relationship. It is because Meursault conveys the truth of the mother. Like her, he is almost without speech, without thought, thinking in closest proximity to this initial lack that is richer than any effective thought, speaking on the order of things, of their muteness, of the pleasures they give, of the certainties they reserve. From beginning to end, his destiny is linked to that of the mother. The trial instituted against him consists in turning the pure lack that is common to them into an offense and, at the same time, in turning the honesty of their relations into a crime: this insensibility in which, without proof and without signs, they lived far from one another, close to one another, indifferent but with a disinterestedness that is the way of having access to the only true solicitude. On the last page of the narrative, we clearly hear how the innocent destiny of the mother speaks through the mouth of the condemned, and how, in their irreducible simplicity, the two lives come together outside judgments of value;[2] just as in the final vehemence—a reversal of indifference to passion—that stirs Meursault, one imagines the inflexible desire to defend, against all moral or religious usurpations, the simple fate of a silent being, and to find finally the language that could give speech to the speech that does not speak. To which one must add that the reader or commentator, the other defender of the soul, insofar as he would like to read, according to the joint views of a dull psychoanalysis and a dull Christianity, the expression of remorse or the feeling of guilt that the author obscurely feels toward his mother in the little comprehensible act of Meursault the murderer and then in his awkwardness at defending himself, and in the strange aggravated circumstances that the tribunal heaps on him—this reader is, in advance, with his morality, his doubts, the delicacy of his feeling, his dubious spiritual inquisitions, denounced in the narrative, where he is figured, either in the robe of the judges or in the soutane of the priest, among all those who falsify the simplicity of our lives (like the simplicity of narratives) by introducing into them the false measure of the depth of conscience and the concerns of the soul.

Thus there are at least three possible readings of this book that is so clear. One is performed "between yes and no," on the level of "the indifference of this strange mother," "an indifference that, alone, the immense solitude of the world can measure." Another reading will grasp the movement of the experience in the narrative with which Camus's youth was enlightened and which he himself put in relation to the experience of the Greeks: the experience of *presence*, of the happiness of presence in the measured harmony with things, with the world, then in the measurelessness to which this presence, over which we are powerless, destines us by opening us to unhappiness. Finally, a third reading will find the hero absurd, he who obstinately maintains, in the face of the promises of heaven and the embellishments of the spirit, his lucid attachment to the solitary condition, his refusal to accept a rule other than that of his earthly life, absurd and happy even in the death that awaits him. Not to indulge in a lot of empty talk was already the affirmation on which the text of *L'Envers et l'endroit* came to its conclusion, here again very close to *L'Etranger*: "Yes, everything is simple. It is men who complicate things. They should not tell us stories. They should not say about a man condemned to die: 'He is paying his debt to society,' but 'He will have his head cut off.' This may not seem like much. But there is a small difference." Not to dress up with words, with reasons, with consolations, the naked truth of our fate; to greet it, if this is possible, such as it is: this is the only moral of the story, a moral that is first and foremost an aesthetic, because it tempts us with the rigor of an exact speech.

In *L'Etranger* itself, this speech oscillates between a retreat and a suddenly exalted affirmation in which refusal is deployed. Sobriety and exaltation, restraint and song are the two measures of the exact language, just as the two poles of the movement are impossible unhappiness, impossible beauty, the two extremities of presence, the two levels of silence. When sober speech and vibrant speech fold in on one another, when the speech of effacement and the speech of evidence, the one beneath the personal mode of expression and the other above it, come to coincide, we have the answer of art to which Camus, who refused the name of philosopher but claimed that of artist, never ceased to be drawn, in the freedom of a risk that he did not separate from mastery. It is true that he had, more than others in our time, a concern for measure, maintaining the necessity of not breaking forms in the vicinity of the twice immeasurable affirmation that, absurdly happy, absurdly unhappy, presence represents in the approach of nature and in life with men. He defends himself against this double attraction by redoubling the constraints, all the more faithful to the purity of distinctions and to the separation of differences in that he remains tied to the reserve of the *strange indifference*—which is sometimes experienced by him as a threat, the loss of the spontaneity that was his youth, the loss of the beautiful, fiery harmony with nature (and he responds to this with sarcastic coldness, the incrimination and speed of *La Chute*),[3] and is at other times recognized as the enigma of the initial depth, the common ground of happiness and unhappiness, the beginning of all agreement and the rupture of all harmony: *that* very thing which always maintains itself as the secret truth of all differences, those which are decided according to the (Greek) necessity of apportionment, as well as those which are achieved by the (modern) violences of power.

~

The moment has not come for us to ask ourselves about the work of Albert Camus, holding ourselves at a distance from it and from ourselves. Perhaps this kind of questioning has ceased to be legitimate in a time that changes and turns back while precipitously pursuing its powerful course. Camus anxiously sensed this turning back that he translates, at times uniting himself passionately with the time, at other times painfully turning away from it; sometimes very close to the present, with the most awakened consciousness of the condition of unhappy men, at other times close to pure presence, in this absolute of light that does not recognize our measures and is unaware of the modest necessities of humanism. An obscure alternative that he calls "the enigma" and that makes him a contemporary of the age even so far as the distance he keeps in relation to it, if the latter contains its own estrangement in the mysterious turn that would be its present. Whence, however, all of the misunderstandings, which arise from a work that is not at all dissimulated, and from a writer so visible who escapes us, not because he is fluid and ungraspable in the manner of Gide, but firm and faithful each time in this double exigency of turning back, the affirmations of which he holds together secretly in himself from his earliest experience.

(The exigency of the "turning back" is expressed in each of Camus's works in a different way, and it is this exigency that undoubtedly orients the whole of his work. It is not a later movement, linked to a crisis of maturity; it is the principle that animates even his earliest books. In *Sisyphe*, Sisyphus turns back because the stone turns back; the turning back is here the refusal to be ruled by the ideal immobility of the sky, the refusal to understand the fatality of the process by accepting the immobile sentence of the gods and their inflexible decisions; it is therefore in accord with the turning back of the stone, and then with the earthly reality that this stone represents: for as long as we have a stone to roll, to contemplate, and to love, we will be able to behave as men. In *L'Etranger*, it is the turning point itself of the narrative, when the measured and happy presence suddenly and as if without reason turns into the immeasurable and gives rise to unhappiness; it is also the passage from the first to the second part, when the most banal and everyday existence, the existence denounced by the moralists as being inauthentic, becomes, by affirming itself *simply* in the face of the travesties of moral and religious ways, what is most authentic and most strange. One must add, as I have noted, Camus's strong conviction that this turning back is not dialectical and that on the contrary it puts the dialectic into question; this will be the subject of *L'Homme révolté*. But the reversal of refusal to affirmation should not be interpreted as a moral decision, and Camus, placed once and for all within the ranks of the moralists, will say, "We live for something that goes further than morality." It is perhaps up to art to bring us closer to the meaning of this movement, to uncover it and to affirm it without giving it *value*. On the condition that art does not claim to escape the movement, and thus, in advance, agrees to be already diverted from all pure artistic realization or else deprived of the detour by its affirmation of itself as pure presence.)

§ 22 The Fall:
The Flight

Clamence, the man so named by *La Chute* and yet anonymous (he cries out in his own desert), converses in hushed tones with someone whose face we do not see, whose replies we do not hear. A "solitary dialogue," it is not, however, the tragic speech that in *Oedipus* is a dialogue with the silence of the gods—the speech of the solitary man, a speech in itself divided and truly cut in two because of the silent sky with which it pursues its invincible discourse—because for Oedipus, from whom gods and men alike have withdrawn, divesting him of his glorious appearance, this void beside which he must henceforth speak by questioning his unjustifiable fate is not empty, being the sign and depth of divinity, suddenly revealed to him by the unhappiness of knowledge.

There is, it is true, some semblance of Oedipus in the man who speaks here. He, too, once ruled within himself and outside himself; a king in appearance, as befits a time without kingdoms, a king by opinion and fallen from this opinion of glory, of contentment and virtue with which he was permitted for a time to make a solid reality. And why does he fall? For the same reasons as King Oedipus, of whom it is said, in a verse attributed to the madness of Hölderlin, that he had "*perhaps an eye too many.*" Lucidity does not permit one to rule innocent for very long.

But it is not with the gods that this other king speaks, nor even with the distance of the gods who turn away, but only with the shadow of a casual companion, invisible behind a curtain of silence; his double, perhaps, but also anyone at all, the ordinary man whose distracted attention and vague presence constantly allow the language that tries to reach him—so well formed nevertheless—to fall back into unreality. The sober malediction of sorts that the narrative brings us is in this partitioned speech. A dialogue enclosed in monologue. There will be no dearth of thoughtful men to make us see the varied ways in which *L'Etranger, La Peste, La Chute* accommodate the confessional narrative—and that the Stranger, speaking of himself by saying "I," speaks of himself with the impersonality of a He already estranged from itself; to see that, in *La Peste*, the central character, writer of the story, recounts the events, which nonetheless directly concern him, in the third person, for in the community of anonymous misery it is unsuitable to mark out the intimacy of one's own memory. And here, in *La Chute*, where the one who speaks, speaks only of himself—not without detours, but apparently without reticence, with all of the resources of a marvelous rhetoric, as the distinguished lawyer that he is—we soon perceive that he is not speaking of his own life but of everyone's life, that this life is without content, that his confidences do not confide anything, just as the interlocutor toward whom he is turned is a wall of fog into which his words sink without having been heard and as if they had not been uttered.

What is left? Irony.

~

In this narrative one will undoubtedly look for the grim movement of a satisfied man who, by dint of adopting a virtuous and happy ego, finally abandons himself to this power of discontent and destruction that is also in the ego. It is dangerous to be too attentive to oneself. This attention is first a spontaneous and happy adhesion that forgets everything, both others and oneself; but the attention becomes reflection; the amiable gaze with which one caresses oneself becomes a suspicious gaze; one is wounded precisely where one thought oneself loved; the wound is clairvoyant in finding everything that wounds; and everything wounds. Lucidity does its work in the end. It judges everything and it condemns everything—ironically, without seriousness and without respite, with the cold flame that it has kindled in the ego.

In *La Chute*, however, I read a narrative very different from this narration prompted by the psychology of La Rochefoucauld. Even less do I think that its purpose is to teach us discontent, the uncomfortable truth and necessary anxiety. First of all, it guards against teaching anything. This is the grace of irony: it gives us only what it takes from us; if it affirms, the affirmation is a fiery place that we are in a hurry to leave. At times the irony becomes heavy. This weight is also its lightness, for irony is without humor.

In this appealing narrative, I perceive the traces of a man in flight, and the appeal that the narrative exerts, an appeal that is strong and without content, is in the very movement of flight. When did he move away? From what did he move away? Perhaps he does not know, but he does know that his whole being is only a mask: from his name, which is borrowed, to the smallest episodes of his life that are so unspecific that there is no one for whom they would not be appropriate. His confession is but a calculation. His "guilty man" narrative is based on the hope of believing himself guilty, for a true offense would be a certainty upon which he could anchor his life, a solid marker that would allow him to determine his course. In the same way, when he seems to reproach himself for his egoistic existence, when he says "Thus I lived without any continuity save that, from day to day, of the me-me-me," it is remarkable, because every time he says Me, no one answers; it is an address that resounds vainly here and there, an ironic reminiscence, a memory that he does not remember.

If he is a masked man, what is there behind the mask? Another mask, Nietzsche says. But the cold and passionate glow that signals his passage and allows us to follow him through the meanderings of confidences always suspended, digressions destined only to evoke his refusal yet carry us along with him, persuades us of his presence, similar to a brilliant fire over a moving expanse of water. There is certainly, in him and around him, a strong supply of absence; but this void, this distance, is but a path in reserve, the possibility of evasion, of always going farther if need be, and of leaving, for whoever might seize him, only a simulacrum and a cast-off. Here we see an example of the manner in which Albert Camus uses classical art for ends that are not at all classical. The impersonality of traits, the generality of characters, the details that correspond to nothing unique, and even the scene of remorse that seems borrowed from one of Stendhal's letters, this "disdainful confession" that confesses nothing in which one could recognize any lived experience, everything that, in classical discretion, serves to depict man in general and the beautiful impersonality of everyone, is here only in order for us to reach the presence of someone who is almost no longer anyone, an alibi in which he seeks to catch us while escaping.

The course of the narrative is constantly doubled by a quasi-nocturnal course—even when it takes place during the day—across the flat expanse, sunless and inhospitable, of a northern land, through the gray labyrinths of water and wet desert where a man without refuge finds his center in a sailors' bar, frequented by men who do not like the law. This second course is essential to the narrative, and the landscape is not a setting. On the contrary, all of reality can be found in it. The story behind which the man dissimulates himself, and which seems painfully hollow and fictitious, has its point of truth here, its moving ending. Something lives here. It is real, it draws us into the real; we know that someone could be there, someone coming and going, looking at the brightness in the sky made by the wings of doves still absent (which are perhaps gulls), a derisory prophet who calls judgment on himself and on others so that the judgment may take hold of him and fix him. Vain hope. He must only flee and serve to sustain this great movement of flight that carries each person away unbeknownst to all, but of which he became conscious, of which he is the bitter, greedy, at times almost lighthearted, drunken consciousness.

~

But what is he fleeing? What is this flight? The word is not well chosen to please. Courage is, however, to accept flight rather than live quietly and hypocritically in false refuges. Values, moralities, homelands, religions, and those private certitudes that our vanity and our self-indulgence generously grant us are so many deceptive abodes that the world develops for those who believe they stand and rest among stable things. They know nothing of the immense rout to which they are put, unaware of themselves, with the monotonous drone of their steps, always quicker, that carry them along impersonally in a great immobile movement. Flight before flight. Clamence is among those who, having had the revelation of the mysterious drift, can no longer accept to live within the pretenses of the abode. At first he tries to take this movement on as his own. He would like to move away personally. He lives on the margin. In the great army's retreat, he plays the sniper, the kind of man who generally is fiercely set upon by malicious opinion and the condemnations reserved for deserters. But this operation does not succeed. The petty life of debauchery that he leads brings him some satisfaction, but not at all that of being discredited and rejected from the whole. Virtue continues to protect him with its appearance. It is not good for someone who wants to carry the banner of evil to have learned a beautiful language, good manners. Meursault was condemned, innocent, because an imperceptible difference set him apart, a deviation that was his offense. Clamence is unable to pass for guilty because everything he does to separate himself is but one form of the general discordance. In the void, it is said, heavy bodies and light bodies fall together with equal motion and consequently do not fall. It is perhaps this, the fall: that it can no longer be a personal destiny, but the fate of each in everyone.

∼

Believers will say that Clamence does nothing but flee God, just as humanists will say that he does nothing but flee men. Each will thus express himself according to his own language of flight. There is in the book a remarkable page. Evoking his life as a man satisfied with himself, the narrator says, to our surprise: "Was this not Eden in effect, my dear Sir: life without mediation? It was mine." Or, further, "Yes, few beings were more natural than I. My harmony with life was total, I adhered to what it was, utterly, refusing none of its ironies, its greatness or its servitudes." A strange confidence, for the man who speaks, or at least the character he borrows in order to speak, is a man of vanity and self-love, very removed from any natural spontaneity, and the very manner in which he confides without confiding, in a movement of irony and ruse, further increases the impression of affectation or artifice that his character wants to give us. How are we to believe that he ever was in harmony with life? Or else are we to think that the masked man is here unmasking himself? Would he be betraying someone else? I am not trying to suggest that Albert Camus suddenly remembered himself, suddenly remembered the natural man it was his happiness to be and whom he would have ceased to be, because a man who writes must first, like Oedipus, have "perhaps an eye too many." But it is true that *L'Etranger* and *Noces* enabled us to touch the pleasure of immediate life. The Stranger was indeed a stranger in this, because of a simplicity and an innocence so assured that they could only render him guilty. It is as if the tortuous, bitter man, all equivocation, of *La Chute* were opening onto another man and another life that he evokes as the pagan dawn of the world. The fall would thus be only suspicion with regard to happiness, the need to be not only happy but justified for being happy. The search is a dangerous one. The justification passes by way of the offense. One becomes guilty through the same feeling of happiness that was at first the substance of innocence. One was happy, therefore innocent. One is happy, therefore guilty; then unhappy and still guilty; finally, never guilty enough in the eyes of this lost happiness that was without authority and without justification. The search for offense henceforth constitutes the whole of life, an offense that one would like to share with everyone in a community that heightens the solitude.

But this way of seeing things is but a momentary marker that, in the perspective of the infinite movement of the fall, has no real value. We fall. We console ourselves for falling by determining in our imagination the point at which we would have begun to fall. We prefer to be guilty than to be tormented without fault. A suffering without reason, an exile without kingdom, a flight without vanishing point cannot be tolerated. The imagination comes to help us fill the void in which we fall, by establishing a certain beginning, a certain starting point, that lead us to hope for a certain point of arrival and, although we do not believe in them, we are relieved by these markers that we fix for a moment. And then we speak of them. Speaking is essential here. This speech is itself without end, like the fall. It is the sound of the fall, the truth of this movement of error, which speech has as its object to make one hear and to perpetuate, by revealing it without betraying it. Here, rather than the monologue of a man who is fleeing the world, the deceptive consideration, the false virtue, the happiness without happiness, I hear the monologue of the fall such as we might perceive it were we able for a moment to silence the chatter of the stable life in which we maintain ourselves out of necessity. The character who speaks would willingly take on the figure of a demon. What he murmurs grimly behind us is the space in which we are invited to recognize that we have always been falling, without respite, without knowing it. Everything must fall, and everything that falls must drag into the fall, by indefinite expansion, all that means to remain. At certain moments we realize that the fall greatly exceeds our capability and that we have in some sense further to fall than we are able. It is at this point that the vertiginous feeling begins with which we split ourselves off, becoming, for ourselves, the companions of our fall. But sometimes we are fortunate enough to find beside ourselves a true companion with whom we converse eternally about this eternal fall, and our discourse becomes the modest abyss in which we also fall, ironically.

§ 23 The Terror of
Identification

In the essay written in the form of an introduction to Gorz's "biographical" book, Sartre says of Gorz: "I rank him among the Indifferents: this subgroup is of recent origin, its representatives are no more than thirty years old; no one yet knows what they will become." According to what he tells us of himself, Gorz is of Austrian origin; his father, Jewish, his mother, Christian; after the *Anschluss* he lived in Switzerland, in the solitude of adolescence and exile, deprived even of his language, to which he prefers, in a surprising decision, the French language in which he writes this book.[1] I do not cite these details in order to give an identity card to someone who does not like to be identified, but to recall that forty years before him, an Austrian writer, also condemned to exile, made of the passion of indifference the truth of his life and the theme of his work. That Gorz and Musil should have been born in Austria, that they should both have been separated from themselves by analogous political difficulties: this is not the comparison that seems important to me, but rather, in a social and literary context that is very different, the return of the one, same, singular experience—that of a man impassioned by indifference in a desperate refusal of differences and particularities.

Is this surprising? Undoubtedly. But the surprise is the very one caused us, every time we encounter it, by modern literature: it is the surprising fact of this literature.

One must nonetheless immediately add—the error is quickly

208

committed—that this "indifference" is in no way a fact of character or sensibility, that it only indirectly concerns the individual who writes, that it is even secondary to discover whether it is his task, his drama, or his truth; certainly, it is also important, but if one begins by asking oneself about the difficulties specific to the writer struggling with indifference, one will very quickly forget the essential: that it is not the writer who is indifferent (he is rather the complete opposite), nor does this way of being come from the work as it strives for a certain impersonality of indifference—which is not a matter of style or lack of style, of formalism or classicism: were this the case, everything would be simple, we would be in aesthetics, we would know how to judge and be judged, admire and be held for admirable, fortuitous abilities that we are lacking because we have not acquired the right to reach the place in which they are exercised. However, when we sense that literature is "intimately bound" to a neuter speech, we know that we are before an affirmation that is very difficult to situate (and even to affirm), for it precedes everything that we can say about it.

~

At the beginning of his essay, Sartre evokes "this muted, steady, courteous voice," inviting us to hear it behind Gorz's book: "To whom does it belong? To No One. It seems as if language were beginning to speak on its own. Here and there it happens that the word 'I' is pronounced, and we think we hear the Speaker of this Speech, the subject who chooses the terms. A pure mirage, the subject of the verb is itself only an abstract word." A little further on, he says of this speech that it is almost deserted, elsewhere that it is the voice of Concern. "There is this voice, that is all: this voice that searches and does not know what it searches for, that wants and does not know what it wants, that speaks in the void, in the darkness." It is not without reason that Sartre should have heard this voice precisely in Gorz's book, but it is also because this voice has not ceased to make itself heard for some time in those books that are barely books, and I think, above all, in Samuel Beckett: yes, there, with Molloy, Malone, the Unnameable, for the first time without pretext and without alibi, we encountered the obstinate, weary, indefatigable speech, circling around a fixed point only to descend toward the point of its springing forth, of its desiccation; a monologue in which one does not know who is speaking; there is a presence, tormented, suffering, though incapable of suffering, that is no longer altogether someone; it comes and goes; in the beginning there was perhaps a real vagabond and, in that room, a real dying man, but the tramping has taken the place of the tramp, the agony has worn away the power to die. Confined within an oriental vase in an apartment, spread out on roads, immobilized in the empty corner of an empty house, always more infirm, more crippled, more reduced, an irreducible remains of humanity affirms itself: a powerlessness without name, without face, a fatigue that cannot rest, an empty, vague waiting that nothing stimulates, that nothing discourages. To such a semblance of existence, what could happen? What is still there, and how can one help it to be no longer there? How can this speech be silenced when it has already fallen below silence without ceasing to speak?

The thought and the hope of Sartre, as he formulates it to rejoin Gorz's book, is that behind the cold, remote, insistent murmur that observes, reasons in our place, and speaks to us, that is, expresses us by occupying us with an alien speech that responds perfectly to us behind the impersonality of the indifferent He, there would subsist, inalienable, even in the most radical alienation, the power to speak in the first person, the transparency of an I that has only been obscured, obfuscated, "devoured by others," as Teste says, or worse, devoured by itself, seduced [*sic*] to the consistency of a borrowed singularity. "Here is the moment. . . . The Voice recognizes itself: the action discovers itself in it and says, I. *I* am making this book, *I* am looking for myself, *I* am writing. Somewhere, a guy with hollow eyes sighs, intimidated: 'How pompous it is to speak in the first person!' and then dissolves: Gorz appears: I am Gorz, *it was my voice* that spoke, I write, I exist, I suffer myself and I make myself, I have won the first round."

~

Does Gorz's book authorize such commentary? It is a strange and passionate work, well devised to deceive us. A precipitous reader will not fail to see in it a philosophical work or even an attempt to apply to oneself the method that Sartre has applied to Baudelaire, to Genet. And it is true that this kind of bizarre narrative seems only to consist in a series of reflections and in a movement that is perfectly reasoning: one is constantly arguing in it, one speaks, with extreme agility no less, a language that commentators will easily equate with that which is in use, or so they believe, in the school of a certain Morel. This is true and this is an illusion. Everything here is mere semblance, all is imitation. The language spoken by the narrator is not the language of thought, it only resembles it; its movement only appears to be dialectical; its intelligence is so marvelously intelligent only because it knows that it imitates itself, an image of itself forced into indefinite reflections of lucidity by its inability to stop at anything that could guarantee it.

One will conclude: if the language is imitated, if the thought is borrowed, then the book can only be written after, without any original value. Yet there is almost no book in which a more authentic search affirms itself, a search more necessary and more unrelenting against inevitable deception. This is, first of all, because the enterprise is a vital one: Gorz, in a wager more total than that of Pascal, has staked everything on the truth of this exigency to write. It is also that he has put himself under conditions such that he cannot deceive himself as to the assumed being he chooses to be, openly and deliberately building his life on a fake, as we all do, but without the concern that we have of dissimulating from ourselves, through natural alibis, our tenderly and familially alien existence. Refusing his mother tongue, beginning not only to write but to think, to dream in French, and then beginning to think as Sartre, Gorz does not for a moment forget that he is outside himself, without anything that is specific to him, in the image of the adolescent that he is, exiled from himself, disappropriated, neuter in a neutral country. Such strange and frightening abstract purity! Such a decision made, as if suddenly, by a solitary child: to be in no way what one is, to be only another, to be another only by a resolution that is voluntary, disciplined, always fictitious, artificial, alert to its own falsehood, in order to keep, at the very least, this falsifying conversion true, by which one refuses one's natural particularity. "He decided that the total man was French, that the body of true thought and Reason was the French language." "He decided . . ." Who is this He? Gorz does not say "I decided"; he cannot say it—why? And what is this He? Is it not simply an ancient Ego, the Austro-Germanic-Judeo-Christian ego from which he has strayed in his sudden resolution? But if this "He" were then simply his always particular being, the being inherited from childhood and from the origin, and if he were the one to have made the decision, the decision to become "other" is necessarily "altered" by a movement that has remained particular and cannot reflect anything other than this particularity: the need to be oneself while pretending to cease to be it, or else the need to place oneself under the guarantee of Sartre and Valéry, to "defuse" one's own experience by translating it into a foreign language with a universal vocation; flight, thus, before a self divided, unhappy, inconvenient, but a flight that is, of course, only the self that flees and follows itself and sticks to itself in this pursuit of an Other.

It is not enough—we know this—to lose oneself in order to take leave of oneself, nor is it enough to elevate oneself to some sort of abstract or indefinite existence to separate oneself from this too-well-defined ego that one was. One wants to become other, but in this one confirms oneself in the Same and in the Me-Myself that is still altogether in the flight toward the other. Gorz's book is the cold, methodical, passionate search, a search without order for the distant choice, rooted in his personal being, that later deployed itself in the decision to impersonalize itself. What speaks, therefore, in his book is the falsely disincarnate voice, falsely false, actual and yet inactual, a voice that is the cold necessity to speak while being still but a speaking imitation, the feint of what is distant, indifferent, and neuter in the foreign language, the relentless beginning-again that psychoanalysis has taught us to rediscover in what is closest to us and always behind us.

What is particular to such a voice—its power of enchantment and fascination—is that it claims to speak in the name of an initial event toward which, were we able to follow its call, it would return us in such a way that suddenly, with liberating clarity, with an obviousness capable of shattering us, we would believe that we were discovering the first step that oriented our life: the originary project in relation to which we could get a hold of ourselves by welcoming it in order to discharge it better. Gorz also experiences this fascination and, at the conclusion of the book, in a sudden illumination that is the shock of revelation, finally comes up against himself, recognizing with surprise what he has never ceased to be in a position to know: that the first disposition that organized all others for him was the terror of being identified. This is the point of departure: a profound, constant terror of being identified by others with an I that had come from others; the refusal, out of the fear of adhering to this foreign I, of any I, then the rejection of all character, the challenging of all affective preference, the banishing of all taste and distaste, the passion for a life without passion, without naturalness, without spontaneity, the disgust at saying anything that is not neuter in order never to say more, or something other than what one says; and finally the silence, the terror of assuming a role and acting, the escape into an existence that is purely intelligent, always occupied with ridding itself of itself, with disidentifying itself.

Gorz has no trouble finding in his family history everything he needs to understand such a movement—the terror of being oneself out of a desire to be only oneself—on the basis on his childhood experiences: this is because his entire childhood was lived under the constraint of his mother, "always called on by her to identify himself with a role, the 'I' she intended him to play, that she *imputed* to him by force because that was the way she wanted to see him. She saw him as she would have liked for him to be, she presented his imaginary 'I' to him as in a mirror, and this 'I' was an Other, a fake, unless the opposite was true: that he was himself an Other, a fake." Whence, one day, the need to free himself from the mother tongue, the realm of the mother out of which he has to escape; whence at the same time, in order to fight the obscure modification that she imposed on him, the almost intelligible decision to go all the way in this modification and to give himself a completely other ego by identifying with a borrowed thought and a learned language.[2] A vertiginous move at the end of which, because of the effort he makes to grasp it, he will arrive, not back at his old terrorized ego but at an I, free of the terror of identification and identical to disidentification itself, the I of almost pure transparency. This is why the narrative, begun under the power of a speech that is neuter and without subject, is in the end reconciled with the narrator when the latter, having recognized himself in the foreign speech, believes he has acquired the right to write in the first person, or at least seeks to make himself responsible, by writing, for this I that is no longer afraid of losing itself when relating to others.

~

A happy ending, consequently, and almost edifying. I will not say that it persuades me, but the energetic concern to live again that is revealed in it is moving, and I admire, in this methodical search for a path, the ruse that allows Gorz to accept the path he chose blindly the first time (in the terror of being taken for an other) by choosing it a second time resolutely, and then, each time again, with a stubbornness of a design that is vaster and enriched with significations more essential. But what is this first choice on which all would depend? What is the beginning from which our entire life would make sense? Gorz indeed senses that the return to the origin for which he strives, as if to find at the very beginning the key phrase capable of giving him the word on himself, attracts him only by the illusion of a beginning that always has a further beginning, that refers to another, indefinitely: behind the phrase he hears and would like to unlock in order to reach the univocal meaning of this phrase (the event or the complex "signified" by it), there is always another uttering of the same phrase, the same and yet completely other, as the earlier echo of itself, the repercussion of what has not yet been said. Or else, peering over ourselves in an effort to see the model that the childhood of our history seems to conceal, what we find is never our original but our double and our image, and then the indefinite reflection of this double, the fascinating movement of a resemblance that is nothing other than the slippage from semblance to semblance at the heart of a similitude where everything resembles everything without there being anything to resemble.

In Gorz's case, it is at the end of his narrative, as we have seen, that the shock occurs with which he suddenly reads what he knows to be the originary text, the complex that the "terror of identification" is for him. Yet, in the first twenty pages of the book, he had already formulated it in the most precise manner: "the horror he has of letting himself be identified with his acts or works, the need to escape the figure that his acts convey of him, by affirming himself as their overcoming." Why does this phrase not speak to him at this moment? Why is it not the revelation that, two hundred pages later, will return him to himself? What we have here, no doubt, is the proof of the movement that is accomplished in writing. At the same time we are able to discern that if he does not receive the communication of the phrase he nonetheless writes in all lucidity, it is because he is not truly there to hear it, not knowing that it concerns him as ego, for it is still but a neuter statement in a foreign language in which what appears of him only causes him to appear as other and in the indifference of the He without face, mask behind which there is still only his absent figure, a figure still to come. Everything depends on the reversal that occurs, in a way that is always a little mysterious, at a certain moment: it is when Gorz agrees to be identified with the one he now is—that is, to recognize that the "original" is not to be sought in the past but in the present, and that the revealing phrase can be heard only from the current versions that present the only meaning for which he must be responsible—that, by an abrupt and dazzling superimposition, all of the variations are able to coincide, all of the modifications of the same phrase, which is always other and always the same. And then, for an instant, he understands everything, understanding that there is no other origin of himself than his decidedly present ego (present, it is true, and already gathered in a book), and that it is now that all can begin: *hic Rhodus, hic salta.*

∼

We perceive what is at stake here: How can the movement of writing (that literature demands), this speech that speaks before any other, cold, without intimacy, without happiness, which perhaps says nothing and in which it nonetheless seems that profundity speaks, always speaking for a single person but impersonal, speaking entirely from within though it is the outside itself—how can this nonspeaking speech, ignorant of the true, whose flux is alien to dialectical power, ever become the language of truth, of happy mediation, of a dialogue once again possible? Between the two languages, will Gorz offer us the reality of an itinerary? What is striking in his attempt is the great distrust with which, wanting to speak the neuter speech, he goes along with its movement under the appeal of which he indeed wants to write, while keeping open, however, the possibility of returning to himself. He never severs the moorings. He says "He," but it is always about the I. He lets the foreign voice speak in him, but on condition that it not lose itself in the hollowness of indifferent chatter. There is a remarkable page in the book where he describes himself as being "paralyzed, ter- rorized" by all banal conversations about rain and good weather: he does not feel equal to banality. A moving avowal. What this tells us is that he is not able to accept inauthentic speech, which is, however, all that speaks when "one" speaks. Not having accepted it, nor even perhaps suffered it, he succeeds in saving himself from it, which leaves the experience inconclusive. This, I think, is the problem of nihilism—we do not know whether its power comes from our retreat before it or whether its essence is to withdraw before us: that is to say, whether this essence is always posed, deposed by the very question of the detour.

§ 24 Traces

Presence

What Jacques Dupin has written on Alberto Giacometti is fitting to a work as clear as it is unapparent and always ready to escape whatever it is that might attempt to measure it. After reading these "texts," I can better understand why such a work is close to us—I mean close to writing—to such an extent that every writer feels himself implicated by the work—although it is in no way "literary"—experiencing the need to question it constantly and knowing that he cannot repeat it in writing.[1]

"Surging forth of a separate presence," "incessant work," "discontinuity of the line" ("a line constantly interrupted, opening the emptiness, but dispelling it"): in each of these designations, dissociated and linked, that Jacques Dupin proposes to us, we are called toward the place from which we might see such a work (*Woman Standing, Woman in Venice*), if seeing were suited to the relation the work asks of us. This relation is one of distance. This distance is absolute. At this absolute distance, what appears before us, but as if without us, is the "surging forth of a presence"; presence is not something present; what is there, not approaching, not withdrawing, ignorant of all the games of the ungraspable, is there with the abrupt obviousness of presence, which refuses the gradual, the progressive, the slow advent, the insensible disappearance, and yet designates an infinite relation. Presence is the

217

surging forth of the "separate presence": that which comes to us as incomparable, immobile in the suddenness of the coming, and offers itself as other, as is, in its strangeness.

Jacques Dupin says to us: "There is, there always was, above all, for Giacometti, an instinct of cruelty, a need for destruction that strictly conditions his creative activity. From his earliest childhood the obsession with sexual murder provokes and governs certain imaginary representations. . . . He has a passion for war stories. The spectacle of violence fascinates and terrifies him." Whence the experience he had of presence. It is out of reach. One kills a man, one does violence to him; this has happened to all of us, either in act, or in speech, or as the result of an indifferent will; but presence always escapes the power that does violence. Presence, in face of the destruction that wants to reach it, disappears but remains intact, withdrawing into nullity, where it is dissipated without leaving any traces (one does not inherit presence; it is without tradition). To the experience of violence there corresponds the evidence of the presence that escapes it. And the attack of violence has become, for Giacometti, the gesture of the former-deformer, the creator-destroyer of whom Jacques Dupin speaks to us in this way: "The gesture of Giacometti: its repetition, its renewal, refute the disfiguring brutality of every particular intervention. Doing and undoing incessantly amounts to diminishing, deadening each gesture. . . . Thus the figurine that I see being sculpted first seems indifferent to the cruel attentions that the sculptor inflicts on it. Formed by an imperious, violent touch, it would seem that such a fragile apparition must inevitably return to the chaos from which it arose. Yet it resists. The destructive assaults it endures only bring imperceptible modifications to its graceful being. Their multiplication immunizes and protects it. . . . It lends itself to it and becomes accustomed to it. . . . Its autonomy and its identity proceed, in fact, from such torture, *on condition that it be without limit.*"

Presence is only presence at a distance, and this distance is absolute—that is, irreducible; that is, infinite. The gift of Giacometti, the one he makes us, is to open, in the space of the world, the infinite interval from which there is presence—for us, but as it were, without us. Yes, Giacometti gives us this, he draws us invisibly toward this point, a single point at which the present thing (the plastic object, the figured figure) changes into pure presence, the presence of the Other in its strangeness, that is to say, also radical non-presence. This distance (the void, says Jacques Dupin) is in no way distinct from the presence to which it belongs, just as it belongs to this absolutely distant that is others, to such an extent that one could say that what Giacometti sculpts is Distance, surrendering it to us and us to it, a moving and rigid distance, threatening and welcoming, tolerant-intolerant, and such that it is given to us each time forever and each time is swallowed up in an instant: a distance that is the very depth of presence, which, being completely manifest, reduced to its surface, seems without interiority, yet inviolable, because identical to the infinite of the Outside.

Presence which is not that of an idol. There is nothing less plastic than a figure of Giacometti's, to the extent that the reign of plastic art wants to make a beautiful form out of manifestation and a full and substantial reality out of form, to the extent that the presumptuous certainty of the visible is established through the reign of plastic art. One can call *Woman Standing* a figure or even a figurine, one can describe it in its nakedness; but what is it, this figure? Not what it represents, but the place of nonpresent presence; and its nakedness is the affirmation of naked presence that has nothing, is nothing, retains nothing, that nothing dissimulates. Presence of human transparency in its opacity, "presence of the unknown," but of man as unknown, turning toward us that which always turns away and putting us in the presence of what is between man and man, absolute distance, infinite strangeness.

Thus, each time, we receive from Giacometti this double discovery that is, each time, it is true, immediately lost: only man would be present to us, only he is alien to us.

Wakefulness

Roger Laporte's narrative is—it seems to me—an attempt to lead thought as far as the thinking of the neuter.[2] An attempt that is a reflection, and a reflection that is a moving, controlled, dominating experience. It must be given our full attention. I have written this on occasion, not without a great excess of simplification: the entire history of philosophy could be seen as an effort to domesticate the neuter or to impugn it—thus it is constantly repressed from our languages and our truths. How does one think the neuter? Is there a time, a historical time, a time without history, in which speaking is the exigency to speak in the neuter? What would happen, supposing the neuter were essentially that which speaks (does not speak) when we speak?

These are questions! And here are others: the neuter, being that which cannot be assigned any gender, escaping position as well as negation, also does not belong to any questioning that the question of being might precede, to which we are led by so many contemporary reflections. Being is not a neuter; it is but a screen for the neuter. How does one designate it? In *La Veille*, if one accepts that what is in play is the postulation of the neuter, "it" is marked from the first word precisely as the he, a he that has *obviously* always already disappeared and is nonetheless such that, outside the game of presence and absence, it seems, day and night, to propose itself, to withdraw itself from access in a manner that is frightening, ravishing; but—and at the same time—it seems destined to a proximity or to a distance that would emerge, through a privileged turn, from the *fact of writing*, the possibility of an *I* that *writes* (in the necessary contradiction of these two terms) and of a *work* to be written. Why? These are the givens of an experience. The writer can "give" himself only this affirmation: that by writing, by not writing, the "I" who writes remains at an inappreciable distance from a "he."

Thus we have three terms defined by a certain relation: writing, an I, a he; and the entire narrative stems from a constant and dramatic inversion of these three terms, an inversion maintained between them by the dissymmetry and infinity of their relation. But we immediately perceive, in this formidable game, that one of the factors risks predominating, even if it erases itself: it is the "I." It alone, apparently, is certain; the others are not; to write, one never knows if one writes, and the "he" never coincides with any identification, it is the non-coincident. This is why we are present—these movements are described with trembling sobriety, a mastery on the edge of chaos—before the movements of the "I" that tenses itself, anguishes itself, defends itself, restrains itself, yet exposes itself. The danger, for the search, is to transform the "he" into He, favorable Presence, formidable Absence—that is, into a power that is perhaps "separate from everything," yet unified, unifying. The danger comes from the tension of the "I": the I, in this surprising dialogue, besides its own unity, can project onto this region that is other only the legitimate desire not to lose itself, its reserve, in face of the mystery that is played out when, writing, not writing, it devotes itself to a work. And there is also the danger of hypostasizing the Work, of making it sacred, in such a way that the writer, once the work is written and he has been dismissed, will be ascetically rewarded by the sacrifice he accords in advance to an impersonal glory in which he will not participate, solitary Party where the *He* would be celebrated without anyone's knowledge and in its non-appearance.

The neuter is a threat and a scandal for thought. The neuter, were we to think it, would free thought of the fascination with unity (whether the latter be logical, dialectical, intuitive, mystical), turning us over to an exigency that is altogether other, capable of failing and of escaping all unification. The neuter is not singular, nor does it tend toward the Singular; it turns us not toward what assembles but equally toward what disperses, not toward what joins but perhaps disjoins, not toward work but toward idleness, turning us toward that which always diverts and diverts itself, in such a way that the central point toward which we would seem to be drawn when writing would only be the absence of center, the lack of origin. To write under the pressure of the neuter: to write as if in the direction of the unknown. This does not mean to speak the unspeakable, to recount the unrecountable, to remember the immemorable, but to prepare language for a radical and discreet mutation, as can be foreseen if we recall the following statement that I will be content to repeat: the unknown as neuter, whether it is, whether it is not, could not find its determination there, but only insofar as the relation to the unknown is a relation that light will not open, that the absence of light will not close—a neuter relation; which means that to think in the neuter is to think, that is, to write while turning away from all that is visible and all that is invisible.

It seems to me that it is in relation to such a search that one must read Roger Laporte's book, a major book (rich in other unsuspected books), and not by asking it whether it teaches us something about inspiration or if it disappoints us by refusing to teach us anything about it. Approach of the neuter, *La Veille* is without clarity, without obscurity; neither diurnal nor nocturnal; waking without awakening; and helping us, outside of any image and all abstraction, to decide what the presence of the unknown would be if, in this presence infinitely distant and infinitely dispersed, the presence of speech, the unknown were made present, and always unknown: a vigilance of the before-waking, the "watching over the unwatched."

The Book of Questions

I had promised myself to say nothing about the book, the books of Edmond Jabès (a silence I prefer to keep in regard to certain austere, even remote works that have been talked about too quickly and, as a result of their strange renown, are reduced to a fixed and categorized meaning). There are thus certain works that trust in our discretion. We do them a disservice by pointing to them; or, more exactly, we take from them the space that had been that of reserve and friendship. But in the end, there comes a moment when the austerity that is the center of every important book, be it the most tender or the most painful, severs the ties and takes it away from us. The book no longer belongs to anyone; it is this that consecrates it as book.[3]

In the totality of fragments, thoughts, dialogues, invocations, narrative movements, and scattered words that make up the detour of a single poem, I find the powers of interruption at work, so that the writing, and what is proposed to writing (the uninterrupted murmur, what does not stop), must be accomplished in the act of interrupting itself. But here, in *The Book of Questions*—the very title speaks of its insecurity, its painful force—the rupture not only is marked by poetic fragmentation at its various levels of meaning, but is also questioned, suffered, regrasped, and made to speak, always twice, and each time doubled: in history, and in the writing at the margins of history. In history, where the center of the rupture is called Judaism. In the writing, which is the very difficulty of the poet, the man who wants to speak justly—but which is also the difficult justice of Jewish law, the inscribed word that cannot be played with, and which is spirit, because it is the burden and fatigue of the letter.

A rupture suffered in history, where catastrophe still speaks, and where the infinite violence of pain is always near: the rupture of violent power that has tried to make and mark an entire era. Then, the other, the original rupture, which is anterior to history, and which is not suffered but required, and which, expressing distance in regard to every power, delimits the interval where Judaism introduces its own affirmation: the rupture that reveals "the wound . . . invisible at its beginning," "this wound rediscovered in a race that has issued from the book," "nothing but the pain whose past and continuity merge with those of the book." For this interval, this gap, previously affirmed in relation to the pressure of things and the domination of events, precisely marks the place where the word is established, the word that invites man to no longer identify himself with his power. The word of impossibility. And then we understand that the meditation of the poet Jabès on the poetic act and its demands can be coupled with the meditation on his recent and ageless ties to the Jewish condition.[4] "I have spoken of the difficulty of being a Jew, which is inseparable from the difficulty of being a writer, for Judaism and writing are but the same hope, the same wait, and the same wearing away." In such a way that *The Book of Questions* is always written twice—the book that interrogates the movement of the rupture, by which the book is made, and the book in which "the virile word of the renewed history of a people folded in on itself" is designated—a double movement that Edmond Jabès supports: supports without unifying it, or even being able to reconcile it.

There is the empty, desertlike waiting that holds back the writer who works at the threshold of the book, making him the guardian of the threshold, his writing a desert, and from his very being the void and absence of a promise; and if this waiting is answered by another waiting (another desert) in which the first ten words of interdiction were pronounced, there is also, nevertheless, between the one and the other, a void, a divergence, a rupture. Because, first of all, the Tables of the Law were broken when still only barely touched by the divine hand (a curse consistent with the removal of interdiction, not with punishment), and were written again, but not in their originality, so that it is from an already destroyed word that man learns the demand that must speak to him: there is no real first understanding, no initial and unbroken word, as if one could never speak except the second time, after having refused to listen and having taken a distance in regard to the origin. Secondly—and this is perhaps the most important teaching of the "virile word"— the first text (which is never the first), the written word, the scripture (how strange the way this induces reflection, the first word, which is not uttered but written, whose advent is the strictness of the letter, with only itself as precedent, and with no other meaning but that of a graven and continually aggravated demand), is also, at the same time, a commented text that not only must be reuttered in its identity but learned in its inexhaustible difference. "The homeland of the Jews," says Jabès, "is a sacred text in the middle of the commentaries it inspired." The dignity and importance of exegesis in the rabbinic tradition: the written law, the unoriginal text of the origin, must always be taken on by the commenting voice—reaffirmed by the oral commentary, which does not come after it, but is contemporary to it[5]—taken on, but unjoined, in this dis-junction that is the measure of its infinity. Thus, the simultaneity of the first scriptural text and the context of the second word that interprets it, introduces a new form, a new interval in which it is now the sacred itself, in its too immediate power, that is held at a distance, and, if we dare to say it, ex-ecrated.

By the arduous and scathing experience that Judaism carries with it—a shattering that continually rises, not only up to the Tables of the Law but on this side of creation (the breaking of the Vessels) and up to loftiness itself; by a tradition of exegesis that does not worship signs but that sets itself up in the gaps they indicate—the man of words, the poet, feels involved, confirmed, but also contested, and in his turn, contesting. We can do nothing concerning his inter-ruption. On the one hand, we cannot answer his austere criticism, because he is the guardian of strictness and has denounced poetic affirmation, the neuter word that attests to no one, neither recognizes nor leaves any traces, and dwells without guarantee. But, on the other hand, how can the poet—the man without authority and without control, who accepts as his most personal duty the task of answering this interruption that continually breaks the seal of his word and makes it faithfully unfaithful—rely on a first message, the reference to the Unique, the affirmation of the Transcendent Being that, through the distance between Creator and created, pretends to give us the exact dimension of the interruption, and thus its foundation, while at the same time intercepting the message? And doubtless the poet is neither the support nor the substitute of multiple gods, nor the unseeing face of their absence. And neither is he the one, dedicated to the word, who would turn this vocation and devotion into something arrogant, an idolatrous power, a privilege of enchantment, or a kind of magic that could be manipulated, even in illusion, with absolute freedom. He is neither free nor in heteronomy, or more exactly, the heteronomy he is in is not that of a moral law. His discourse is dis-course. And this dis-course makes him responsible for the interruption on all its levels—as work; as fatigue, pain, unhappiness; as inaction of the work's absence—and constantly urges him to carry through the act of breaking (a rupture that is the skill of rhythm), for he knows that the word, too, can become power and violence, a power, even though forbidden and bearing interdiction, that risks becoming the simple power that forbids (as perhaps comes to pass in all ethical systems).

"Do not forget that you are the essence of a rupture." The two experiences, that of Judaism and that of writing, at once joined and separate, which Jabès expresses and affirms, the one through the other, but also through the patience and generosity of his double vocation, have their common origin in the ambiguity of this rupture that, even in its explosion, reveals the center (essence, unity) while leaving it intact, but that is perhaps also the explosion of the center, the decentered point that is center only in the shattering of its explosion. "The way I have taken is the most arduous. . . . It begins in difficulty—the difficulty of being and writing—and ends in difficulty." A difficulty that he succeeds in maintaining, without attenuating it, in the measure of a just voice. This is perhaps the book's most important characteristic: this holding back, even when it must reply to the most painful blows. It is a book of discretion, not because he refrains from saying all that must be said, but because he holds himself back in the space or the time of pause, where the Law, the pure arrest of the forbidden, comes to ease its severity, and where the cry becomes "*patience*," "*the innocence of the cry*." The tender endurance of the song. A cut and broken word; but the gap becomes a questioning decision, and then a narrative in which the separated beings it evokes, Sarah and Yukel (separated, because between them they bear the affirmation of a profound community: separated, because they are united), are evoked so discreetly, either spoken of or not spoken of, that they live, maintained beside each other in the folds and refoldings of the book, in the expectation of their meeting and their always deferred separation. It is interesting to mention here—precisely because it seems that Jabès has been in no way influenced by them—the marvelous Hasidic tales, and *Gog and Magog*, of Martin Buber, which we can now read, collected, rewritten, and almost reinvented by him, in a French version that I find extremely illuminating.[6] The relationship between the contemporary poet and these legendary stories is not due solely to the medium of the Eastern tale, that is to say, to genre and tradition. I can explain myself better by what Martin Buber tells us of one of the last representatives of Hasidism, who was a contemporary of the crisis, a crisis whose essence is still very much with us: he was, we are told, capable of a modest silence without pretension, but which, nevertheless, was infinite; neither the authority of ecstasy nor the effusion of prayer was expressed in the silence, only "a voiceless cry," the holding back of "mute tears." This voiceless cry, adds Buber, is the universal reaction of the Jews to their great suffering: when "it's going badly," the cry "is fitting." It is also, at all times, the word that is fitting for the poem, and it is in this word, its hidden solitude, its feverish pain, and its friendship, that Edmond Jabès has found, precisely, the fitness.

> *From one word to one word*
> *a possible void*

TRANSLATED BY PAUL AUSTER
AND ELIZABETH ROTTENBERG

§ 25 Gog and
Magog

In truth, what does the word *Hasidism* evoke in us? Almost nothing: certain memories of medieval Jewish devotion, the Golem, the
mysteries of the Cabala, the powers of occult men bound to the
divine secret, the hidden knowledge of the ghetto. But precisely all
of these evocations are already false. The Hasidism of the eighteenth century has almost nothing to do with the Hasidism of the
Middle Ages. If it receives certain themes from the Cabala, it does
so by popularizing them and by retaining their most common
aspects. The Cabala is an esotericism.[1] Hasidism, on the contrary,
wants everyone to have access to the secret. And the teacher of the
Hasidim is not a learned, solitary man, who remains in contemplation of the august mysteries; he is a religious leader, responsible
for a community, which he has participate in his experiences and to
which he teaches these experiences through his life and in a simple
and living language. Here, personality counts more than doctrine.
It is by spiritual power, the vitality and originality of strong individuals, that the Zaddikim (the Righteous Ones or the Saints), at least
for the first five generations, impose themselves and show the
authenticity of the religious movement. Their knowledge is in no
way comparable with that of even the most ordinary teachers of
rabbinical erudition. It is not science but the gift of grace, the
charismatic force, the prestige of the heart that marks them out
and assembles students, believers, pilgrims around them. "I did not

go to the 'Maggid' of Meseritz to learn Torah from him, but to watch him tie the laces of his shoes." This remark by a disciple is of a far stranger nature for the Jewish faith than it is for either the Christian or Far Eastern faith. A hidden Zaddik, speaking of the rabbis who "say Torah" (that is, interpret the written words with their spiritual knowledge), declares: "What is this, to say Torah? Each must act in such a way that his conduct is a Torah, and he himself a Torah." Here, we clearly see how Hasidism offers points of encounter with a doctrine of existence. Of the founder of this movement, the Baal-Shem, it is said that what he did, he did with his whole body, and he himself formulated this recommendation: "Everything that your hand finds to do, do it with all your might." Perhaps it is the distinctive feature of any religious teacher to teach profound truths with the most ordinary gestures rather than with doctrine. In the accounts of wisdom, we find countless reminders of this; the following, for example: a Zen master, when the student who has served him for years complains that he has still not been initiated into wisdom, answers him, "From the day of your arrival, I have not stopped teaching you wisdom."—"How is this, Master?"—"When you brought me a cup of tea, did I not take it? When you bowed before me, did I not return your reverence?" The student bows his head and understands. Hasidism thus follows in a tradition that does not belong to it. But precisely in relation to Jewish faith and even to Jewish mysticism, it brings new features that we should perhaps not receive as representative.

～

Our ignorance of the important movements of Hebraic mysticism is obviously great, commensurate with the prestige with which we regard it. It is a phenomenon worth reflecting upon. One whole part of the literary nineteenth century—not to go further back—lived in the frightened admiration of the mysteries of the Cabala, about which no one was in any position to have an accurate idea. This is the counterpart to anti-Semitism. A secret knowledge, a hidden power, deeply buried in anonymous heads, offers to the vague unbelief of writers resources of oneiric compensation

from which they would like to make literature profit. There is
something that attracts them in the strangeness of surprising mythological imaginations, in the force of a very ancient, very occult,
and very cursed knowledge, and finally in the power attributed to
certain written words. All this is very tempting. That there should
be books unknown to all, capable of a mysterious life, containing
the highest secrets stolen from the mystery itself: this is a literary
opportunity that every writer must jealously admire.

To this must be added, it is true, a discretion that the writer does
not suspect and that he would imitate perhaps only reluctantly
himself. Yet this is one of the proudest features of Jewish mysticism.
The mystics of other religions are always ready to reveal at great
length the greatest experiences they have had; the Christians are
not the least talkative (one must naturally make an exception for
Meister Eckhart). The teachers of Cabalism show an extreme
aversion to speaking about themselves; they hold themselves aloof
from all autobiography; of the great ecstatic movements, from
which they have benefited no less than others, they do not wish to
make a subject of confidences, nor even of instruction (with the
exception of Abulafia and his school), and it has taken the accident
of centuries to preserve personal documents for us, not destined to
be published, in which we find explicit testimonies. This is because
they have no interest in their own movement, being more ashamed
of their personal adventure than prepared to be exalted by it, and
are concerned only with connecting the revelations they take from
it to the objectivity of "tradition." Is this out of powerlessness? Out
of a concern not to reduce what does not let itself be said to words?
Rather, out of a respect for language itself, the divine origin and
sacred value of which they recognize. The Hebrew language can
speak of God, because God speaks in it, and it can reach God
because it comes from God. But it is not made so that we can slip
our little individual stories into it, be they in praise of what is not
ourselves. There is, in the whole immense Jewish mystical production, a striking search for anonymity. Authors slip away under
august names. The Zohar is the best-defended example of this
pseudepigraphy. The need to be an author is obviously not nearly

as strong as the need to be the impersonal place in which the tradition is affirmed par excellence. Private, "subjective" revelations have no significance; the more authentic the revelation, the more what it reveals belongs to the originary foundation of common knowledge—common but mysterious, and mysterious both because it concerns what is hidden and because it does so only for a few. Anonymity is here the cloak of invisibility. An incognito of sorts hides the mastery and makes it more essential. The number of Cabalists whose teaching bears the mark of a personality is very small, remarks G. G. Scholem, and one must arrive precisely at the Hasidic movement in order to find, through a kind of degeneracy, individuals and leaders.

~

One might attribute the fundamental predisposition to disappear to the hatred of the "I am," proper to all mysticism.[2] But another feature of Hebraic mysticism is precisely that it does not lay claim, except in very rare cases, to a concrete union, which would cancel out all difference, between God and man. The feeling of a distance never abolished, but on the contrary maintained pure and preserved, belongs to the ecstatic movement itself. If, as Buber says, the great feat of Israel is not to have taught one God, but to have founded history upon a dialogue between divinity and humanity, this concern for reciprocal speech, in which the I and the You meet without erasing one another, is at the heart of the most fervent divine exchange. Speech alone can cross the abyss; the voice of God alone, God as voice, as power that addresses without letting itself be addressed in turn, makes this separation the locus of understanding. In every religion, no doubt, there have been relations between Creator and creature through sacrifice, prayer, inner rapture. But in Israel, a unique relation of familiarity and strangeness, of proximity and distance, of freedom and submission, of simplicity and ritual complication comes to light, a relation whose speech—the mystery and friendship of speech, its justice and reciprocity, the call it conveys and the response it awaits—constitutes the principle or the substance. In the Christian West, where the tendency to a monologic life is pressing, there is always the secret conviction that a God to whom one speaks and who speaks to one is neither pure nor divine enough. This is because the conversation seeks to be altogether interior, of a uniquely spiritual essence, a vanishing symposium in which the soul alone seeks to have dealings with God alone—and not a fundamental dialogue of a real nation, representing real humanity, with the One who is essentially speech. To say *you* to God in the tradition of Israel is thus not a pure doing of the solitary soul or the pretension of poor lyricism; it is first of all to hold oneself to the truth of a concrete relation that passes by way of history and seeks to bring about the possibility of a total and living encounter in the world. A movement that, it is true, the fact of exile comes to obscure, a phenomenon of painfully inexhaustible significance, whose immense scope both reduces human initiative and solicits it without measure.

Before quickly proceeding to Buber's book, which describes, in connection with an episode of modern history, this cosmic dimension in which the mix of earthly and heavenly planes causes us to live, one must remember that Cabalism, this strange creation, admired and certainly admirable, was almost always greeted with reserve in places of Jewish faith, often with disgust and even shame. G. G. Scholem, to whom we owe a knowledge of these things that is finally somewhat precise, and who judges them with an impartial assurance,[3] says exactly this: "If we consider the writings of the important Cabalists, we are constantly torn between admiration and disgust." The reason for this is clear. The Jewish religion, marked from its origin by moral exigencies, by the concern with having the distinction between Good and Evil superimposed on and in agreement with the distinction between the Sacred and the Profane, affirmed itself in a world of mythology by a coherent refusal of all mythical idolatry. However, with Cabalism, the myth takes its revenge on its victor. "The principle symbols of the Cabala," says Scholem, "arise from an authentic religious feeling, but at the same time are invariably marked by the world of mythology." The gnosis that took form precisely through contact with Judaism, in its sphere of influence and by fighting against it, finally succeeds in invading Jewish mysticism by proposing to it its own figures of expression (schemata of very bizarre appearance, superb remnants of the old Oriental religions), which the Cabalists use to approach theological problems of importance and to elaborate a living grasp of them. The result is a surprising mix of profound thoughts and extravagant myths, strange figures and pure ideas, fiery images and simple, painful visions. That such creations should have been successful in closed places of pious erudition might be explainable. But the immense repercussion of the Cabala for centuries among the people and finally in universal culture is a mysterious phenomenon, a sign of the creative forces that affirmed themselves in it and that had ties to the popular mythology of the Jewish universe; a sign also of the appeal, impossible to vanquish, of a certain mythical imagination, when it gives form to intense themes, halfway between religion and thought (here is a subject of reflection for our own inner vagaries).

～

Indeed, to grasp the quality of enchantment at work in Buber's book, one must make it clear, I think, that Buber is almost not the author of the book.[4] This is not to diminish its merits; on the contrary, it is to admire the naive assurance with which the book has succeeded in making us live in the marvelous world of the narration, this tradition of narratives and stories in which events and gestures of real people take place. The two protagonists of the narrative, the Rabbi of Lublin, the "Seer," and his student, the "saint Jew" (who oppose each other like two modes of spiritual action, the one desiring to produce certain effects magically, the other holding himself to a pure inner conversion), both belong, as do all of the figures of their entourage, as do the principal incidents of their lives and even the words that are attributed to them, to the living community of stories told and transmitted from generation to generation. This is one of the wealths of Hasidism. Naturally, it is not of absolute originality, since one of the creations of rabbinical thought is, besides the Halakah (the Law), the Haggadah (the Narration); and Jewish faith has always succeeded in keeping alive the narrative force that allows any believer to participate, in his real life, not only in the great biblical stories but also in a prodigious profusion of narratives in which earth and sky are mixed in a spirit of familiarity and marvel. In Hasidism, where doctrine is almost nothing and the glamour of concrete action almost everything, narratives are a part of religious existence. Not only do disciples constantly tell a superabundance of stories about their teachers, but the Zaddikim barely express themselves except by means of anecdote and, what is more, live in some sense in the mode of narration. From this results a very striking feature of literary enchantment: when, in their lifetime, one attributes to the great teachers of a generation acts that belong to a tradition much more ancient, the smallest details of which everyone knows and recognizes, what is told appears neither less spontaneous nor less true—on the contrary: something very ancient is, again, reproducing itself, affirming the unweakening continuity of tradition, the intact state of its power, its truth always in anticipation, the ability to realize itself once again from the inexhaustible event.

History here is curiously divided among the cycle of immutable religious celebrations; the appearance of men of great stature, with their very characteristic personal features, who belong to a new community in the process of creating its own legend; and finally the events of the profane outside world that cannot remain alien to the destiny of faith. Whence a subtle mix of legendary actions, singular psychological features, and historical tension. That we should be in the presence of an original version—and, all in all, spiritually much richer—of *War and Peace*, this is what the reading discovers with a start of interest and surprise. There is something moving in the manner in which the formidable events of the West—the French Revolution, the wars of Bonaparte, and then his monumental glory as master of the century—come to be inscribed, as from the greatest distance and reduced to a few minuscule points on the retina of the Seer of Lublin, who, from the occult window of his cell, silently contemplates them and tries to make them serve his own designs. Tolstoy sought to humble historical individualities by ascribing the most glorious initiatives of military art to chance.

Here the change of perspective is even more impressive. In this separate world of the Jewish communities, what takes place on the outside is so remote, so deprived of reality, and so outside the realm of true life that it is the obscure Rebbe who becomes the figure of gigantic proportions, whereas the enigmatic man of war who traverses history in the name of a mission he does not suspect acquires his grandeur simply as an allusion to several prophetic verses.

The story, told by Buber, may also seem like the illustration of the theme of Doctor Faustus, itself obviously derived from Hebraic models. The relations between mysticism and magic have always been extremely entangled in Cabalism. The Hasid of the Middle Ages, the pious German Jew, is the true master of magical power: without resources, abandoned, deprived of himself, sublimely indifferent, he is capable of dominating all forces; he can do everything because he is nothing, an idea of which Greek stoicism and cynicism had already taken advantage. Of the Hasid, one could say what Eleazer of Worms said magnificently of the All-Powerful: "He keeps silent and carries the universe." Later, in the prophetic Cabala of Abulafia, mysticism, which has the great divine names as its principal object of meditation, naturally associates itself with the magical disciplines that invoke the terrible powers of names. As for the Cabalism of the Zohar, it is, to a certain extent, too haughty to use mystery toward private ends, but magic then becomes metaphysical: just as man has the power to penetrate the secrets of the contradiction of Being, so he has the power to embrace the means proper to suspend this contradiction. If the common belief of Cabalism consists in interpreting the problem of the world as a problem of divinity, then it seems that "earthly reality must mysteriously react upon that of the heavens, for everything, including our activity, has its *deep roots* in the kingdom of the Sephiroth." Whence this maxim of the Zohar: "The impetus from below calls forth that from above."

Following the expulsion from Spain, when the miseries of exile are transformed into an unbearable spiritual drama, the Cabalists, who had until then been more interested in the beginning than in the end of the world (the mystical path toward God being but the reversal of the process through which we have departed from God; this is the originary movement that first had to be grasped), will bring all of their power of elucidation to bear on the doctrine of return. This will be the part of Isaac Luria, whose influence was prodigious and perpetuated itself (by popularizing itself) in Hasidism. One might think that the thought of exile, exile of man, exile of Israel condemned to separation and dispersion would definitively bring to a close the divine and earthly plans and deliver man to the powerless wait. But exile cannot be only a local event; it necessarily affects all powers; it is also the exile of God, the separation of one part of God from himself, the suffering of particles of light maintained captive in obscurity. One recognizes here the ancient conception of gnosis as it remained surprisingly alive: it is Sophia, the light fallen into darkness, a being abandoned and yet divine, separated from its origin and yet not separated, for separation is called *time* and reunion, *eternity*. In most gnostic doctrines, it is through the sky alone that the divine soul, fallen to earth, can be recalled: there is only one possible action, that which is directed from above to below. However, notes Buber, in Jewish mystical thought, founded upon a relation of reciprocity, upon a free dialogue between the earthly I and the divine You, man remains the auxiliary of God. The spheres are separated so that man can bring them together. All creation and God himself lie in wait for man. It is he who must complete the enthronement of God in his kingdom, unify the divine name, return the Chekhina to its Master. This anticipation on the part of God, who shares in the exile, is profound and moving: it illustrates the responsibility of man, the value of his action, his sovereign influence in the destiny of the Whole. "The Righteous Ones increase the power of the Sovereignty Above." A strong belief, but one that offers the Righteous Ones the greatest temptations of pride and spiritual domination.

~

How, in Buber's story, is Napoleon called on to collaborate in the hope of salvation? There are two levels of interpretation. According to the letter, things are simple. Since a prophecy proclaims that the victory of Gog, from the land of Magog, will immediately precede the coming of the Messiah, there is great interest in letting the man from the West become the demonic force capable of raising the abyss and of dragging the seventy peoples into it. But for this, he must truly be Gog, the being of unlimited darkness, and for him to become it, it is necessary for the great Zaddikim, those who read in the sky and who are in touch with the powers, to cooperate in his destiny and help him take on a suprahuman dimension. Indeed, one understands that what is at issue here is a very risky and very questionable intervention. Should one favor Evil, carry it to its paroxysm, precipitate the catastrophe so that deliverance might also be brought nearer? Should one hasten the end? The horrible memory of Sabbateanism, to which no allusion is made in Buber's narrative out of a revealing sense of discretion, is certainly in the background of this entire action. I will recall the story briefly. Sabbatai Zebi is the Messiah of the seventeenth century who, in the end, converted to Islam. What is strange about his appearance is that his apostasy, far from discrediting him, became the sign of his redemptive mission. To profoundly vanquish Evil, one must descend to the unhappy depths and array oneself with Evil itself. The apostasy, the renunciation of self, the obligation to live internally in the refusal of one's truth (which was precisely what was imposed on the Morranos by the Church) is the supreme sacrifice of which the Messiah becomes capable. Here we have, taken much further than in Christianity, the paradox as mystical foundation of salvation. The disciple of Christ, to recognize the Savior in a poor man condemned to death and crucified, certainly had a great effort of faith to accomplish, but what must it be then when the Savior is an apostate, when the act to glorify is no longer only an infamous death but betrayal, when the Christ makes himself Judas? Scholem says it well: the paradox becomes horrifying, it leads straight to the abyss. What profound despair, what energy of belief must have been gathered and abruptly tapped for so many men to have rallied around such an oddity and upheld it.

The adventure of Sabbatai Zebi was a painful catastrophe. It marked the advent of religious nihilism, the rupture with traditional values, under the justification that at the end of the world, Evil is sacred and the Ancient Law without force; finally, it gravely altered authentic Jewish messianism. Although Hasidism is, as it were, the heir of this aberrant movement, it constitutes its purified image, in the margins of orthodoxy and struggling against it, without, however, ever breaking with the faith of tradition. Whence the dramatic nature of the debates between Rebbes on the possibility of having Evil serve Good without the latter being engulfed, on the right to intervene in the depths, and finally on the meaning of the authority that the great Zaddikim assume for themselves, very tempted as they necessarily are by dreams of power. Their role is singular, their mission indecisive; they form a compromise of sorts between the visible Messiah, as Sabbateanism made him appear, and what is perhaps the true Hebraic tradition: a tradition according to which the messianic force is not expressed in a single being but is at work in everyone, in a hidden manner, everyday and anonymous, in such a way that each person, obscurely and without privilege, is responsible for the ultimate event that is realized invisibly, also, at every moment. The Zaddikim do not claim the role of Messiah by any means: on the contrary, they defend against it, and the most prideful with a movement of piety and fear. First of all, there are a number of them, thirty-six manifest and thirty-six hidden, and although the disciples are always ready, as is natural, to place their teacher alone above all others, this plurality, as if given by law, forms a secret defense against the vertiginousness of the one. However, they are individuals who are surprisingly strong, rich with an unlimited spiritual authority and often embodying a dangerous will to power. The Zaddik is a man apart. He is very close to the simplicity of ordinary man (whence his influence and often his grandeur) and he is the exception: the man capable of seeing, who has dealings with Good and Evil, who conveys the blessing from below to above and from above to below, the privileged being who with more concentration than all others is turned toward the salutary task. However, he is but a man; indeed, he is the man par excellence, the "true man," as is said of the Seer of Lublin, and the true man is more important than an angel, because the angel stands immobile, whereas the man passes, and in passing, contributes to maintaining, renewing the movement of the world. It is this incessant renewal that is the principle of life of the Zaddik, in whom is gathered, freed from the arbitrary and in order to return to its origin, the process of creative becoming: the man thus endowed with great powers who acts in view and in virtue of divine unity, but not through himself alone, to the extent that, as a man of exception, he remains bound to the community of simple men, of whom he is but the representative and guide.

Buber's narrative speaks to us of this world, surprising, remote, and close, with simple persuasiveness. It has all the charm of the stories, their ambiguous innocence, which, in transforming teaching into image and image into truth, makes reading a kind of mysterious dream from which one still awakens from time to time, wondering if a mystery so perfectly recounted were not solely fated to be realized in tales.

§ 26 Kafka
and Brod

Max Brod saw something in Kafka's glory that was not very reassuring, something that made him regret having helped it come into being. "When I see how humanity refuses the salutary gift contained in Kafka's writings, I suffer sometimes for having torn the work from the obscurity of destruction into which its author wanted to see it fall. Did Kafka sense the abuse to which his work might be exposed, and is this why he did not want to authorize its publication?" It was perhaps a little late to be asking oneself the question. The posthumous years having done their work, Brod was not grappling with the discreet fame he might have wished for— but, from the beginning, had he not wanted it to be dazzling? Did he not suffer when Werfel read the first writings of their common friend and said, "Outside of Tetschenbodebach, no one will understand Kafka"? Did he not recognize a part of himself in the glory of which he complained? Was it not also in keeping with him, in his image, not close to Kafka's reserve but close to Brod's swiftness of action, close to his honest optimism, his determined certainty? Perhaps there had to be Brod beside Kafka for the latter to overcome the discomfort that prevented him from writing. The novel that they write in collaboration is a sign of this joint destiny: a collaboration about which Kafka speaks with uneasiness, which engages him, in every sentence, to concessions from which he suffers, he says, in his very depths. This collaboration ceases almost immediately, but it resumes after Kafka's death, closer than it had even been before, heavier also for the living friend who has dedicated himself with extraordinary faith to bringing to light a work destined, without him, to disappear. It would be unfair—and frivolous—to say that there is, in every writer, a Brod and a Kafka, and that we write only insofar as we satisfy the active part of ourselves, or else that we become famous only if, at a certain moment, we abandon ourselves completely to the unlimited devotion of the friend. The injustice would consist in reserving for Kafka all the merit of literary purity—hesitation before the act of writing, refusal to publish, decision to destroy the work—and in charging the powerful, friendly double with all the responsibilities connected to the earthly management of a work too glorious. Kafka dead is intimately responsible for the survival of which Brod was the obstinate instigator. Otherwise, why would he have made Brod his legatee? Why, if he had wanted to make his work disappear, did he not destroy it? Why did he read it to his friends? Why did he share many of his manuscripts with Felice Bauer, with Milena, not, no doubt, out of literary vanity, but to show himself in his dark realms and in his lightless destiny?

Brod's fate is also moving. At first haunted by this admirable friend, he makes him the hero of his novels—a strange metamorphosis, a sign that he feels himself bound to a shadow, but not bound by the duty to leave the shadow undisturbed. Then he undertakes the publication of a work, of which he was the first and for a long time the only one to recognize the exceptional value. He must find publishers, and the publishers evade him; he must collect the texts, which evade him no less; affirm their coherence, discover in the scattered manuscripts, almost none of which is finished, the completeness that is hidden in them. Publication begins, it too is fragmentary. Of the big novels, certain chapters are held back, one does not know why. Here and there, one does not know how, a certain page torn from the whole comes to light, a certain ray escapes from a hearth still unknown, shines, and is extinguished. Because one must protect the living, one excludes from the *Diary* documents that are too direct or notes that seem insignificant; one confines oneself to the essential, but where is the essential? However, the glory of the writer quickly becomes powerful, soon all-powerful. What is unpublished cannot stay unpublished. It is like a greedy force, irresistible, a force that digs about in even the most protected reaches, and little by little, everything that Kafka said for himself, about himself, about those he loved, could not love, is handed over, in the greatest disorder, to an abundance of commentaries, themselves disorganized, contradictory, respectful, insolent, tireless, and such that the most impudent writer would hesitate to stand up to such curiosity.

There is nothing, however, that one should not approve of in this terrible bringing to light. Once the decision to publish is made, it follows that everything must be. Everything must appear, this is the rule. He who writes submits to this rule, even if he rejects it. From the time that publication of the complete works was undertaken—it is reaching its end—the part left to chance and to the arbitrary is reduced as much as possible. We will know everything, in the order in which it is reasonable—though always contestable—to know it, with exceptions as far as the letters are concerned: for example, passages that implicate certain living people have still been deleted from a few letters, but the living quickly disappear. Already, the ordeal of the war and the persecution, to an extent that it is not necessary to recall, has wiped out witnesses and the consideration that they are due; it has also wiped out, it is true, the testimonies and destroyed a large part of the work, already in part destroyed by Kafka during his lifetime, and then, after his death, according to the instructions he had left, by Dora Diamant, especially with regard to the *Diary*. (The *Diary* is missing precisely for the last part of his life, from 1923 on, when he found, as we are told, peace and reconciliation. This is what we are told, but we do not know it, and when, in reading his *Diary*, we see just how differently he judged himself from the way his friends and those who were close to him judged him, we must recognize that the meaning of the events that marked the coming of his end remain for us, for the moment, unknown.)

But who is Kafka? While he began to bring to light the manuscripts of his friend according to his means, and because fame, with "its misunderstandings and falsifications," was already trying to decipher the mysterious face, Brod decided to write a book that would better explain him, a biographical book, but also a book of interpretation and commentary in which he attempted to bring the work into the proper light, the light in which he wanted it to be seen.[1] A book of great interest but, concerning the events in Kafka's existence, necessarily reserved, a little disorganized, and allusive— in short, incomplete, because a single witness does not know everything. Brod, while recognizing the great complexity and the central mystery of genius that inhabited his friend, always protested against the very dark colors in which posterity, with a black preference, was immediately pleased to see this figure and this work. Kafka's other friends have, moreover, all recognized, loved, and celebrated the living force in him, the gaiety, the youthfulness of a sensitive and wonderfully just spirit. "Was Kafka in perfect despair?" Felix Weltsch asks himself, and answers: "It is very hard, even impossible, to see this man who was open to all impressions and whose eyes gave forth such a succoring light as someone in despair." "In general," says Brod, "all those who have created an image of Kafka for themselves on the basis of his writings have before their eyes a tonality that is essentially darker than those who knew him personally." This is why the biographer acknowledges having accumulated in his biography all of the features capable of correcting this conventional picture. Important testimony that everything indeed confirms. But should one forget the other face, "the man with too big a shadow," forget his profound sadness, his solitude, his estrangement from the world, his moments of indifference and coldness, his anguish, his obscure torments, the struggles that brought him to the edge of distraction (especially in 1922 in Spindlermühle)? Who knew Kafka? Why is it, then, that the latter rejects, in advance, his friends' judgments of him?[2] Why are those who knew him, when they pass from the memory of a young man, sensitive and gay, to the work—novels and writings—surprised to pass into a nocturnal world, a world of cold torment, a world not without light but in which light blinds at the same time that it illuminates; gives hope, but makes hope the shadow of anguish and despair? Why is it that he who, in his work, passes from the objectivity of the narratives to the intimacy of the *Diary*, descends into a still darker night in which the cries of a lost man can be heard? Why does it seem that the closer one comes to his heart, the closer one comes to an unconsoled center from which a piercing flash sometimes bursts forth, an excess of pain, excess of joy? Who has the right to speak of Kafka without making this enigma heard, an enigma that speaks with the complexity, with the simplicity, of enigmas?

~

After he published and annotated Kafka, after he made him the hero of one of his novels, Brod, in an attempt to push the double life still further, tried to insert himself into Kafka's world by transforming what is perhaps the most important work, *The Castle*, so as to make what was an unfinished narrative into a completed play. A decision that cannot be compared with that of Gide and J.-L. Barrault, who had done the same thing for *The Trial* several years earlier. Gide and Barrault, wrongly, no doubt, had wanted the space of theater to encounter a space of ambiguous dimensions—all surface, without depth, as if deprived of perspective but bottomless, and because of this, very deep—which was that of the world of infinite distraction represented by *The Trial*. Brod seems to have yielded to a more intimate temptation, that of living off the life of the central hero, of bringing himself closer to him, also of bringing him closer to us, to the life of this time, by humanizing him, by giving him the existence of a man who struggles, with indiscreet despair, to find work, resources, and existence in a place where he can be but an unwelcome stranger.

Thus Brod adapted *The Castle* for the theater. Let us leave aside the decision itself, though this manner of having a work pass from one form to another, of creating a work with the work, of forcing it to be what it cannot be by imposing another space of growth and development on it, is a kind of abduction that prohibits the one who engages in it from being too severe with the enterprises of modern nihilism. Let us leave aside the certainty that any adaptation of one of Kafka's works, even if the adaptation is faithful and because it can be too faithful only to certain moments and not to the dissimulated whole of the work (which escapes all faithfulness), must not only falsify the work but substitute a trick version for it, from which, henceforth, it will be more difficult to return to the offended and as if extinguished truth of the original. Let us forget, finally, the right that the adapter has taken upon himself, pursuant to what he believes to be dramatic necessities, to add a conclusion to a narrative that does not resolve itself, a conclusion that was perhaps, at a certain moment, in Kafka's mind, and about which he undoubtedly spoke to his friend, but that, precisely, he never resolved to write, that never entered into the life and intimacy of the work: it remains, furthermore, that this scene in which we are present at the interment of K., an interment that symbolically corresponds to his reconciliation with the earth upon which he had desired to dwell, this scene in which each person comes to throw a word and a handful of dust on a body that is finally at rest, is one of the best in the play, although it is the complete invention of Brod, which goes to show that this play would have had much to gain by owing nothing to Kafka. But why did Brod think it good to insert himself thus into the secret of a work, to which he had contributed, more than any other, to maintaining intact? Why did he, who had so forcefully criticized Gide and Barrault for committing an "unprecedented error" in their dramatization, change the center of the work in a way that was no less manifest, substitute for the central character a character who no longer has anything in common with him except a kinship of words—and this not in order to make the spiritual meaning of his actions any more precise, but to bring him down to a pathetic human level?

This remains an enigma. Certainly the adapter wanted to make the story work on a level that, according to him, was most able to touch us; he wanted to make us understand that Kafka was not a bizarre author, the demon of the absurd and the disquieting creator of sarcastic dreams, but a profoundly sensitive genius whose works have immediate human significance. A commendable intention, but what was the result? From the standpoint of the story, the complex myth of the land surveyor has become the unhappy fate of a man without employment and position, a displaced person, who does not succeed in being accepted into the community to which he would like to belong. From the standpoint of the demand that the central hero must face, of the obstacles he encounters and that lie outside of him only because he is already entirely outside and as if in exile from himself, on this level the transposition is such that it is a true mockery to pass K. off as the bloated character who expresses everything he feels with a paroxysm of emotion, as he rages, shouts, collapses.

The price is certainly great in the effort to create the human at all costs.

Brod reproached Barrault-Gide for having travestied *The Trial* by making its hero a "persecuted innocent" and the novel "a detective story in which fugitive and detectives pursue one another through the games of a superficial dramatization." But what re-proaches should he not have directed at himself, he who not only makes the flaw, to which K. is perhaps doomed, disappear from his fate, but has reduced K.'s step outside the true to a crudely pathetic struggle, without hope and without strength, against adversaries who symbolize the modern world, a step itself erroneous, marked by the serious flaw of impatience, yet nevertheless, at the heart of error, ceaselessly tending toward a great goal.

What can a man do who is entirely taken over by the necessity of wandering, a man who, because of an obscure impersonal decision has renounced his native land, has abandoned his community, has left his wife, his children behind, has even lost the memory of them? The man of absolute exile, of dispersion and separation? The man who no longer has a world and who, in this absence of world, nonetheless tries to find the conditions of a real dwelling? This is K.'s fate, of which he is very conscious, in this very different from Joseph K., who, in his negligence, his indifference, and his satisfac-tion of the man provided with a good position, does not realize that he has been rejected from existence and whose whole trial is the slow coming to consciousness of this radical exclusion, of this death by which, from the very beginning, he has been struck.

The spirit of the work has disappeared from Brod's play as the result of a spell; with the show of pathos and of humanity, everything that makes it so moving and, in effect, so human has disappeared, but the emotion is one that slips away, refuses cries, vehemence, vain complaints, that passes by way of a silent refusal and a certain cold indifference, in connection with the loss of all inner life, the initial wound without which the search that animates the work cannot be understood.

In such a way that everything that could be "positive" in the work has disappeared from Brod's play—not only the background of the Castle, which no longer offers even direction to the efforts of the exhausted vagabond (the Castle appears, at most, as an arbitrary concentration of power, a quintessence of authority and meanness, under the influence and fear of which the larvae of the village develop their own little tyrannical activities)—and furthermore, everything has been lost that radiates strength on the level of powerlessness, a concern for the true in the depths of distraction, an inflexible determination at the heart of the loss of self, a clarity in the empty and vague night in which everything already disappears.

Where does this come from? Why is it that Brod, who is so convinced of the nonnihilistic meaning of the work, has emphasized only its superficially unhappy side?

~

One of his errors is to have deliberately—out of a concern for humanity and actuality—reduced the myth of *The Castle* to the story of a man who searches in vain, in a foreign country, for employment and the happiness of a stable family. Is this what K. wants? No doubt, but he wants it with a will that is not content with it, an avid and dissatisfied will that always exceeds the goal and always reaches beyond. To misjudge the nature of his "will," this need to wander, which is extreme in him, is to put oneself in the position of not understanding anything about even the superficial intrigue of the narrative. For, otherwise, how can one explain that every time K. achieves a result, he pushes it away rather than hold on to it? No sooner does he obtain a room at the village inn than he wants to stay at the Herrenhof. No sooner does he obtain a small job at the school than he neglects it and is disdainful of his employers. The hotelkeeper offers him her intervention, he refuses it; the mayor promises him his kind support, he does not want it. He has Frieda, but he also wants Olga, Amalia, Hans's mother. And even at the end, when he receives an unexpected interview from a secretary, Bürgel, during the course of which the latter gives him the keys to the kingdom, an hour of grace when "everything is possible," the slumber into which he then slips and which causes him to pass up this offer is perhaps just another form of the dissatisfaction that always pushes him to go further, never to say yes, to keep a part of himself in reserve, secret, that no visible promise can satisfy.

In a small fragment that does not belong to the edition of *The Castle*, but obviously refers to the same theme, Kafka writes: "When you want to be introduced into a new family, you seek out a common acquaintance and you ask this person to intercede on your behalf. If you do not find this person, you are patient and you wait for a favorable occasion. In the small country where we live, this occasion cannot fail to present itself. If one is not found today, it will be found tomorrow, and if it is not found at all, you will not threaten the columns of the world for so little. If the family can manage without you, you can manage without the family just as well. This is obvious; however, K. does not understand it. He has gotten it into his head recently to make his way into the family of the master of our estate, but he refuses to employ the ways of life in society, he wants to reach it directly. Perhaps the usual way seems too tedious to him, and this is right, but the path that he is trying to follow is impossible. It is not that I want thus to overstate the importance of our master. An intelligent, industrious, honorable man, but nothing more. What is it that K. wants of him? An employment on the estate? No, he does not want this, he himself has property and leads a life free of such worries. Is it that he loves his daughter? No, no, we cannot suspect him of this."

K., too, wants to reach the goal—which is neither the employment that he nonetheless desires nor Frieda, to whom he is attached—he wants to reach it without passing through the tedious paths of patience and measured sociability, but *directly*, an impossible path, with which he is not familiar and, furthermore, which he only senses, a feeling that leads him to refuse all other routes. Is this, then, his error, a romantic passion for the absolute? In one sense, yes; but, in another sense, not at all. If K. chooses the impossible, it is because he was excluded from everything possible as the result of an initial decision. If he cannot make his way in the world, or employ, as he would like, the normal means of life in society, it is because he has been banished from the world, from his world, condemned to the absence of world, doomed to exile in which there is no real dwelling place. To wander, this is his law. His dissatisfaction is the very movement of this error, it is its expression, its reflection; it is itself thus essentially false; yet, nonetheless, always to move further in the direction of error is the only hope that is left him, the only truth that he must not betray and to which he remains faithful with a perseverance that makes him thus the hero of inflexible obstinacy.

Is he right? Is he wrong? He cannot know, and we do not know. But he suspects that all the opportunities granted him are temptations from which he must escape, especially the more advantageous they are: questionable is the promise of the hotelkeeper; malicious, the benevolence of the mayor; the small job that he is offered, a chain destined to captivate him. And is Frieda's affection sincere?[3] Is it not the mirage of his half-slumber, the grace that is offered him through the interstices of the law by the smiling secretary Bürgel?[4] All of this is appealing, fascinating, and true, but true as an image can be true, illusory as an image would be, were one to become attached to it with the exclusive devotion from which the most serious of perversions, idolatry, arises.

K. senses that everything outside of himself—himself projected on the outside—is but an image. He knows that one cannot trust images nor become attached to them. He is strong with a power of contestation without measure, whose only equivalent is a passion without measure for a single, indeterminate point. If such is his situation, if, in acting with the impatience that is his own, he is only obeying the rigorous monism that animates him, whence does it come that this impatience is precisely his flaw, as negligence would be the flaw of Joseph K.? It is because these images are nonetheless images of the goal, because they participate in its light and because to misrecognize them is already to close one's eyes to the essential. The impatience that escapes the temptation of figures also escapes the truth of what they figure. The impatience that wants to go straight to the goal, without passing through the intermediaries, succeeds only in having the intermediaries as goal and in making them not what leads to the goal but what prevents one from reaching it: obstacles infinitely reflected and multiplied. Would it thus suffice to be good, patient, to follow the advice of the hotelkeeper, to remain beside Frieda with a peaceful and amiable heart? No, for all of this is but image, emptiness, the unhappiness of the imaginary, loathsome phantasms born of the loss of self and all authentic reality.

~

K.'s death seems to be the necessary term of this progression in which impatience pushes him to the point of utter exhaustion. In this sense, the fatigue from which Kafka intimately suffered—fatigue, coldness of the soul no less than of the body—is one of the forces of the intrigue and, more precisely, one of the dimensions of the space in which the hero of *The Castle* lives, in a place where he can only wander, far from all conditions of true rest. This fatigue that the actor, too vigorous for the role, tried to represent in the play with a spectacular exhaustion does not, however, signify the fatal slip toward failure. It is itself enigmatic. Certainly, K. tires himself out because he goes back and forth without prudence and without patience, spending himself when he should not, in activities destined not to succeed, and having no strength left when he needs it to succeed. This fatigue, the effect of a dissatisfaction

that refuses everything, the cause of the stupor that accepts everything, is thus another form of the bad infinity to which the
wanderer is doomed. A sterile fatigue, which is such that one
cannot rest from it, such that it does not even lead to the rest that is
death, because for the one who, like K., even exhausted, continues
to act, the little strength that would be necessary to find the end is
lacking.

However, at the same time, this lassitude, which is secret, moreover; which he does not display; which, on the contrary, he dissimulates through the gift of discretion that belongs to him—
would it not be, as well as the sign of his condemnation, the way of
his salvation, the approach of the perfection of silence, the gentle
and insensible slope toward deep sleep, the symbol of unity? It is at
the moment at which he is exhausted that he has, with the benevo-
lent secretary, the meeting during the course of which it seems he
will be able to reach the goal. This takes place in the night, like all
interviews that come from over there. Night is needed there, the
deceptive night, the succoring night in which mysterious gifts are
enveloped in oblivion. What is it, therefore, in this case? Is it
because of the exhaustion of fatigue that he misses the wondrous
occasion? Or is it because of the solace and the grace of slumber
that he is able to approach it? No doubt, both one and the other.
He sleeps, but not deeply enough; it is not yet the pure, the true
sleep. One must sleep. "Sleep is what is most innocent and a man
without sleep what is most guilty." One must sleep, just as one
must die, not this unfulfilled and unreal death with which we are
content in our everyday lassitude, but another death, unknown,
invisible, unnamed, and furthermore inaccessible, to which it may
be that K. arrives, but not within the limits of the book: in the
silence of the absence of book, which, through a supplementary
punishment, Brod's play has unfortunately come to disturb.

§ 27 The Last
Word

Because they made up the last volume of the *Complete Works* when they were published in the German edition (in 1958), the *Letters* seemed to constitute Kafka's last word. We were prepared to expect from these ultimate writings the final revelation that, as on the day of the Last Judgment, would give form to the enigma. Whence our naively anxious reading, childishly disappointed. This is because there is no Last Judgment, no more than there is an end. The strange nature of posthumous publications is to be inexhaustible.

Although the war, the persecutions, the changes in regime have made a void around him, destroying witnesses and testimonies, there will certainly be, and will hardly cease to be, many documents, perhaps important ones, perhaps insignificant ones. Inquiries have been made about his childhood and his adolescence, the results of which have begun to be collected. In a certain way, the biography remains to be written.[1] Until now, what we know is the face and the life as Max Brod knew them; and this knowledge is irreplaceable. The letters only confirm this to us: to no other was he so close, with such a lasting trust—I will not say through an impulse of his nature. "Max and I [are] radically different." But it is this difference that makes their friendship a strong and virile understanding; even if Kafka admires Brod for his power of life, his ability to act, his force as a writer, if Kafka thus puts Brod far above himself, he never humbles himself before him and in relation to him, with the passion for self-abasement that he displays with others. But precisely he was other with others; and with himself, what was he? It is this invisible self that, in staying hidden from us, remains the object of our naive curiosity and our search, necessarily disappointed.

The letters cover twenty years of his life. If they reveal to us less than we had hoped, there are several grounds for this. First of all, they were already partially known, because Brod used them in his biography and his other books. Furthermore, they remain very fragmentary, such publications being always painfully subject to the chance that preserves and destroys without reason. Thus we have almost nothing of the letters exchanged with his family. From his adolescence a little of the passionate correspondence was saved: with his fellow student, Oskar Pollak, and then slightly later with a young lady, Hedwige W., encountered during a stay in Moravia in 1907, the early stages of his tormented relations with the feminine world. Later, the essential part is made up of the letters to Brod, F. Weltsch, O. Baum, the friends of a lifetime (almost nothing of the letters to Werfel); still later, to R. Klopstock, the young medical student, who, with Dora Diamant, was present at his end. As chance would have it, the sparsest years of the *Diary* are the richest in important letters: we now have a more precise account of the stay in Zürau when the tuberculosis declared itself, of the stays in Matliary, in Plana, and the years 1921, 1922, when he writes, then abandons *The Castle*; certain allusions become clearer, certain obscurities deepen; we feel ourselves confirmed in the mysterious nature of certain moments. We have a better sense of the curve of this rare existence; the negative side of the revelation is more perceptible to us.

Nothing, however, that by force of the unexpected could be compared with the letters to Milena.[2] Also nothing that gives us the feeling of being close to crossing the threshold, as it happens in the *Diary*. This is because, as close as he is to his correspondents, revealing to them what is most secret to him, speaking of himself with ruthless candor, he maintains an insensible distance intended to spare both their truth and his own. "You must not say that you understand me," he repeats to Brod. His friends are always ready, convinced of his admirable personality, to represent to him all the reasons he has not to despair. But it is precisely in this that they drive him to despair: not that he should be happy only with complete unhappiness, but because any interpretation that is too favorable by those who know him the best, by showing the inaccessible nature of the illness (unhappiness and pain) that is specific to him, also shows the depth of this sickness and the poor worth of the solutions with which one soothes him. "What you say about my case is right; from the outside, it presents itself thus; it is a consolation, but, when the moment comes, also a despair; for it shows that nothing of these dreadful things shows through and that everything lies hidden in me. This obscurity that I alone see, and I myself do not always see it; already the day after that particular day I could no longer see it. But I know it is there and that it waits for me."

One must add that Kafka always had an extreme respect for the truth of others; he keeps them at as much of a distance as possible from the dark experience in which he finds himself and, in the advice he gives them, in the judgments he forms about them, just as in the radiance of his light gaiety, persuades them of an opening onto hope, which he immediately impugns as soon as anyone wants to make him participate in it. In a late letter to Klopstock (July 1922), I find these lines: "If we were on the right path, to renounce would be a despair without limits, but because we are on a path that only leads us to a second, and the latter to a third, and so forth; because the true way will not come forth for a very long time, and perhaps never; because, therefore, we are completely given over to uncertainty, but also to an inconceivably beautiful diversity, the fulfillment of hopes . . . remains the always unexpected miracle, yet always possible on the other hand." Here we have, rarely described by Kafka, the positive aspect of a search that appears only negative (because the true way, which is unique, is not given to us; there is not one path but an infinite number, and we have something that is infinitely varied and scintillating, the incomparably beautiful scintillation of reflections, which brings us an aesthetic joy); however, I doubt he would have accepted to have this consolation, which he shares with his discouraged friend, applied to himself.[3] Another example. Brod always called attention to this aphorism as the center of Kafka's faith: "Theoretically, there is a perfect possibility of earthly happiness: to believe in the indestructible in itself without striving to reach it." But we see, in a letter, that this thought refers to one of Max Brod's essays (*Paganism, Christianity, Judaism*): "Perhaps one would come closest to your conception were one to say: 'There is theoretically a perfect possibility of earthly happiness: to believe in what is decidedly divine without striving to reach it.' This possibility of happiness is as impious as it is inaccessible, but the Greeks perhaps came closer to it than anyone else." Would this then be Kafka's truth, a truth proper to the Greeks? And what is more, a "blasphemy"? This commentary would suffice to recall us to a prudence, which the generous optimism of Brod sometimes made him forget.

~

Kafka's life was an obscure fight, protected by obscurity, but we clearly see its four aspects, represented by his relation with his father, with literature, with the feminine world, and these three forms of struggle can be retranslated more profoundly to give form to the spiritual fight. Naturally, with each of these relations, all the others are called into question. The crisis is always total. Each episode says everything and withholds everything. The concern of his body is the concern of his entire being. The insomnia, this dramatic difficulty of each of his nights, expresses all of his difficulties. The only interest in constructing his biography around these four more or less hidden centers would be, therefore, to make us perceive it momentarily according to the greater or lesser insight that we have into each of these enigmas, the quality of which is very different. We would observe, for example, that the problem of the father with which he is occupied in such an obvious manner, and although it develops along with the three others (we notice immediately how he complicates the problem of his marriage to an extreme, how he forms one of the obsessive themes of his writings, how finally he finds himself implicated in all of the questions of Judaism), is probably the least burdened with secrets and the one that accompanies him the least far. The most far-reaching is the problem of the writer. The most dramatic, the one that provokes him at his darkest moments is that of feminine relationships. The most obscure, that of the spiritual world, necessarily hidden, because it is shielded from any direct grasp: "I cannot speak of the essential; it is, even for me, enclosed within the obscurity of my breast: there it lies next to the illness, on the same common bed."

The letters bring us, if not insights, at least the possibility of a more prudent and more nuanced understanding of each of these forms of himself. Above all, we have a better sense of the movement of this entire life, a life that, although it is rooted from youth in extreme affirmations from which he no longer seems to depart, will not cease to transform itself. It is this movement in the immobile that makes it rich and enigmatic. The words of adolescence, those of maturity may appear superimposed on one another; they are the same, they are very different, and yet not different, but somehow the echo of themselves at more or less profound levels of agreement; and at the same time, the becoming is not purely internal; history is important, a history that, on the one hand, is his personal history, his encounter with Felice Bauer, Julie Wohryzek, Milena, Dora Diamant, with his family, with the countryside at Zürau, books, illness, but that, on the other hand, is the history of the world, of which the voiceless rumblings have not ceased to precede him through the tragic problems of Judaism.

Of course, this history and this movement come together in the movement of literary creation, which will always remain the truth toward which he tends. Until the end, he will remain a writer. On his deathbed, deprived of strength, voice, breath, he is still correcting the proofs of one of his books (*The Hunger Artist*). Because he cannot speak, he notes on a piece of paper for the benefit of his companions: "Now I am going to read them. This will perhaps agitate me too much; yet I must live it one more time." And Klopstock reports that when the reading was finished, tears rolled down his face for a long time. "It was the first time that I saw Kafka, always so master of himself, let himself be overcome by such a movement of emotion." The only severe and almost fierce letter that finds its place in the collection he wrote to protect his solitude as a writer. I will quote it in order to show that in spite of his wonderful attentiveness to others, there is a limit that he cannot allow to be crossed. Klopstock, the young medical student whose acquaintance he had made in Matliary and whom he likes, moreover, almost with tenderness, seemed to have desired a more intimate friendship, wanted to see him more often, found that he had changed since the first days of their encounter: "I will concede that between Matliary and Prague there is a difference. During that time, after being tormented by periods of madness, I began to write, and this activity, in a manner that makes it very cruel for all of the people around me (unspeakably cruel, I will not say more), is for me the most important thing on earth, as his delirium can be for the one who is mad (were he to lose it, he would go 'mad') or pregnancy for a woman. This has nothing to do with the value of the writing, I know its value all too well, but rather with the value it has for me. And this is why, in a trembling of anguish, I protect writing from anything that might disturb it, and not only writing but the solitude that belongs to it. And when I told you yesterday that you should not come Sunday night, but only Monday and when twice you asked: 'So, not in the evening?' and I had to answer you, at least the second time: 'Get some rest,' this was a perfect lie, for my only aim was to be alone."

～

On the central problem of the necessity of writing, which is both a fatality and a threat, we find in the *Letters* two of the most important texts. They are dated July and September 1922. Important in themselves, they are also important because they reveal to us the circumstances in which *The Castle* was abandoned. I will partly summarize and partly quote these texts, which are rather long. I will begin with the more recent: "I have been here [in Plana] for a week once again; I did not spend it gaily, for I had to abandon, manifestly for ever, the story of the Castle; the latter could not be taken up again because of the 'collapse' that began a week before the trip to Prague, although what I have written in Plana is not as bad as what you know." Kafka tells how his sister Ottla (who lived with him) was soon obliged to return to Prague for good and how the servant had offered to prepare his meals for him so that he might continue his stay in a place he liked so much. He accepts, everything is decided: "I will stay the winter, I am still thankful." "Immediately, I was barely at the top of the stairs leading to my room when the 'collapse' occurred. . . . I need not describe the external side of such a state, you are also familiar with it, but you must think of what is most extreme in your experience. . . . Above all, I know that I will not be able to sleep. The force of sleep has been gnawed away to its very center. I already anticipate the insomnia, I suffer as if last night had already been without sleep. I go out, I cannot think of anything else, nothing occupies me but a monstrous anguish and, at clearer moments, the anguish of this anguish. . . . What can this be? As far as I am able to penetrate it with thought, there is only one thing. You say that I must meet with bigger subjects. This is right . . . but I also find myself tried by my mouse hole. And this one thing is: fear of complete solitude. Were I to remain here alone, I would be fully solitary. I would not be able to speak to people, and were I to do it, the solitude would only be increased. And I know, at least in an approximate way, the frights of solitude—not so much of solitary solitude but of the solitude among men, the first times in Matliary or a few days in Spindlermühle, but I do not want to speak of this. How is it with solitude? Solitude is my one goal, my greatest temptation, my possibility, and, admitting that one could say that I have 'organized' my life, then it has been organized in order that solitude be at home in it. And, in spite of this, anguish before what I love so much."

This desire, which is anguish—anguish before solitude when it is there, anguish when it is not there, anguish again before any compromise solution—this, it seems, is what we understand well, but let us not be in a hurry to understand. In a slightly earlier letter,

Kafka clarifies, but in a more enigmatic way, the entanglement of all of these relations. Once again it is a matter of a serious crisis. He was supposed to go to Georgental to stay with his friend Baum. He had just written to him to say that he accepted. Everything pleased him about his trip, or at least he did not see any reasonable objection to it. And yet "the collapse," the infinite anguish, the night without sleep. "While these thoughts were coming and going between my pained temples during this night without sleep, I was again conscious of what I had almost forgotten in the past rather peaceful days: the weak or even inexistent ground upon which I live, above the darkness from which the tenebrous power emerges at its whim, a power that, without regard for my stuttering, destroys my life. Writing sustains me, but would it not be more correct to say that writing maintains this sort of life? Naturally I do not wish to claim that my life is better when I am not writing. It is much worse, altogether unbearable, and can only lead to madness. And yet, it is true, it is incumbent on me even if, as is the case at the moment, I am not writing, to be a writer nonetheless; and a writer who does not write is all the same a monstrosity that calls forth madness. But what is it, then, about this, being a writer? Writing is a charming and wonderful reward, but who is paying us for what? At night, with the clarity of a child's lessons, I saw distinctly that it was the salary for services rendered to the demon. This descent into the dark powers, this unleashing of spirits normally under control, these dubious embraces and everything that can happen down there, about which one remembers nothing when one writes stories in the light of the sun. Perhaps there is another way of writing, I know only this one; in the night, when the anguish does not let me sleep, I know only this one. And what is diabolical in it seems very clear to me. It is vanity and concupiscence that ceaselessly circle around my person or around an unknown person and derive pleasure from it, in a movement that only multiplies itself, a real solar system of vanity. The wish of the naive man: 'I would like to die and see how I will be mourned,' such a writer constantly accomplishes it, he dies (or he does not live) and constantly mourns himself. Whence his terrible anguish before death, which does not necessarily express itself as the fear of dying, but also manifests itself in the fear of change, fear of going to Georgental."

But why this fear of dying? Kafka distinguishes two series of reasons that, he says, may perhaps become confused. And, in effect, they seem to come down to this thought: the writer is afraid of dying because he has not yet lived, and not only because he has missed out on the happiness of living with a woman, children, fortune, but because, instead of entering the house, he must be content with admiring it from the outside and crowning its rooftop, excluded from the pleasure of things by a contemplation that is not possession. Here is this writer's kind of interior monologue: "What I played at will really happen. I did not redeem myself through writing. I have spent my life dying, and what is more, I will really die. My life has been gentler than others' lives, my death will only be more terrible. Naturally, the writer that is in me will die immediately, for such a figure has no ground, no reality, it is not even made of dust; this figure is possible, only a little possible in earthly life at its most senseless, and is but a construction of concupiscence. Such is the writer. But I myself cannot continue to live, because I have not lived, I have remained clay, and the spark that I could not turn into fire, I have only made it serve to illuminate my corpse." "It will be a strange burial," adds Kafka: "the writer, something that does not exist, conveys the old corpse, the lifelong corpse to the grave. I am writer enough to want to enjoy this fully in the full oblivion of myself—and not with lucidity; the oblivion of self is the first condition of the writer—or, what amounts to the same, to want to tell it; but this will no longer happen. And why only speak of true death? In life, it is the same thing. . . ." A little further on, Kafka makes these two remarks: "I must add that in my fear of traveling the thought that for several days I will be separated from my writing desk plays a role. This ridiculous thought is in reality the only legitimate one, for the existence of the writer really depends on his table, he does not have the right to move from it if he wants to escape madness, he must hang on to it with his teeth. The definition of the writer, of such a writer, and the explanation of the action he exerts (if there is one): he is the scapegoat of humanity, he allows men to take pleasure in a sin innocently, almost innocently."

~

Without claiming to give a commentary on these lines, what one can nonetheless remark is that the affirmations that follow one another here are not all on the same level. There are clear affirmations: to write is to put oneself outside life, it is to take pleasure in one's death through an imposture that will become a frightening reality; the poor, real ego to whom one offers the prospect of a short trip is literally beaten, tormented, and thrashed by the devil; henceforth, the world is forbidden, life is impossible, solitude inevitable: "With this, it is decided that I no longer have the right to leave Bohemia, soon I will have to limit myself to Prague, then to my room, then to my bed, then to a certain position of my body, then to nothing. Perhaps then I would freely be able to renounce the happiness of writing—yes, freely and with rejoicing, this is what is important." The anguish of being alone here is almost captured. Writing is thus a bad activity, but not only for these reasons: also for others more obscure. For writing is a nocturnal thing; it is to abandon oneself to the dark powers, to descend into the regions down there, to give oneself to impure embraces. All these expressions have an immediate truth for Kafka. They evoke the tenebrous fascination, the dark glow of desire, the passion of what is unleashed in the night in which everything ends with radical death. And what does he mean by "the forces down there"? We do not know. However, increasingly he will associate words and the use of words with the approach of a spectral unreality, greedy for living things and capable of exhausting any truth. This is why during his last year he will almost cease to write, even to his friends, and above all he will cease to speak of himself: "It is true, I am not writing anything, but not because I have something to hide (insofar as this is not my life's vocation). . . . Above all, as I have made it a law for myself these last years for strategic reasons, I do not have confidence either in words or in letters, neither in my words nor in my letters; I am perfectly willing to share my heart with men but not with the specters that play with words and read letters, tongues hanging out."

The conclusion should thus categorically be the following: no longer to write. Yet it is altogether different (and for twenty years it did not vary): "Writing is for me what is most necessary and most important." And he did not fail to make the reasons for this necessity known to us, and even to repeat them to us in his different letters: that if he did not write, he would go mad. Writing is madness, is his madness, but this madness is his reason. It is his damnation, but a damnation that is his only way to salvation (if there remains one for him). Between the two certainties of losing himself—lost if he writes, lost if he does not write—he tries to create a passage for himself, and this by way of writing again, but a writing that invokes the specters in the hope of warding them off. In the letter to Brod in which he speaks in such a disquieting manner about his words being in the hands of ghosts,[4] he adds the following in passing, which greatly clarifies for us perhaps his hopes as a writer: "It sometimes seems to me that the essence of art, the existence of art, can be explained only by such 'strategic considerations': to make possible a true speech from man to man."[5]

∼

I would like to translate the impression left by the letters written during the last year. Kafka, whom the least move disrupted, made the decision to live in Berlin, far from his family and friends, with Dora Diamant, whose acquaintance he had made in Müritz in July 1923 (he died in June 1924; thus he lived with her for only a few months). Until then, it indeed seemed that, although ill, he was not yet dangerously ill. The illness was worsening, but slowly. It is the stay in Berlin that proved fatal to him. The harsh winter, the unfavorable climate, the precarious conditions of existence, the scarcity of this big city starved and agitated by civil war represented a threat that he could only be very conscious of, but from which, despite the entreaties of his friends, he refused to remove himself; it took the intervention of his uncle, "the country doctor," to make him decide to change residences several weeks before the tubercular laryngitis declares itself. This indifference to his health is a new phenomenon. It is also marked by this feature: whereas until 1923 his least discomforts occupy him greatly, he almost refrains from speaking about them as soon as the situation becomes more serious; and it is with a remarkable sobriety and discretion that he makes his condition known, henceforth disastrous: "If one comes to terms with the tubercular laryngitis, my condition is tolerable, I can swallow again, for the time being." And in the last sentences of his last letter to Brod, after the latter had come from Prague to see him one last time, he is anxious to point out that there are still joyful moments: "Aside from all these subjects of complaint, there are also naturally several minuscule gaieties, but it is impossible to describe them or they have to be saved for a visit like the one that was so miserably spoiled by me. Good-bye. Thank you for everything." This refusal to complain, the silence about himself that, in their reticence, almost all the Berlin letters make sensible, is the only sign of the change that has occurred in his life. A silence that is tense, watched over, voluntary. "There is little to tell about me, a life somewhat in the shadows; he who does not see it directly will notice nothing about it." "In reality it is very calm around me, never too calm, moreover." And to Milena: "My state of health is not essentially different from what it was in Prague. This is all. I will not venture to say more; what is said is already too much."

One can interpret this silence.[6] Does he refuse to speak of himself because his fate is too close to the fate of another being of whom he does not consent to speak? Does he want henceforth to keep his secret for this being? Or else, with greater force and coherence than ever before, has he closed himself in on his solitude, become even for himself the "man buried in himself, imprisoned within himself by foreign locks" of whom he speaks to Klopstock in 1922? Does he truly distrust written words and the ghostly way of communicating that wears away truth by entrusting it to deceitful and unfaithful messengers? This last point, though it does not explain everything, is certain. Even on the subject of his literary writings, he remarked that fiction shows reality the way. Thus, in the *Country Doctor*, in which he describes a strange bloody wound, he sees the anticipation of his hemoptyses, which occur shortly thereafter. An even more impressive coincidence when, in March 1924, the terminal phase of the illness begins with an extinction of the voice: he has just completed his narrative *Josephine*, in which he writes about a singing mouse who believes herself blessed with an exceptional gift for chirping and whistling, because she is no longer capable of the means of expression that are in use by her people. He then says to Klopstock: "I think I undertook my research on animal chirping at the right moment." How not to evoke here his remark about the anguishing discovery of the writer when the latter, at the last moment, sees himself taken at his word by reality? "What I played at will really happen." Was it like this for him? The play of speech coming visibly and painfully to its end, did he refuse to speak further of it, henceforth applying all of his attention to greeting in silence the silent approach of the event? Yet this distrust of words does not prevent him from pursuing his task of writing to the end. Much to the contrary, no longer able to speak, he is permitted only to write, and rarely has agony been so written as his. As if death, with the humor that is particular to it, had thus sought to warn him that it was preparing to change him entirely into a writer—"something that does not exist."[7]

§ 28 The Very
   Last Word

Commenting one day on Kafka's letters that had just appeared in their original text, I said that the *Complete Works* would always be missing a last volume because the nature of posthumous publications was to make them inexhaustible. Why? First of all, for reasons of fact. Missing at the time were the letters to his fiancée, Felice Bauer, letters that a difficult negotiation had momentarily excluded from the edition. Information that was capable of shedding more light on the encounter with Dora Diamant, the encounter with which his life ended, was also missing and no doubt will be missing for a long time, not to say forever. (By this I mean not the outside testimonies that can still be gathered, but Kafka's judgment, his speech, the notes of his *Diary*.)

This commentary is approximately ten years old.[1] Now (since October 1967) that we are in possession of all of the letters to Felice B., with few exceptions, including those to Grete Bloch, the enigmatic friend of the couple (that is to say, a volume of more than 700 pages); now that we have in hand the documents collected slowly and conscientiously by Klaus Wagenbach (the first volume of the biography he is working on appeared in 1958 and was translated in the Mercure de France Editions; then there is the *Kafka-Symposium* edited by him with several authors, which brings together documents on diverse and unelucidated points, in particular a chronology of the texts, as well as a long and important

letter, addressed to the sister of Julie Wohryzeck, the second fiancée; and finally there is the little book from Rowohlt Editions, a
sort of Kafka by Kafka [and by Wagenbach], the restricted form of
which makes it easier for us to recognize what is known, what is not
known, or what is not yet known of a life henceforth too manifest),
we are closer, but also almost deflected from asking the true questions, because we no longer have the strength to let them come to
us in their innocence, to hold them away from the biographical
reports that attract and engulf them by giving them fuel.

    1. Let us try to bring together several features in order to free
ourselves of them. After reading the letters as if in a single movement, we should perhaps ask ourselves if they teach us anything
new, other than the always hidden becoming of what is said in the
hope of being clear. First, what is confirmed: every time Kafka
enters into a relation with the feminine world, it is a sort of grace,
levity, a seductive and seducing temptation. His first letters are
borne by a desire to charm, which charms. Even when he writes to
Mlle. Bloch, of whom, at least in the beginning, he asks for nothing
except a friendly sympathy or a contact in confidence, he does not
fail to write in such a way that the young lady, still very young, will
be visibly troubled by them to the point, voluntarily, involuntarily,
of contributing to the rupture of the first engagement, and then
later, of perhaps inventing a strange episode, an imaginary child
that she attributes to Kafka. (Let us just say that this is a hypotheti-
cal episode that K. Wagenbach makes the mistake of transforming
into a certainty when it remains at the limit of the probable-
improbable.)*
    Even if the difficulties come very quickly—and in some sense
almost immediately—they are at first part of a movement of young
passion, which does not lack a certain happiness. It is during this
relatively happy period (with utterly black moments) that he writes
The Metamorphosis (of this narrative he says to F., "It is such an
exceptionally repulsive story that I am putting it aside to rest and
think of you: it is more than half finished, and on the whole, I am

* See the end of the chapter.

not displeased with it, but it is infinitely repulsive, and, you see, such things come from the same heart in which you reside and which you tolerate as your residence"). He met her, who will twice be his fiancée, in August 1912 (in Prague, at his friend Max Brod's parents' house); he writes to her a few weeks later (end of September) and soon thereafter almost every day or several times a day. It is at the beginning of 1913 that relations all of a sudden become more gloomy. On several occasions, Kafka confirms this change: "I am different from the way I was in the first months of our correspondence; this is not a new transformation, but rather a relapse and one that threatens to last. . . . I was different in the beginning, you will concede this; it is not anything that could not be repaired except that it is not a human development that has led me from here to there, but, on the contrary, I have been entirely transported back onto my old path and between roads there is no direct connection, not even a zigzag communication, but a sad path through the air followed by specters." Why? To this question we can give only inconclusive answers.

It is approximately at this time that, prompted by his feelings and no doubt solicited by his friend, Kafka considers traveling to Berlin, after evading an encounter at Christmas: a trip that appeals to him, repels him, and will nonetheless take place on March 23. Almost all the encounters will be disappointing. Reading the letters (we do not know those of the young lady except indirectly), we have the feeling that Felice appears more reserved than affectionate and, as socially vivacious as she proves to be when she is with others, she seems lifeless, distraught, or tired when, rarely, they happen to be alone. This, at least, is Kafka's impression, as he formulates it to her (but that should not be accepted too readily; just as when he declares himself incapable of social relations, he contradicts the testimony of his friends who saw him, amiable, at ease, and often warm, although sometimes, it is true, withdrawn and strangely absent). About Felice, he always said he recognized in her the qualities he thinks he does not have: she is a young woman who is sure of herself, active, courageous, knowledgeable in business; from which it would be too easy, and no doubt deceptive, to conclude that she attracts him through what he lacks; physically, she is far from pleasing him right at first; in his Diary, he describes her in terms of an almost cruel objectivity and, what is worse, he will speak of her to Mlle. Bloch with a certain repulsion (her spoiled teeth, her spotted, rough skin, her bony skeleton). And at the same time he loves her—passionately, desperately. At the same time: *in the same time*; this is all that can be said about it without falling into psychological futility. Should it be added that she represents life, the chance to live? The possibility of a reconciliation with the world? This is true, but according to what truth? I would say instead—and this is the feature she has in common with Milena and perhaps with Julie Wohryzeck as well as with the unknown woman from Zuckmantel and the adolescent girl from Riva—that she bears, in the manner of a memory, the trace of the absence of trace, that is, of a non-culpability, which does not signify innocence exactly. On the first day of the first encounter, when he notes in his Diary, "Mlle F.B., . . . bony and empty face openly bearing its emptiness," the word *empty*, here not only repeated but bared, not as a feature of insignificance but as the discovery of an enigmatic possibility, makes him feel the attraction of a flaw that is like the absence of error, this "outside error" whose obviousness the feminine world incarnates, but also already incarnates, in its presence, the equivocal separation. From this world, in effect, all temptations come (which should not, however, be understood in a naively Christian sense as seduction of the flesh, although Kafka has here, too, as we know, his difficulties).[2] It is rather the temptation of a life that attracts him because it seems so strange in its remoteness from guilt, but such that the attraction immediately makes the one who is subject to it forever guilty by turning him away from himself, doomed henceforth to the deception of the turning away and fated to the enchantment of oblivion: this will be one of the meanings of *The Trial* and also, in part, of *The Castle*, both of which were written under the provocation of the strangeness of the feminine.

(In a letter to Weltsch, at a particularly unhappy moment, Kafka explains himself with his unfailing lucidity on what his friend, also very lucid, calls Kafka's happy feeling of guilt: "You think that my feeling of guilt is an aid, a solution, no, I have a feeling of guilt only because for my being it is the most beautiful form of remorse, but one does not need to look at it very closely to see that the feeling of guilt is nothing but the exigency to go backward. But immediately, much more formidable than remorse and far above any remorse, the feeling of freedom, of deliverance, of measured contentment already rises." To feel guilty is to be innocent because it is to strive, through remorse, to erase the work of time, to free oneself from error, but hence to render oneself twice guilty, because it is to devote oneself to the idleness of the absence of time, where nothing more happens and is thus hell or, as Kafka himself says in this letter, the inner courtyard of hell.)

2. Yet why, after the first months of an alliance passionately in search of itself, does everything become more unhappy? I spoke of the trip to Berlin; nothing can be explained by this. What does he himself say about it (for our task is only to repeat him)? During the same period, as he wrote in tormented but impetuous bursts, and an almost timeless regularity (every night in the infinity of the night: *The Verdict*, just one month after having met F.B. and two days after sending her the first letter; then the continuation of his novel, *Amerika*; and at the same time, *The Metamorphosis*), suddenly the writing stops and comes to an end. Not only this, but in rereading the "notebooks of the novel," he is convinced that, with the exception of the first chapter, which does not depart from an inner truth, "all of the rest was written only in memory of a great but radically absent feeling and must be scrapped, that is to say, of the more than 400 pages only 56 have the right to remain."

It is a commonplace to show Kafka struggling for the solitude of writing and Kafka struggling for the exigency of life, which passes by way of the necessary relations with men, which thus passes by way of marriage or salvation in the world. Numerous passages of the correspondence—numerous: let us say almost innumerable— would confirm it. He has barely begun to write to her with whom he is not yet on familiar terms, than he confides in her without reserve: "My life consists and has in fact always consisted in trying to write and most often in failing. But were I not to write, I would remain stretched out on the ground, deserving nothing more than to be thrown away. . . . As thin as I am . . . there is nothing in me that, with regard to writing, is not already superfluous and superfluous in the good sense. . . . Even the thought of you is related to writing, only the ups and downs of writing determine me, and surely, during a barren period, I would never have had the courage to turn to you." Felice soon takes fright at such outbursts and advises him, as a reasonable person, more moderation: "My heart [he responds] is more or less in perfect health, but it is not easy for any human heart to hold out against the melancholy of bad writing or against the happiness of good writing. . . . Were you to consider my relation to writing, you would cease to advise me '*Maß und Ziel*,' moderation and limitation: human weakness is but too drawn to setting limits to everything. Should I not engage everything I have in the one thing I am able to do? . . . It may be that my writing is nothing, but then and certainly I am truly nothing."[3] Then comes the surprising letter of January 15, 1913, in which, to her whom he already considers to be his life companion, he describes the ideal existence that he proposes to her: "One day you wrote that you would like to sit beside me while I wrote; but think of it, then I would no longer be able to write (as it is, I barely can), but in that case I could no longer write at all. Writing means opening oneself to measurelessness; the extreme openness in which a person already feels he is losing himself in human relations and from which, if he is a being of reason, he will always try to withdraw, stricken—for every person wants to live for as long as he is alive—this openness and this gift of heart are not enough for writing, not by far. What from the surface is recovered below by the act of writing—unless it goes otherwise and the sources of the depths are silent—is nothing and collapses the moment a true feeling comes to shatter this ground situated above. This is why one could never be alone enough when one writes; this is why there is never enough silence around one, when one writes; night is still not night enough. . . . I have often thought that the best way for me to live would be to set myself up, with my writing material and a lamp, in the innermost room of a spacious locked cellar. I would be brought food, but always far away from the place in which I would be sitting, behind the cellar's outermost door. My only walk would be to fetch this food, in my bathrobe, through the many vaults of the cellar. Then I would return to the table, I would eat slowly and solemnly, and immediately after I would begin writing again. The things I would write! The depths from which I would tear it! Without effort! For extreme concentration knows no effort. The only reserve being that I would not be able to keep it up for long, and at the first failure I would fall into a grandiose fit of madness, perhaps impossible to avoid even in these conditions. What do you think, my dearest? Do not shrink from your cellar dweller!"

This narrative (for it is one) is impressive, but at this date, still enlivened by the illusions of youth: Kafka first seems to believe (does he believe it?) that when Felice understands the necessity of the underground life, she will be happy with it, happy with the cellar, because the cellar will also belong to her ("*a cellar*," he will say a little further on, "a sad possession for you all the same"); then he seems to believe (but does he believe it?) that the cellar might suffice for his isolation and bring him aid: the cellar, the emptiness of a presence full in its retreat, habitable and comfortable; in other words, madness itself, but well converted and as if protected (in the years 1915–1916, when he looks for a room in the city in which to work, he cannot even tolerate that it should be deprived of a horizon, but this is because he is then in the truth of solitude, no longer in his musing). It is indeed true that almost all of his behavior with Felice seems capable of being explained by his sole desire to protect his work and by the wish not to deceive his fiancée about the conditions of their future together, if ever there is a future: barely, he says, will they see each other for an hour a day. Later, after the rupture of July 12, 1914 (when he is brought to trial), when, in November, he again takes up his explanation with the young lady, it is this truth that he will propose to her with new authority and austerity: "You were unable to see the power that work has over me; you saw it, but only incompletely, very in-completely. . . . You were not only the greatest friend, you were at the same time the greatest enemy of my work, at least considering things from the point of view of work, and as the latter loved you at its center beyond all limits, it had to defend itself against you with all its might in order to protect itself. . . . You want me to explain why I behaved thus,[4] and this explanation consists in this: your fear, your disgust were constantly before my eyes. It was my duty to watch over my work, which alone gives me the right to live, and your fear showed me and made me fear (with a fear much more intolerable) that here was the greatest danger for my work. . . . This is when I wrote the letter to Miss Bloch. . . . Now, you can turn the whole thing around and say that you were no less threatened in your essence than I and that your fear was no less justified than mine. I do not believe that this was the case. I loved you in your real being and it is only when it touched my work with hostility that I feared it. . . . Even if this is not altogether true. You were threatened. But did you not want to be? Ever? In no way?" (A questioning traversed by the movement of sovereignty that was also the least visible, the least contestable part of Kafka: of the writer in him.)

3. The conflict of writing and life, reduced to such simplicity, can offer no sure principle of explanation, even if to explain here is but the deployment of affirmations that call forth one another in order to put themselves to the test without limiting themselves. To write, to live: how could one hold oneself to this confrontation of terms that are precisely so poorly determined? Writing destroys life, protects life, demands life, is ignorant of life, and vice versa. In the end writing has no relation to life, if it is not through the necessary insecurity that writing receives from life, just as life receives this necessary insecurity from writing: an absence of relation such that writing, as much as it gathers itself in the absence of relation by dispersing itself in it, never refers to itself in this absence, but to what is *other than* it, which ruins it, or worse yet, disrupts it. Kafka is made aware of this "*other than*"—the other in the neuter—that belongs to writing insofar as writing cannot belong to itself, cannot designate a belonging, through the obstinate, interrupted, never broken, never questioned attempt to be united with Felice, to

rejoin her (rejoin the disjunction). His relations with the young woman are first and foremost established on the level of written words, consequently in the place that words control and under the truth of the illusion that they necessarily provoke. When he tells her (and before they meet in Berlin for the first time), "It sometimes seems to me that this exchange of letters, which I almost incessantly long to get beyond in order to arrive at reality, is the only exchange that corresponds to my misery (my misery, which naturally I do not always experience as misery) and that were we to cross this limit that is imposed on me, we would be led to a common unhappiness," he is still only expressing the apprehension of an encounter frightening in all regards, but he also senses the contradiction to which he is exposing himself. Through letters— this mixed communication, which is neither direct nor indirect, neither of presence nor of absence (he designates it as a hybrid or bastard, *Zwitter*)—he shows himself, but to someone who does not see him (one night, he dreams that Felice is blind), and if he thus wins the young woman, it is in the mode of non-possession and also of non-manifestation, that is, of non-truth ("I am going to Berlin for no other reason but to tell and to show you, who have been misled by my letters, who I really am").

In a certain sense, at least in the dramatic course of the year 1913, which will lead, even before the official engagement, to a first rupture, the only thing at stake for him is the truth: the truth about him or, more precisely, the possibility of being true. How to avoid deceiving the young woman? How to convince her of what he is, as he is in the depths of solitude that he reaches only in the nights of writing? How to unveil himself in such a way as to be seen as he searches for himself through invisibility which is outside of all veiling and all unveiling? "My letter today will arrive torn; I tore it on my way to the station in a movement of impotent rage at not being able to be true and precise when I write to you, such that even when I write, I am never able to hold you firmly or to communicate to you the beating of my heart, there being nothing from this moment on to expect from writing." And a little earlier, in a manner that is even more striking: "Naturally, I cannot forget you when I am writing to you, because I can never forget you at all, but I would like in some way not to rouse myself from the dizziness of the reverie without which I cannot write to you, by calling your name." Practically speaking, this movement can be translated in this way: to say everything (and not only to her, but to the father of the young woman, as to the higher authority), which means to tell how he will make her unhappy or, more precisely, the impossibility of communal life to which he is condemning her; and this with nothing to make up for it, so that she may accept it and see it precisely as impossible, from which it will follow that none of the answers that she gives him can satisfy him. For if she says to him, perhaps out of levity, out of affection, perhaps also out of a proper concern for nuances: "you speak too abruptly about yourself," or else "things are perhaps as you say, but you cannot know that they will not change when we are together," this hope that she maintains despairs him: "What do I have to do? How can I make you believe the unbelievable? . . . "There exist hindrances that you know to a certain extent, but you do not take them seriously enough and you would still not take them seriously enough, were you fully aware of them. No one around me takes them seriously enough or one neglects them out of friendship for me. . . . When I see how much you change when you are with me and the indifferent fatigue that takes hold of you then, the young woman normally so self-assured, whose thinking is quick and proud . . . the result of this is: I cannot assume the responsibility, for I see that it is too great, you cannot assume it, for you hardly see it."

This on the one hand. But on the other hand if, convinced or eventually hurt, she takes her distance, becomes reticent, formulates doubts, writes less, then he becomes all the more despairing, for he has the feeling that she misjudges him precisely because she knows him, thus deciding according to the knowledge he gives her of himself, instead of deciding, not blindly, not by weighing the reasons, but in all clarity under the attraction of the impossible. There are, he says, three answers; there are no others that she can make: "It is impossible, and therefore I do not want it." "It is impossible, and for the time being, I do not want it." "It is impossible, and therefore I want it." This third answer, the only correct one (which might, inspired by Luther, take this form: "I cannot do otherwise, in spite of everything"), Kafka will one day deem to have received it—he, too, out of lassitude, from her whom he then calls his "dear fiancée," not without adding: "I will say for the last time that I am insanely afraid of our future and of the unhappiness that may arise as a result of my nature and my faults in our life together and that must first affect you, for I am at bottom a cold, egoistic and insensible being, in spite of my weakness that dissimulates but does mitigate it." Where the impossible speaks, a relation of strangeness (of transcendence?) is introduced that cannot be designated as such, a relation in which it would be deceptive to see any trait of the sublime (in the romantic manner), but which Kafka nonetheless refuses to perceive in terms of practical reason. When Felice, overwhelmed, and perhaps rightly so, writes to him: "Marriage would lead us both to give up many things; we do not want to weigh the side on which the greatest weight would be; for both of us, it would be great," he is deeply hurt, precisely because she reduces here the impossible to a sum of possibles, producing thus a sort of bargaining of accounts. "You are right, we must keep accounts; unless this is, not unjust, but deprived of meaning. . . . This is, in the end, my opinion." And finally the exigency of truth always returns: "A lasting life together is impossible for me without deception, just as it would be impossible without truth. The first glance I would cast upon your parents would be deceptive."[5]

4. Before going on, I would like to quote two or three texts that are among the most serious. I quote them as if in parentheses, not because they are of secondary importance but because of their seriousness. They explain why (this is not the only reason; it is even a reason that Kafka expressed himself, to himself, only at very critical moments), when he believes he is losing the young woman who seems so remote from him, he is immediately certain of losing himself. "In my letters, my perpetual concern is to free you of me, and as soon as I have the appearance of success, I go mad." It is not the madness of a lover split between movements of opposing

passions, it is madness itself from which she, Felice—and she alone, because she forms his only and essential human bond—can still protect him, for she is still capable, when he is not writing and at times when he is, of keeping him away from the monstrous world that he carries in his head, a world that he does not dare confront except in the nights of writing. "Traversing the nights in a fury of writing, this is what I want. And to perish thus or to go mad, this is also what I want, because it is the long-anticipated consequence." But immediately the other affirmation, the desire to find in her, against this threat, a recourse, a protection, a future: "It is a justifiable anguish that prevents me from wishing you were coming to Prague; but more justified still and much exceeding it, the monstrous anguish that I will perish if we are not together soon. For if we are not together soon, my love for you, which does not tolerate any other thought in me, will direct itself to an idea, a ghost, something altogether unattainable, altogether and forever necessary, that would, in truth, be capable of tearing me from the world. I tremble as I write this." Which I will permit myself to translate in this way: I tremble with writing. But what writing? "You do not know, Felice, what a certain literature can be in certain heads. It creates constant havoc like monkeys in the treetops instead of walking on the earth. It is being lost and not able to be otherwise. What should one do?" Whence, again, no longer the desire or the hope of being protected by Felice, but the fear of being exposed to a more serious threat while under her protection and the worse fear of also exposing her to a danger he cannot name: "At present, I only torment you in my letters, but as soon as we lived together, I would become a dangerous madman fit to be burned. . . . What holds me back is, in some sense, a command from heaven, an anguish that cannot be appeased; everything that seemed of greatest importance to me, my health, my small resources, my miserable being, all this, for which there is some justification, vanishes before this anguish, is nothing compared to it and is used by this anguish only as a pretext. . . . It is, to be perfectly frank, and so that you are able to recognize the degree of my madness, the *fear of the union* with the most beloved being and precisely with her. . . . I have the definite feeling that I will be exposed to doom, through marriage, through this *union*, through the dissolution of this nothingness that I am, and I will not be exposed alone, but with my wife, and the more I love her, the swifter and more terrible it will be."[6]

5. When, in Berlin for the first time, he sees her whom he had approached only through the detour of letters, he will be as if repelled from all living relations. And, upon his return, he writes to her: "My true fear—certainly nothing more grievous could be said or heard: never will I be able to possess you. In the most favorable case, I would be limited to kissing your casually abandoned hand in the manner of a crazily mad dog, which would not be a sign of love, but of the despair that you would feel for an animal condemned to muteness and eternal separation. . . . In short, I would remain forever excluded from you, were you to lean toward me so far as to be in danger." To Brod, he will confide the next day: "Yesterday, I sent the big confession." Thus it is a confession. We must not give it too simple a meaning, however, one that would contradict what we know of his various brief affairs about which his friends speak. In 1916 in Marienbad, when he sees in Felice a being he could love, more than from at a distance, he writes again to Brod. I will recall three features of these very controlled reflections that he then composes for the benefit of his friend. "I did not know her at all" [until the final days in which he established intimate relations with her],[7] "what bothered me [prevented me], other scruples not with-standing, was, essentially, the fear of having to regard as real the one who writes letters to me." Here, therefore, and very distinctly, the retreat before the reality of presence is expressed, not as such but through the relation of writing (the non-presence of writing), that is, the refusal to pass from one to the other, the impossibility of this passage. Second indication: "When [at the moment of the official engagement ceremony] she crossed the great hall and came to my encounter to receive her engagement kiss, a terrible shudder ran through me; the matter of the engagement, accompanied by my parents, was for me and at every step a constant torture." From

which one must remember, however, that what is disagreeable to
him to the point of horror is not contact with a feminine face but
rather, through it, the approach of conjugality, the falsehood of his
institutional obligations and also, certainly, of everything that the
word *marriage* evokes for him, and first of all, conjugal intimacy,
which in his parents always filled him with disgust, because it
reminded him that he was born of it and still always had to be born
in connection to those "distasteful things."[8] It is the very idea of
marriage—the law, in other words—both solemn, sovereign, but
also sovereignly impure (and sovereign because impure) that, as
Felice crosses the great space of the hall to make her way toward
him, an infinite insurmountable space, rises up and imposes its
sanction on him, a sanction that is like a punishment in advance.[9]
Finally, and this is the third feature—the strongest, perhaps—he
will say to Brod, evoking his new familiarity with Felice: "I have
now seen the confident intimacy in the gaze of a woman and could
not remain closed to it. A laceration as a result of which many
things that I had always wanted to keep protected (it is not
anything in particular, but a whole) are brought to light [*aufge-
rissen*, are torn from me] and, through this laceration [*Riß*] so
much unhappiness will emerge, this I also know, that the entire life
of a man cannot suffice, but I did not call forth this unhappiness, it
was imposed on me." I think this passage is important. It gives not
only the meaning of what happened in Marienbad in 1916[10] (this
finally changes nothing as to the difficulty of their relations, which
confirms that this difficulty had yet another origin), but perhaps
the meaning of the entire story with the young woman, a story the
decisive nature of which Kafka never misrecognized, even apart
from his own feelings, for he knew that it helped change him
almost radically, in the sense that it unveiled him before his own
eyes and constituted a warning that it was his duty never to forget.
Through it, in effect, he was put to the test of "the laceration"; the
circle in which he had thought he could keep himself pure, as
much by the constraints of isolation as by the pressure to write—
pure, this means without falsehood, which does not mean true
(this he never thought but, rather, outside falsehood, just as outside
truth)—was broken, and with a break that did not take place at

such and such a moment or because of particular events, but revealed itself as always having taken place, as if beforehand, before any place and before any event. A revelation that, in turn, did not occur at a specific moment or progressively, no more than it was empirically or internally experienced, but was implied, put into practice in his work and in his relation to his work.

6. This, then, was the great "warning." The letters to Felice only confirm it, in my opinion, and they do this in two ways.

A) During his entire youth as a writer—a youth that came to an end (markers are still needed, however indecisive and however deceptive they may be) with the "failure" of his youthful novel (*Amerika*)—he had confidence in writing, a tormented confidence, most often unhappy, but always intact again. His thought was that writing—if ever he could write—would save him, this word under-stood not in a positive sense but negatively, that is, would defer or delay the sentence, would give him a possibility and, who knows? Provide a way out: who knows? Who knows? To live in the cellar, to write in it endlessly and without any end save writing itself, to be the inhabitant of the cellar and thus dwell (live, die) nowhere but in the outside of writing (but, at this moment, for Kafka, this outside is still an inside, an intimacy, a "warmth," as he writes in this very revealing sentence: "I cannot be thrown out of writing, for I have sometimes thought that I am already settled at its center, in its greatest warmth."). "Ah, if only I could write. This desire consumes me. If above all else I had enough freedom and health for this. I don't think you have understood that writing is the only thing that makes my existence possible. It is no wonder, I express myself so badly, I only begin to awaken in the space of my inner figures." From which one must conclude that in this space, he maintains the hope of reaching a certain awakening. However, little by little and always suddenly, without ever renouncing the exigency of writing, he will have to renounce the hope that this exigency seemed to carry: not only is writing essentially uncertain, but to write is no longer to maintain oneself intact in the purity of the closed circle, it is to attract the dark powers toward the upper reaches, to give oneself to their perverse strangeness, and perhaps to join oneself to what destroys. I am not saying that he needed the interminable failure of his story with Felice (he certainly needed much more, much less as well) to arrive at this insight—hidden, moreover—about his future as a writer, but these two movements point to one another by way of each other, not because they are directly linked but because they repeat at different levels the condition of absence—of alterity—(the rupture, but in the rupture, the impossibility of breaking it off) that precedes and ruins and supports any possibility of a relation, be it the very relation engaged in the movement, removed from any affirmation of presence, that is the movement of writing.

B) Barely has he begun to correspond with Felice than he makes her this essential confidence: "It is one of my failings that I cannot write down in the flux of a single continuous movement what has gathered itself in me according to a preestablished order. My memory is definitely bad, but even the best memory could not help me to write down even a short part of what had been premeditated [thought out in advance] and simply marked, for within every sentence, there are transitions that must remain suspended [in suspense] before the actual writing." In truth, if he thus confides himself to her whom he still does not call Felice, it is because six days earlier he had been victorious in his attempt at uninterrupted writing, having completed *The Verdict* in an eight-hour stretch, in a single nocturnal stroke, an experience for him decisive, which gave him the certainty of a possible contact with the unapproachable space, and he noted in his *Diary* immediately: "My certainty is confirmed, *it is only thus* that one can write: with such a flow of coherence, with such perfect openness of the body and soul." Search for absolute continuity—the uninterrupted in all senses: how to maintain an outside of writing, this lack where nothing is lacking but its absence, otherwise than by a perpetuity without dissidence—a transparency, as it were, compact, or a compactness, as such, transparent—given in time as outside of time, given in one time as infinite repetition? "I need isolation in order to write, not like a 'hermit' but like a dead man. In this sense writing is a deeper slumber, thus a death, and just as one will not tear a dead man from his grave, at night I cannot be torn from my table. This has no immediate bearing on my relations with men, but it is only in this rigorous, continuous, and systematic manner that I can write and thus also live." Yet, the characteristic of such a movement—the interminable according to all dimensions—from which it first seemed to him that only his manner of living (the office work) kept him at a distance, but with which he indeed had to recognize that this distance was in a relation of "essence," always deferred because continual and, by this continuity, united with difference; Kafka was only slowly persuaded and always had to persuade himself that he would never possess this movement except as lack (rupture or absence), and that it is on the basis of this movement as lack that he might also—perhaps—be given to write: no longer, then, the uninterrupted in its becoming, but the becoming of interruption. This was his eternal struggle. All of his unfinished works—and first of all the first novel, the incompletion of which was as if his condemnation as a writer, and thus also his condemnation as a living man, incapable of living with Felice[11]—put in some sense before his eyes their own completion, this new way of completing themselves in and by interruption (under the spell of the fragmentary). However, unable to be anything but *blind* to what could be read there, unable to reach it except through an exigency that he came up against in order to destroy himself and not confirm himself in it, he had to agree (and so it is every time for the writer without indulgence) to see the power to read himself taken away from him, unaware that the books he believed not to have written and that, from that point on, he intended for definitive destruction, had received the gift of being almost freed from themselves and, by erasing all idea of a masterpiece and all idea of a work, of identifying themselves with the *absence of book*, thus suddenly for a moment offered to our own powerlessness of reading, *absence of book* soon itself deprived of itself, overturned, and finally—become work again—reestablished in the assurance of our admiration and our judgment of culture.

7. Kafka—the correspondence confirms it—did nothing (except at certain moments when he lacked the strength) to break, by means of a deliberate initiative, with Felice: contrary to certain biographical affirmations, when he stands trial in Berlin in the

Askanischer Hof, in face of a tribunal consisting of his fiancée, the sister of his fiancée (Erna), the friend of his fiancée (Grete Bloch), and his only ally and friend, Ernst Weiss (but hostile to Felice and to this marriage), in no way is it his design to be done with a situation by which he sees himself condemned, whatever the result. Before leaving for Berlin, he writes to his sister Ottla: "Naturally I will write to you from Berlin; for the moment nothing certain can be said either about the thing itself or about me. I write not as I speak, I speak not as I think, I think not as I should think, and so forth into the greatest depths of obscurity." Nothing can be interrupted, nothing can be broken off.** The illness itself (which intervenes barely a month after his second engagement; the official engagements never lasted more than a few weeks), to which he gave the all too clear meaning of a spiritual symptom, could decide nothing: all still depended upon the young woman ("Do not ask me why I draw a line. Do not humiliate me thus. One word, and I am again at your feet."). The tuberculosis is only a weapon in this fight, a weapon that is neither more nor less effective than the "innumerable" weapons he has used until this point and that he enumerates in the next-to-last letter of the correspondence, when summing up all the events of the past five years: the names by which he designates them, not without a certain irony, include "physical incapacity," "work," "avarice," designations that all tend toward what cannot be designated, even when he adds, "Moreover, I am telling you a secret that for the moment I do not believe (although the obscurity that falls around me as I try to work and think might convince me of it), but that must be true: I will never be in good health again. Precisely because it is no longer the tuberculosis that is being stretched out on a deck chair and tended to, but a weapon the external necessity of which will survive for as long as I am alive. And the two cannot remain alive together."

However, he also says the most likely would be *eternal struggle*, that is, the impossibility of putting an end to it. When, a year later, in the Stüdl pension in Schelesen, he meets Julie Wohryzeck, with

** See the end of the chapter.

whom he becomes friends the following season under conditions of extreme physical and moral deprivation, through a new engagement immediately broken; when, almost at the same date, he abandons himself to Milena's passion and to his passion for her, and would like to bring the young woman to break up her marriage in the prospect of a very uncertain union; when, finally, he appeals with Dora Diamant to the sky itself, through the intervention of a very revered rabbi (Gerer Rebbe, friend of the young woman's father), for the authorization of marriage and receives, with a shake of the head of absolute denial, a silent refusal, ultimate response and, as it were, consecrated (yet, all the same, a response that indicated, be it negatively, in the form of an impugnment, a recognition of sorts from above), it is always to the same rupture that he exposes himself, experiencing it each time at the limit, as the impossibility of breaking off or, more profoundly, as the exigency of exclusion, which, having always already been pronounced, must always again be solicited, repeated, and, through the repetition, erased, in order—by perpetuating itself—to reproduce itself in the powerlessness, infinite and always new, of its lack. Is it therefore the world and life with which he would like to be reconciled by these attempts at marriage, the real nature of which he does everything in advance to exhaust? It is rather with the law that he pursues the tragic game (provocation and interrogation), the law, which his obstinacy—gentle, that is, inflexible—expects to pronounce itself, not by authorizing him or even by striking him, but by designating itself as that which cannot be made attributable, in such a way that he might be able to sense why writing—this movement from which he had hoped for a kind of salvation—has, always and as if forever, put him *outside* the law or, more precisely, has led him to occupy this space of the *outside*, radical (aorgic) exteriority, about which he cannot know—except by writing and by writing to the point of non-writing—whether, exterior to the law, it indicates the limit of the law or indicates itself in this limit, or else, provocation of provocations, exposes itself as disturbing or preceding all law. It remains striking that even before the marriage with Dora Diamant has been challenged by the highest court,

Kafka carries on regardless and, in opposition to social mores, arranges with the adolescent girl a sort of conjugal life together. Dora is nineteen years old, he is forty: almost his daughter or his very young sister (precisely, he never hid his preference for the young Ottla, about whom he said, in all innocence of language, that she was his sister, his mother, and his spouse). As always, the transgression—the decision to fail in what could not exist—precedes the promulgation of the interdiction, thus rendering it possible, as if the limit were to be crossed only insofar as it is impossible to cross and reveals itself to be uncrossable only by the crossing itself. The "No" of the rabbi briefly precedes his death. Was Kafka finally allowed to break off? Liberated, could he finally write, that is to say, die? Finally. But already eternity was beginning: the posthumous hell, the sarcastic glory, the exegesis of admiration and pretension, the great sealing off of culture and, precisely here, once again this last word offering itself only in order to simulate and dissimulate the anticipation of the very last.

  * Obscure and unhappy story. This is what we know of it, at least what I know of it. Grete Bloch, 22 years old at the time and a recent friend of Felice, went to Prague on Felice's behalf and met Kafka in October 1913. She lived and worked in Vienna. Kafka begins to write to her, and what results is a correspondence made up of approximately 70 published letters, from October 29, 1913, to July 3, 1914. On July 12, the engagement is broken off. In the month of October 1914, the young woman writes to Kafka in an attempt to reestablish relations between the formerly engaged couple, relations she had contributed to ruining; Kafka answers on October 15; it is the last letter (to G.B.) that we have. According to the editors, Erich Heller and Jürgen Born, there is no proof that Kafka continued to write to her. (I find, in the *Diary* for the date October 8, 1917, when, having fallen ill, he must take back his "word" from his fiancée: "accusatory letters from F.; G.B. threatens to write me.") He sometimes speaks of her to Felice, either to ask for news or to send his regards, even advice, and also, at a painful moment, signs of deep sympathy. We know that Felice, Grete Bloch, and Kafka took a vacation trip together in Bohemia on May 23 and 24, 1915. Let it be added that the letters, published today, although marked by a desire to please, often with

very affectionate, almost seductive words, remain at the same time rather ceremonious: "Dear Miss Grete" is the most tender address. What else do we know? This: Max Brod published parts of a letter that Grete Bloch, on April 21, 1940, sent from Florence to a friend in Israel. She reveals to him that she had a son who died suddenly in Munich in 1921, when he was seven years old: an "illegitimate" child whose father was not named, but the addressee of the letter (Brod's only guarantor in this story) maintained that Grete Bloch regarded Kafka as the father of the child. What is there to say? In a certain manner, obviously nothing. Let us indicate the reasons for doubt, reasons that are themselves dubious. Wagenbach asserts that beginning in the fall of 1914, a regular and intimate correspondence is established between Grete B. and Kafka, but no doubt he is making a mistake; the only known correspondence lasted from the fall of 1913 to the summer of 1914, and was never such that it would allow one to conclude that there was a relationship between the two correspondents. Naturally, we do not know everything. If one recalls the rule of absolute candor that was always Kafka's (when he has broken with Felice for the first time and spends several days of intimacy with the young Swiss woman in Riga, he does not fail, as soon as relations have been reestablished, to tell everything to her who is no longer his fiancée), it seems very unlikely that he could have kept silent about such a relationship, one that would also have been a double betrayal. Nonetheless, one could imagine that he kept silent in order not to compromise G.B. Such a strangely equivocal situation. The following testimony must also be mentioned: friends of Grete Bloch said that the young woman, during her stay in Florence (thus at the moment when she revealed the story of the child), gave signs of profound melancholia or delirious distress. But what is such an assertion worth? It is as vague as it is grievous. Imaginary or not, the child of which Kafka was unaware had this spectral existence, real-unreal, that does not allow one, for the moment, to give it life outside dreams. Grete Bloch and Felice remained friends until the end. When she had to leave Germany, Grete confided to her friend one part (approximately half) of the letters she had received from Kafka. The rest she deposited in Florence with a notary who later put photostats of them at the disposal of Max Brod. Twelve of these letters had been torn in two in a "rather bizarre manner," but with the exception of one, they were able to be put back together because one of the halves was in the hands of Felice, the other with the notary in Florence. Grete Bloch, who lived in Israel from the time she left Germany, had the misfortune to return to

Italy and, when the country fell under Nazi occupation, she was taken away with many other Jews and died during the deportation or in a camp: an inquiry by the Red Cross has not allowed it to be known with certainty. Felice escaped from such a fate: married, she lived first in Switzerland and then in the United States, where she died in 1960. I will also add: in Kafka's *Diary*, in January and February 1922, during his solitary and very tragic stay in Spindlermühle—he is still friends with Milena, but without hope—certain notations can be read in which the initial G. appears; thus on January 18: "A little peace; on the other hand, G. is arriving. Deliverance or aggravation, one or the other." On February 10: "New attack of G. Attacked from the right and from the left by extremely powerful enemies, I cannot escape." And on January 29, although no name intervenes and in a manner that is enigmatic, which led me some time ago, perhaps rashly, to read these passages in the light of an almost "mystical" obscurity: "Attack on the way, at night, in the snow." "I got away from them," and later, on March 24: "How I am spied on; for example, on the path on the way to the doctor, on the path constantly." Texts of an oppressive strangeness. Wagenbach, who knew the manuscript of the *Diary*, seems to have read: "New attack by Grete." I give this indication, without knowing more.

** To offer better proof of this to myself, I would like to establish a short chronology of the ruptures, at least during the course of the first two years. They begin almost at the same time as the correspondence, which begins, it should be recalled, on September 20, 1912. Already in mid-November, Kafka writes (the young lady had remarked without malice that she did not always understand him or that certain traits of his made him strange to her): "Let us be done with it, if our life is dear to us." Distraught, the unfortunate Felice then appeals to Brod, who answers her: "I beg you to let many things pass with Franz, given his pathological sensitivity; he obeys his mood [*Stimmung*] of the moment. He is someone who wants the absolute in everything. . . . He never accepts a compromise." On November 20, Kafka writes again: "But I do not have any news from you. I must therefore openly repeat the adieu that you silently gave me." Following which their written relations take up their passionate course once again.

In the beginning of January 1913, the change, which is no longer one of circumstance or of mood, begins to take place in Kafka, one that will not cease to aggravate itself without, however, attenuating the relationship—

deepening it, on the contrary. On March 23, meeting in Berlin. After which, the letter of confession: "My true fear: never will I be able to possess you," which for him does not at all signify that he is moving away from her, but she seems to take it otherwise: she spaces out her letters, takes advantage of a trip to Frankfurt to interrupt them, with a casualness that almost drives Kafka mad. On May 11, another meeting in Berlin during the vacation of Pentecost. This meeting gives him a little hope, the hope that one day, at least, he "will be able to seriously discuss with her [about their future] a certain number of dreadful things and thus little by little to reach fresh air." All the same, he adds: "When I was packing my bags in Berlin, I had a completely different text in my head: 'Without her, I cannot live, nor with her either.'" The torment of the truth comes, and at the same time, in a letter begun on June 10, which is interrupted, then courageously finished on the sixteenth: "Would you like to think it over and consider if you want to become my wife? Do you want this?" Following which there is a debate that will come to an end on July 1 (1913) with these words: "So you want, in spite of everything, to take the cross upon yourself, Felice? To attempt the impossible?" It is after this that the first serious breakup occurs. The couple—engaged out of intimate feeling, not officially—do not meet up to spend their vacation together. Felice has a rather cheerful stay in Westerland ("What awaits you is not the life of the happy people you see in Westerland, not a joyful chatter arm in arm, but a cloistered life at the side of someone who is morose, sad, silent, discontented, sickly, bound to literature by invisible chains"), Kafka goes off to Vienna under the pretext of a congress, then to Italy, where he writes that he will stop writing to her: "I can no longer go forward, it is as if I were ensnared. We should separate" (September 16, 1913). He remains for some time in Riva, becoming friends with the very young G.W., the "Swiss woman."

Back in Prague, he will receive Grete Bloch's visit; she is sent by Felice to try to clear up the misunderstandings. The correspondence is far from starting up again with the same impetus. On November 8, he goes to Berlin for an interview and manages to catch only a glimpse of her in effect, F. escaping out of intention or negligence, we do not know. At the beginning of March 1914, still in Berlin, an explanation leaves him altogether discouraged, and he notices that Felice tolerates him with difficulty. Meanwhile, the correspondence with Miss Bloch continues to become more and more cordial: "You are too important to me. . . . Your little card made me happier than anything I received from Berlin. . . . Dear Miss

Grete, I have an ardent desire to see you and as if a manifest nostalgia. . . . Who in Berlin, for the love of God, can have designs on your head other than to caress it?" And when Felice says to him, "You seem to be very attached to Grete," he does not defend against it. However, on the twelfth and thirteenth of May, the encounter takes place during which the official engagement is decided. (The ceremonial celebration, with invitation, kiss, and congratulations, will be observed on June 1.) Kafka comments on the event for Grete: "Berlin was neither good nor bad, but in any case as was necessary for my undeniable feeling." And for Felice: "In spirit, I am united with you in a manner so indissoluble that no blessing of any rabbi could touch it." But Kafka continues to write to Grete, sharing with her his disenchantment, even his repulsion: "Sometimes—you are the only one to know it for the moment—I really do not know how I can assume such a responsibility, nor how it came to my getting married." This is one of the letters that Grete (with what intention?) communicates to Felice, as we learn on July 3, 1914, when he writes to Miss Bloch, breaking in so doing, or shortly thereafter, with her: "You should not have quoted letters. . . . Well then, I have therefore convinced you, and you begin to see in me not Felice's fiancé but Felice's danger." There are also painful debates on the material conditions of their future; Felice desires an apartment to her taste and comfortably furnished (the apartment, moreover, will be rented), just as she does not wish to give up a normal social life. Kafka is finally brought to trial at the Askanischer Hof on July 12, 1914, and the official break of the engagement occurs, much to the horror and surprise of both families.

I will stop here with this short history of the ruptures. The correspondence resumes in November 1914, again through the mediation of Grete Bloch (in the *Diary*, on October 15: "Today, Thursday . . . letter from Miss Bloch, I do not know what to do about it, I know it is certain that I will remain alone. . . . I also do not know whether I love F. (I think of the disgust I felt at seeing her while she was dancing . . .), but in spite of everything the infinite temptation returns," but never again at any moment will the exchange of letters regain the same flow as in the beginning. Kafka has changed and is changed: since July 29 (thus fifteen days after his condemnation) he has begun *The Trial,* writing every evening, every night, for three months. In January 1915, he will see Felice again in Bodenbach, without any real inner rapprochement. It will take the happy reunion of Marienbad in July 1916 for it to be again a question of engagement and, with the engagement, also a question of new ruptures.

§ 29 Friendship

How could one agree to speak of this friend? Neither in praise nor in the interest of some truth. The traits of his character, the forms of his existence, the episodes of his life, even in keeping with the search for which he felt himself responsible to the point of irresponsibility, belong to no one. There are no witnesses. Those who were closest say only what was close to them, not the distance that affirmed itself in this proximity, and distance ceases as soon as presence ceases. Vainly do we try to maintain, with our words, with our writings, what is absent; vainly do we offer it the appeal of our memories and a sort of figure, the joy of remaining with the day, life prolonged by a truthful appearance. We are only looking to fill a void, we cannot bear the pain: the affirmation of this void. Who could agree to receive its insignificance—an insignificance so enormous that we do not have a memory capable of containing it and such that we ourselves must already slip into oblivion in order to sustain it—the time of this slippage, the very enigma this insignificance represents? Everything we say tends to veil the one affirmation: that everything must fade and that we can remain loyal only so long as we watch over this fading movement, to which something in us that rejects all memory already belongs.

~

I know there are the books. The books remain, temporarily, even if their reading must open us to the necessity of this disappearance into which they withdraw themselves. The books themselves refer to an existence. This existence, because it is no longer a presence, begins to be deployed in history, and in the worst of histories, literary history. Literary history, inquisitive, painstaking, in search of documents, takes hold of a deceased will and transforms into knowledge its own purchase on what has fallen to posterity. This is the moment of complete works. One wants to publish "everything," one wants to say "everything," as if one were anxious about only one thing: that everything be said; as if the "everything is said" would finally allow us to stop a dead voice, to stop the pitiful silence that arises from it and to contain firmly within a well-circumscribed horizon what the equivocal, posthumous anticipation still mixes in illusorily with the words of the living. As long as the one who is close to us exists and, with him, the thought in which he affirms himself, his thought opens itself to us, but preserved in this very relation, and what preserves it is not only the mobility of life (this would be very little), but the unpredictability introduced into this thought by the strangeness of the end. And this movement, unpredictable and always hidden in its infinite imminence—that of dying, perhaps—arises not because its term could not be given in advance, but because it never constitutes an event that takes place, even when it occurs, never a reality that can be grasped: ungraspable and henceforth entirely in the ungraspable is the one destined to this movement. It is this unpredictable that speaks when he speaks, it is this which in his lifetime conceals and reserves his thought, separates and frees it from all seizure, that of the outside as well as that of the inside.

I also know that, in his books, Georges Bataille seems to speak of himself with a freedom without restraint that should free us from all discretion—but that does not give us the right to put ourselves in his place, nor does it give us the power to speak in his absence. And is it certain that he speaks of himself? The "I" whose presence his search seems still to make manifest when it expresses itself, toward whom does it direct us? Certainly toward an I very different from the ego that those who knew him in the happy and unhappy particularity of life would like to evoke in the light of a memory. Everything leads one to think that the personless presence at stake in such a movement introduces an enigmatic relation into the existence of him who indeed decided to

*speak of it but not to claim it as his own, still less to make of it an event
of his biography (rather, a gap in which the biography disappears). And
when we ask ourselves the question "Who was the subject of this
experience?" this question is perhaps already an answer if, even to him
who led it, the experience asserted itself in this interrogative form, by
substituting the openness of a "Who?" without answer for the closed and
singular "I"; not that this means that he had simply to ask himself
"What is this I that I am?" but much more radically to recover himself
without reprieve, no longer as "I" but as a "Who?," the unknown and
slippery being of an indefinite "Who?"*

$\sim$

*We must give up trying to know those to whom we are linked by
something essential; by this I mean we must greet them in the relation
with the unknown in which they greet us as well, in our estrangement.
Friendship, this relation without dependence, without episode, yet into
which all of the simplicity of life enters, passes by way of the recognition
of the common strangeness that does not allow us to speak of our friends
but only to speak to them, not to make of them a topic of conversations
(or essays), but the movement of understanding in which, speaking to
us, they reserve, even on the most familiar terms, an infinite distance,
the fundamental separation on the basis of which what separates
becomes relation. Here discretion lies not in the simple refusal to put
forward confidences (how vulgar this would be, even to think of it), but
it is the interval, the pure interval that, from me to this other who is a
friend, measures all that is between us, the interruption of being that
never authorizes me to use him, or my knowledge of him (were it to
praise him), and that, far from preventing all communication, brings
us together in the difference and sometimes the silence of speech.*

*It is true that at a certain moment this discretion becomes the fissure
of death. I could imagine that in one sense nothing has changed: in the
"secret" between us that was capable of taking place, in the continuity of
discourse, without interrupting it, there was already, from the time in
which we were in the presence of one another, this imminent presence,
though tacit, of the final discretion, and it is on the basis of this
discretion that the precaution of friendly words calmly affirmed itself.*

Words from one shore to the other shore, speech responding to someone who speaks from the other shore and where, even in our life, the measurelessness of the movement of dying would like to complete itself. And yet when the event itself comes, it brings this change: not the deepening of the separation but its erasure; not the widening of the caesura but its leveling out and the dissipation of the void between us where formerly there developed the frankness of a relation without history. In such a way that at present, what was close to us not only has ceased to approach but has lost even the truth of extreme distance. Thus death has the false virtue of appearing to return to intimacy those who have been divided by grave disagreements. This is because with death all that separates, disappears. What separates: what puts authentically in relation, the very abyss of relations in which lies, with simplicity, the agreement of friendly affirmation that is always maintained.

We should not, by means of artifice, pretend to carry on a dialogue. What has turned away from us also turns us away from that part which was our presence, and we must learn that when speech subsides, a speech that for years gave itself to an "exigency without regard," it is not only this exigent speech that has ceased, it is the silence that it made possible and from which it returned along an insensible slope toward the anxiety of time. Undoubtedly we will still be able to follow the same paths, we can let images come, we can appeal to an absence that we will imagine, by deceptive consolation, to be our own. We can, in a word, remember. But thought knows that one does not remember: without memory, without thought, it already struggles in the invisible where everything sinks back to indifference. This is thought's profound grief. It must accompany friendship into oblivion.

Notes

Chapter 1

1. Georges Bataille, *La Peinture préhistorique: Lascaux ou la naissance de l'art* (Skira).

2. The word *transgression* certainly does not have the same meaning in each of these two moments. It would require lengthy elaborations to try and justify the use of this word in the first case. It seems, however, that later, when man in progress comes to surround himself with certain prohibitions, it is because of the fortuitous "transgression" of the gaps through which nature has, as it were, exceeded and transgressed itself as far back as the distant *Dryopithecus*. As strange as this may appear, the subsequent possibility of prohibition perhaps always arises from, and forms itself upon, an initial transgression. First we "transgress," and then we become conscious of the way thus opened by establishing bounds, defenses, which often limit us at other points altogether: the law, always breached because it is unbreachable.

Chapter 2

1. This text was written in 1950, when the last of the three volumes of *La Psychologie de l'art* appeared. All three volumes were published by Albert Skira, beginning in 1947, in an edition that Malraux has since substantially revised (*Les Voix du silence*, Gallimard).

Chapter 3

1. Georges Duthuit, *Le Musée inimaginable* (Editions Corti).
2. I refer to the essay *La Bête de Lascaux* (Editions G.L.M.).

Chapter 4

1. These reflections are in the margin of the Encyclopédie de la Pléiade, published under the direction of Raymond Queneau, and more particularly on the occasion of the volumes devoted to *l'Histoire des littératures* (Editions Gallimard).
2. In this he is like the cosmophysicist Milne.

Chapter 5

1. Walter Benjamin, *Œuvres choisies*, translated from the German by Maurice de Gandillac (Denoël, "Les Lettres nouvelles" series).

Chapter 6

1. This text is part of a work published in German under the title *Einzelheiten* (Details).
2. This explains the ban on *Éden, Éden, Éden* by Pierre Guyotat, a book not scandalous but simply too strong (Editions Gallimard).
3. *Mercure de France*, Nov. 1964 (no. 1213).
4. At issue here is the pleasant narrative, in Gilbert Lely's very nice edition, of *Aline et Valcour*, the "philosophical novel" to which Sade gave all of his care in the hope of being taken seriously as a man of letters. With the exception of several scenes, several characteristic traits, and certain forceful ideas that are always worthy of Sade, the book succeeds, in fact, only in making him a perfect writer among others, to such an extent that Mme. de Sade did not fail to praise it. (Today I must nonetheless add that since this note was written, the same series has published Sade's *Les Prospérités du vice* and *Les Malheurs de la vertu*, several editions of which [works prefaced by, among others, Georges Bataille and Jean Paulhan] did not disturb the public powers in the least, but which this time were banned. One will blame the foolishness of a minister. But the foolishness of a minister is the intelligence and truth of a regime.)
5. I would like to cite the following text of Alexander Blok, the great poet of the Twelve, who nonetheless feared the October Revolution:

"The Bolsheviks do not prevent one from writing verse, but they prevent one from feeling oneself a master; a master is one who carries within himself the center of his inspiration, of his creation and who possesses the rhythm." The Bolshevik Revolution first displaces the center, which seems henceforth to be under the control of the Party. Following which the communist revolution attempts, by restoring mastery to the community without difference, to situate the center in the movement and the indifference of the whole. There remains one step, which is perhaps the most surprising, and this is when the center must coincide with the absence of any center. I would like to quote a passage from Trotsky: "With the Revolution, life has become a bivouac. Private life, institutions, methods, thoughts, feelings, everything has become inhabitual, temporary, transitory, everything seems precarious. This perpetual bivouac, an episodic characteristic of life, contains within it an accidental element, and what is accidental bears the stamp of insignificance. Taken in the diversity of its stages, the Revolution suddenly seems devoid of meaning. Where is the Revolution? This is the difficulty." A text that is more enigmatic than it seems, and I think the question that he raises must be asked no less of the most self-assured manifestations of literature and art.

Chapter 7

1. Claude Lévi-Strauss, *Tristes tropiques* (Plon).

Chapter 8

1. Henri Lefebvre, *La Somme et le reste* (Editions La Nef de Paris).
2. *Communism* here is necessarily in quotation marks: one does not belong to communism, and communism does not let itself be designated by what names it.
3. I am leaving aside Comte's different point of view, that of the positivists, of all of those who humble philosophy before science. Nietzsche's point of view takes into account and surpasses this point of view: at the same time, it is radically *other*.
4. Yet does he judge the appearance of surrealism, which is at the turning point of time, according to its true importance? Accidental memories, here, have brought darkness.
5. An abbreviation for "dialectical materialism" in use in countries where Marx is under the control of the government.

6. Hegel also wants to enter more deeply into the thing, but first by eliminating it. Heidegger erases or eludes or denudes the moment of negation. The overcoming: a key word of metaphysics that one claims to "overcome."

7. It must be said here, even in a very brief note, that in his writings Jacques Derrida poses the question of "the end of philosophy" in a new—different (posing it without exposing it)—way.

Chapter 9

1. Dionys Mascolo, *Le Communisme, révolution et communication ou la dialectique des valeurs et des besoins* (Editions Gallimard). It should be recalled that this book appeared in 1953. This is also the date of the review. Note 3 below is more recent.

2. But perhaps it would be more correct (though still very approximate) to say: It is only when man will have completed (*removed*) himself as power that the relation to man will itself cease to be power and will become a possible relation, "communication."

3. But here the question arises: Is it so easy to distinguish between private and collective relations? In both cases, is it not a question of relations that could not be those of a subject to an object, nor even of a subject to a subject, but relations in which the relationship of the one to the other affirms itself as infinite or discontinuous? This is why the exigency and the urgency of a relation through desire and through speech, a relation that is always being displaced, where the *other*—the impossible—would be greeted, constitute, in the strongest sense, an essential mode of decision and political affirmation. I think that Dionys Mascolo would agree with this. Still, the fact remains that the concept of need is not simple, and need itself can be misrepresented, in the same way that in a certain state of oppression, men can fall below their needs.

Chapter 10

1. This was manifest, in a striking manner, in May 1968.

Chapter 11

1. In 1956, Jaspers gave a talk on the atomic peril, which was then broadcast over the radio. It created a considerable stir. Jaspers thought it

necessary to take up the question again and even reexamine all of the problems that arose in relation to this reaction. The result was a book almost beyond measure, which was published in German in 1958 and is now published in French through the efforts of Edmond Saget and the Buchet-Chastel Press (*La Bombe atomique et l'avenir de l'homme: Conscience politique de notre temps*). I will cite the following passage from the preface written by Jaspers after the first edition, which indicates the scope of his project: "The matter of this book is, properly speaking, the political conscience of our time. That the threat of the atomic bomb should necessarily give another structure to political conscience for all time: this fact is what brought about the main title."

2. With exemplary simplicity, Karl Jaspers describes in his autobiography the evolution of his development and in particular of his political development: from Max Weber he inherited a liberalism that was never failing (*Autobiographie philosophique*, translated by Pierre Boudot; Aubier).

3. In order to grasp what is true—partially true—in this idea, one should think of what the *certainty* of being able to destroy the universe would mean. This is, precisely, being certain of one's determinate existence and in some sense creating it.

4. I refer here to André Glucksmann's book *Le Discours de la guerre* (L'Herne).

Chapter 12

1. Response to the inquiry of a Polish magazine: "In your opinion, what is the influence that the war has had on literature after 1945?"

Chapter 13

1. Exceptionally, I will indicate when and where this little text was published for the first time: in October 1958 in *14 Juillet*, no. 2. It was written shortly after General de Gaulle's return to power, brought about not by the Resistance this time but by the mercenaries.

Chapter 14

1. I refer first and foremost to the book *Détruire dit-elle*, by Marguerite Duras (Editions de Minuit).

Chapter 15

1. Louis René des Forêts, *Le Bavard* (Editions Gallimard and Collection 10/18).
2. *La Chambre des enfants* (Editions Gallimard).
3. I would like to recall a note of Kafka's in his *Diary* in which, it seems to me, an allusion is made to one of the hidden truths of the narrative we have just read: "What Milena has said of the joy of chatting with people, without being able to understand fully the truth of what she said (there is also a sad pride justified). Who else but me could take pleasure in chatter?"

Chapter 16

1. *L'Age d'homme* (Editions Gallimard).
2. *La Règle du jeu*: I. *Biffures*, II. *Fourbis* (Editions Gallimard). Since this commentary was written, the third volume has appeared under the title *Fibrilles*; however, the attempt to put an end to the project—were it even with the most direct violence—has still not given us the right to embrace the whole of a life otherwise than as posthumous reader, anachronistic and outdated reader, always late to the meeting set by "poetry," that is, the language to come, in which one's own end as reader is included.
3. This is why the commentator must respond to the candor of the author with an equal reserve. He must be very careful not to make the portrait of a portrait, which, always further simplified, might risk imposing itself on the living model like a death mask. Evidently, it is against the all too accomplished nature of his first book, one that reflected back to him a Michel Leiris in some sense already classical, that the author instinctively reacted by withdrawing into himself in order to rediscover his free truth.
4. Where does the relation, which is almost a relation of constraint, between truth and the author of *La règle du jeu* come from? Why must he seek to be true and to express himself truly? A question that is perhaps naive, yet one that he himself invites us to ask in this form. He thinks that the virtues of physical force and courage, which he believes he lacks, have created a flaw for which he must compensate—so as not to lose his balance—with a punctilious need to know and judge himself. Lucidity would thus spring from a lack, it would be the absence made clear and the void become light. One needs a certain weakness in order to have the self-assured strength of gaze, one needs a laceration and an initial open-

ing in order for the gaze, exerted against oneself, to make this void, by illuminating it and by filling it perfectly, the future—the illusion—of a new plenitude. The author of *Biffures* would be located here, between Benjamin Constant and Proust, both of whom were capable, with regard to themselves, of a clairvoyance originally accompanied by a pitiless sense of their own weakness and by the experience of their lack. But Michel Leiris is well aware that this void, about which he would like to reassure himself by making it clarity and the ability to see clearly, is another aspect of the fear of death, under which he lives and writes: "The prescience of the nauseating moment at which everything will disappear . . . is enough to make me . . . the center of a downy world where only vague forms remain. . . . To my ears nothing sings anymore, and for a number of years dreams have rarely come to animate my nights; one could say that everything that escapes the limits of the serious frightens me." "A collapse" that allowed him "to acquire in return a certain ability to see things in a dry and positive way." However, if the literature of autobiography thus seems to be an attempt to master the force of dissolution, an attempt that turns him away from his obligations as a living man for as long as he has not overcome this force in a virile manner—in particular, the obligation to work toward the economic and social liberation of the world— what will happen on the day when such a literature will have reached its goal and succeeded in silencing in him the empty speech heralding only emptiness, against which he has seemed to defend himself since his "Dostoevsky-like confessions," as he defends himself against the greatest threat that it indeed conveys? That day, not only will he have to give up writing but he will also, probably, have to let himself be petrified by the spirit of seriousness, the other form of imposture to which he could not accommodate himself. It is therefore not possible for him either to conquer or to be conquered. Hence the pact of alliance that, when he writes, he knows full well writing forces him to conclude with the enemy power and that he formulates thus, timidly: "For as long as death does not take hold of me, death is an idea, in short, that must not be pushed aside but rather tamed."

Chapter 17

1. Michel Leiris, *Nuits sans nuit et quelques jours sans jour* (Gallimard).
2. Roger Caillois, *L'Incertitude qui vient des rêves* (Gallimard).
3. For this knowledge, I refer to the book entitled *Les Songes et leur*

interprétation, published in the series "Sources orientales" by Editions du Seuil, under the direction of Marcel Leibovici.

4. "As for the following night, I found myself, as soon as it was over, full of reflections. But I could not grasp them; I was certain only of the fact that I had dreamed. Reflections is saying too much. I retained the feeling in which one seems to oneself to melt" (*Le Pont traversé*). Here, I would like to say that aside from these three nights of Jean Paulhan, I do not know of any words that are closer to the transparency of dreams. From night to day, the bridge crossed. In reading these words, or in reading those of Michel Leiris, I understand how one might write down one's dreams. I also understand how one might not desire to write them down. The only truth that they would like us to understand is perhaps in the speed with which they erase themselves, leaving behind only a trace of light: as if, in these dreams, memory and oblivion were finally coinciding.

Chapter 19

1. *Le Baphomet* (Mercure de France); *Les Lois de l'hospitalité* (Editions Gallimard).

2. This is why when I am in the street, I can brazenly look at a beautiful face or a beautiful knee—Western law is hardly opposed to this—but if I should want to touch either one, immediately I am scandalous, having behaved as a man who is ignorant of a "savoir-voir."

3. Editions Jean-Jacques Pauvert.

4. If there is still God, a god only more silent, or the fascination with Unity, then the sign is no longer but a trace and renounces its exigency as unique sign.

5. Such is the ambiguity of the sign: Unique, does it destroy, does it preserve, does it exceed unity?

6. I would like to recall here, on the same topic, Michel Foucault's fine essay, *La Prose d'Actéon* (N.R.F., no. 135).

7. *Un si funeste désir* (Editions Gallimard).

8. By transforming the legend of the Templars into a myth, *Le Baphomet* translates with baroque sumptuousness this experience of the eternal return—assimilated here to the cycles of metempsychosis and rendered thus more comic than tragic (in the manner of certain oriental tales). Everything takes place in a whirling beyond—a realm of the spirits—where it is natural, under a light of invisibility, for all truths to lose their brilliance; where God is no longer anything but a far-off and

much diminished sphere; where death, especially, has lost its omnipotence and even its power of decision: neither immortals nor mortals, given over to the perpetual change that repeats them, absent from themselves in the movement of intensity that is their only substance and makes a game of their identical being, a resemblance without anything to resemble, an inimitable imitation—such are the "whispers," words of spirit or words of the writer; such are also the figures and the works formed by these words. There remains the inexplicable desire to return to the day, under the pretext of honoring the dogma of final resurrection; the desire to be incarnated, even as a group, in the same body; a desire less to be purified than to be corrupted and to corrupt all purifying work, in which I would readily see a just malediction thrown on the eternity of being. (It is like a new and fascinating version of the myth of Er.) One will pronounce the name *gnosis*; perhaps wrongly, perhaps rightly. If, however, the connection is made, it should not be made in order to age an essentially modern work, but rather, in the same way that Kafka was able, in writing, not writing, to imagine that his work, had he written it, would have given rise to a new Cabala. Let us recall certain traits of the resemblance. Gnosis is not a Manichaeanism, it is often a very nuanced dualism. From the role that the reflection of God plays in it, to the attraction to what is below provided by the gaze of self, it poses the problem of the repetition of the Same and thus introduces plurality in unity. With or without syncretism, it introduces, in many cases, an exigency such that the pagan mysteries and the Christian mysteries succeed in passing into each other. It gives a certain place to the great feminine figures and to sexual elements (androgyny, sodomy). It makes the idea of circular time its own (and even metempsychosis), but in order to fight against what it calls the "cycle of death" with a movement of return, of a rising toward the above, which would require little to be transformed into an eternal return. It makes room for the oblivion that appears as a more profound memory: here suddenly a God learns—he had forgotten it—that he is not the first God, that there is, above him, a God more silent still, more ungraspable (and it would be tempting to add "and so forth"). It is essentially a narrative, a cosmic narrative ruled by complexity, an immobile narrative in which truths are engendered by being recounted through an indefinite multiplication. It is true that it lacks, as the Gospels lack, the "supreme manifestation of the divine": laughter, the laughter that "bursts forth from the depths of the truth itself" and that is the gift of the work of Klossowski.

Chapter 20

1. These reflections were almost given to me by the work of Clémence Ramnoux, *Études présocratiques* (Editions Klincksieck), a book of wisdom, erudition, simplicity, in which the encounter of these opposing qualities also makes one think. In the margin of this book, I am still tempted to add: if the myth can be interpreted when it gives rise to two series whose relation would be the meaning of the myth, we understand that the trilogy of Aeschylus carries with it this debate, among others: Does the child come from the father or does it come from the mother? In the first case, Orestes is almost innocent, guilty of a crime of milk but not the crime of blood; but for the series father/mother, two others, more frightening, can be substituted: Does man come from the father and/or the mother—modern and "Oedipal" belief—or else is he of chthonic origin? The "chthonic" being not simply the Earth but what is beneath the "Threshold" (with ambiguity: Am I carried by the Earth? Am I engulfed by what is below?), the question seems to refer, now and again, to the double series Earth:Chaos, separated absolutely, and yet constantly and dangerously implicated in one another. Aside from this meaning, one could also suggest another: Would it not be the genealogical account itself that tells itself (thinks itself) by letting itself be told under this double series—on the one hand, things and phrases capable of begetting and of consequences, on the other, the obscure and empty, a repetitive beat, capable nonetheless of giving rise to a difference of names (Chaos is repeatedly named as Erebus, Tartarus, Night—the triple Night—then, as Night according to the three names of Death: Moros, Kère, Thanatos; then, as Kère according to the Erinyes: Chaos is then almost there, in our vicinity)? When Hesiod establishes between Chaos (which is below) and existing things, or their limits, sources, or roots, a *threshold* of unshakable bronze, we can see in the threshold the border that is beginning and end, and we can also recognize in it the impassable threshold of the interdiction. We also can retain only the term *Threshold* and strive, as Paul Celan engages us to do, to think from *threshold to threshold.*

Chapter 21

1. In an essay, *Sur un Héros païen* (Editions Gallimard), devoted to *L'Etranger*, Robert Champigny discovers in the latter all of the traits of Epicurean wisdom, which, it is true, at decisive moments extends as far as the great visions of the pre-Socratics.

2. "For the first time in a very long time, I thought of maman. . . . There, there too, in that home where lives were passing away, evening was a kind of melancholic respite. So close to death, maman must have felt herself liberated and ready to relive everything. No one, no one had the right to cry over her. And I too felt ready to relive everything."

3. One of the most expressive passages in this narrative is this one: "Yes, few beings were more natural than I. My harmony with life was total, I adhered to what it was, utterly, refusing none of its ironies, its greatness and its servitude." If this man feels guilty for not having tried to save the drowning woman, the fault is not to be found on the level of the soul but of the body, this body of a city dweller who is afraid of the cold and afraid of water. It is certain that for the Stranger, with his youthful vigor, this heroic act would have been the simplest of acts. One could say (this is one of the "legitimate" readings) that, in this dark narrative, Camus is trying to grasp—in what has separated him from himself, from nature, from his natural spontaneity, and has alienated him by turning him to the work of time (and the task of writing)—a movement that also belongs to the period, a movement that should find its fulfillment in the return to a new perception of the native experience, the return to simplicity. The next chapter ("The Fall: The Flight"), however, proposes another reading of *La Chute*.

Chapter 23

1. André Gorz, *Le Traître*, foreword by Jean-Paul Sartre (Editions du Seuil).

2. How not to evoke here Wolfson's attempt (*Le Schizo et les langues*; Editions Gallimard): an attempt that is, however, very different because, for Wolfson, the work bears precisely on his own language, such that where the relation of words to things has become material and no longer a relation of signification—a reified relation—one finds the means of pushing aside the "bad, sick matter," the harmful maternal object?

Chapter 24

1. Jacques Dupin, *Alberto Giacometti, textes pour une approche* (Editions Maeght). The title I have given these reflections is intentionally borrowed from Ernst Bloch's very rich book, *Spuren*, which appeared thirty or so years ago and was recently reedited in German (and since translated into French; Editions Gallimard). *Spuren*, traces, tracks (for

example, those on magnetic tape, where voices are contiguous yet do not mix), discontinuous words, affirmations, not only fragmentary but related to an experience of the fragmentary.

2. Roger Laporte, *La Veille,* "Le Chemin" series (Editions Gallimard).

3. Edmond Jabès, *Le Livre des questions* (Gallimard).

4. I am alluding not only to a peculiarity of personal history, but to another sort of truth: "to be Jewish" extracts no more from the fatality (or dignity) of being—understood as race, as biological or even biographical vocation—than a power that is unconditionally free. One could even say that it also comes from our belonging to "humanity," no doubt; and that is why both belongings go through the same vicissitudes. One does not become a Jew through gracious consent. One is a Jew before being one, and at the same time this anteriority that precedes being Jewish and, in some way, history, does not root it in a nature (in the certitude of a natural identity), but in an already formed otherness, which, even so, has never yet occurred, and which must be answered, without being able to turn down the responsibility. From this "the condition of the Jew" is the most reflexive, and at all times sealed by an affirmation more inveterate than nature, more necessary than it, and from which one would not be able to hide, even if one ran from it.

5. In the book *Difficile Liberté* (Editions Albin Michel), in which Emmanuel Levinas, with his customary depth and authority in speaking of Judaism, speaks of what concerns us all, I find, among many essential reflections, the following: "The oral law is eternally contemporaneous to the written. Between them there exists a relationship whose intellection is the very atmosphere of Judaism. The one neither maintains nor destroys the other—but makes it practical and readable. To penetrate this dimension every day and to maintain oneself in it was the work of the famous study of the Torah, the celebrated *Lernen* that occupies a central place in Jewish religious life."

6. Martin Buber, *Les Récits hassidiques* (Plon). The translation, worthy of the original—an original without origin—is by Armel Guerne. This is what Buber says about working on the collection: "It was transmitted to me [the legend of the Hasidim] through popular books, notebooks, and manuscripts, but I also heard it from living lips, from lips that had received its stammering message. I have not adapted it as if it were just any piece of literature, I have not worked on it as if it were a fable: I have told it in my turn, like a posthumous son . . . I am only a link in the chain of narrators, I repeat in my turn the old story, and if it sounds new, it is because the new was in it the first time it was ever told."

I would also like to recommend another book, by Robert Misrahi, *La Condition réflexive de l'homme juif* (Julliard), and in particular a chapter titled "The Significance of Nazi Anti-Semitism as the Original Experience of the Modern Jew." From it I take the following passage for consideration: "For the Jew, the enormity of the Nazi catastrophe reveals the *depth* to which anti-Semitism has been 'anchored,' and reveals anti-Semitism to be a *permanent* possibility. . . . Consciousness of the *Catastrophe*, as if derived from a renewed Jewish consciousness, is a sort of sinister conversion, not to light but to darkness. This *past beginning*, this primitive experience beyond which it is impossible to go, constitutes, in effect, for Jewish consciousness a method of somber initiation: it is the apprenticeship of wisdom and fear. "To be a Jew" is something that cannot be defined for the cultured, assimilated Jew, except paradoxically and circuitously: by the *mere fact* of always being susceptible to gratuitous murder "because of being Jewish." The whole of society becomes for him a permanent possibility of mutation and from now on will constitute a latent menace. R. Misrahi adds, "Nazi anti-Semitism is not simply a historical phenomenon for which we can determine the causes and sociological structures. . . . If it is that, it is also something else: the manifestation of pure violence addressed without motivation to the other, simply because he incarnates the scandal of *another existence*."

Chapter 25

1. One would have to qualify this assertion.

2. "Between me and you," says a maxim of Hallaj, "there is an 'I am' that torments me. Ah! Remove with your 'I am' my 'I am' from between us."

3. G. G. Scholem, *Les Grands Courants de la mystique juive*, translated by M.-M. David (Payot). I would like to make it clear that I certainly did not fail to use this remarkable book for this commentary, as well as the following works of Buber: *Die chassidische Botschaft* and *Sehertum* (*Anfang und Ausgang*).

4. *Gog et Magog, Chronique de l'épopée napoléonienne*, translated by Jean Lœwenson-Lavi (Editions Gallimard).

Chapter 26

1. Besides the biography, Brod dedicated several volumes to his friend in which he specifies what were, according to his views, the "belief and teaching" of Kafka.

2. *Diary*, note from May 3, 1915.

3. In a later chapter, Pepi, Frieda's replacement, who tries to seduce K., explains to K. at great length the intrigue in which Klamm's girlfriend has engaged herself by throwing herself around the neck of a stranger, to attract attention through scandal and to recover a little of the prestige that her feeble physical attractions and her disagreeable character have caused her to lose. Moreover, is she Klamm's girlfriend? Everything leads one to think that this is a fable, cleverly concocted by the ambitious Frieda. Such is Pepi's point of view, in keeping with her own miserable little existence. K. himself puts no faith in it, though he is tempted to find refuge in the underground passageways of a sad servant's life. "You are wrong," he says. In the final pages, he tries, not without success, to strike up a new intrigue with the wife of the innkeeper of the Herrenhof. Thus everything begins again, but this incessant beginning-again of situations also shows that everything is stuck, even the book, which can only interrupt itself.

4. In a fragment, an observer from the village makes a mockery of what he calls "the adventure" that K. has had with Bürgel. "It is all too comical," he says, "that it had to be Bürgel." Bürgel is, in effect, the secretary of Frederic, an official of the Castle, who has for some time fallen into disgrace and no longer has any influence. All the more reason for it to be Bürgel, who is but a secretary of the lowest rank.

Chapter 27

1. It is this biography that Klaus Wagenbach has undertaken to write, a work that is very instructive (*Franz Kafka, eine Biographie seiner Jugend,* 1958). Cf. the next chapter, devoted to the letters written by Kafka to his first fiancée, Felice Bauer, letters excluded from this first volume of the correspondence as a result of an editorial agreement.

2. I would remind the reader that the *Letters to Milena* were published as a separate volume in 1952.

3. He writes to Brod: "The bad opinion that I have of myself is not an ordinary bad opinion. This opinion constitutes rather my sole virtue; it is that which I should never, never have to doubt, when I have drawn reasonable limits for it in the course of my life: it puts order in me, and for me, who in the face of what I cannot embrace break down immediately, it makes me passably peaceful." This reflection is from 1912: the bad opinion is still but methodical; moreover, circumscribed and mea-

sured. "What I have written," he says in the same letter, "was written in a warm bath, I did not live the eternal hell of real writers." The letters confirm what we sensed: that the dramatic relations with life begin around his thirtieth year, when on the one hand writing becomes the absolute exigency, and on the other he encounters his fiancée. The year 1912 precisely marks the rupture. Until then, during the years dominated by the father, he is certainly already "in despair," but it is a despair illuminated by humor, scintillating and almost light, threatened by aesthetic pleasure, of which the following is an example: "For I have been, as I saw this morning before washing up, in despair for two years, and only the more or less distant limit of this despair determines my mood of the moment. And here I am at a café, I have read several pretty things, I am doing well, and I do not speak of my despair with as much conviction as I would have liked to at home" (1908). What is there in common with this cry: "In the fields, outside the madness of my head and my nights. Such a being am I, such a being am I. I torment her, and myself to death" (1916)?

4. The same is true in the last letters to Milena, but to Milena with more humor.

5. We also know from many other texts that he does not hold his art originally responsible for the life outside the world to which it dooms him: it was first imposed on him by his relations with his father; it is by him that he was exiled from life, pushed outside the borders, condemned to wander in exile. Art but translated, exploited, and deepened this earlier fatality. Kafka, furthermore, is far from always speaking unfavorably of this life outside the world, which, on the contrary, he sought out with unrelenting strength. In June 1921, to Brod: "The first slightly peaceful day after fifteen days of martyrdom. This life-outside-the-world that I lead is not in itself worse than the other, there is no reason to complain about it, but when the world, desecrator of tombs, begins to scream even into this life-outside-the-world, I come off my hinges and I really knock my head against the door of madness, which is always but half-open. The least thing suffices to put me in this state."

6. One must also mention the circumstances: during this period, Max Brod is in a painful emotional state—married in Prague, he is passionately attached to a young woman who lives in Berlin. Kafka often sees this young woman, and he knows that it is first of all of her that he must speak to his friend.

7. During his last days, Kafka held himself strictly to the orders not to

speak, even in whispers. He conversed until the end with his friends by writing out short sentences in which the sensitivity and originality of his language, always alive, continue to be expressed.

Chapter 28

1. Cf. the preceding chapter.

2. I refer to the letter that Kafka wrote to Milena in which he describes with his implacable candor "his first night" ("L'échec de Milena," postface to volume VIII of Kafka's *Œuvres complètes*; Cercle du Livre Précieux).

3. One day when Felice evokes his "bent for writing": "Not a bent, I have no bent, writing is my whole self. A bent, one could wipe out or reduce. But it is myself. Certainly, one could do away with me, but what would be left for you?"

4. In particular on the day of the trial when he gives up justifying himself and also when he writes a letter to Mlle. Bloch in which, although recently engaged, he speaks of his horror of marriage, a letter that his correspondent wrongly shows to Felice, such that Felice is struck with a feeling of painful duplicity, for the truth, of which she had been warned so many times by Kafka directly, had become a power of deadly objectivity (as it always happens) as soon as it had been communicated to her by someone else.

5. On the relation to "truth," one would have to cite the letter of Sept. 20, 1917—the next-to-last letter, I believe—already partially published in the *Diary*: "For five years you have been kept informed as to the progress of the struggle, by word and by silence and by a combination of the two, and most often it has been a torment for you. . . . If you ask whether it has always been in keeping with the truth, I can only say that with no one else but you have I held myself so strenuously from conscious lies. There have been certain attenuations [*Verschleierungen*], but very few lies, assuming that in what concerns lies it is possible for there to be 'very few.'" The continuation can be read in the *Diary* with, at the end and in form of a verdict, the following: "In summary, it is only the tribunal of men that is important to me, and it is this tribunal, moreover, that I wish to deceive, though without deception."

6. On "literature" and the danger it represents, responding to Felice, who judged herself, in everything, to be less than he: "I would be 'more advanced than you in everything'? A small capacity for judging men and

for putting myself in their place out of sympathy, this I have. . . . I have no memory, not for things learned, or read, or experienced, or heard; it is as if I had no experience of anything; I know less about most things than the smallest schoolboy. I cannot think; in my thinking, I constantly come up against limits; certainly, I am still able to grasp this or that isolated point, but a coherent thought, capable of elaboration, is impossible for me. I cannot even tell a story, or even speak. . . . All I have are certain powers that focus themselves in view of literature at a depth that cannot be recognized under normal conditions, powers to which I do not dare give myself over in my present professional and physical state, because in face of the inner demand of these powers there are as many inner warnings. Were I able to give myself to these powers, they would straightaway carry me, of this I am sure, out of all of this inner desolation" [must one specify? out of life].

7. On these new relations, there is a very brief note in the *Diary* that Max Brod judged himself not authorized to publish but that Wagenbach read in the manuscript.

8. I refer to the letter (on his relations with his family), an important excerpt of which is published in the *Diary* (Oct. 18, 1916).

9. According to convention—convention!—Kafka is obviously the one who should have crossed the great space and gone to his fiancée, but Kafka "is bound like a criminal; had I been put in a corner, with real chains . . . it would not have been worse" (*Diary*, June 1914).

10. About the stay in Marienbad, Kafka also writes in the *Diary*, on Jan. 29, 1922, as he takes fright at the thought that Milena might come: "It remains to solve this one enigma: why I was happy for fifteen days in Marienbad and why, consequently, I might also perhaps be happy here with Milena, after the most painful breaking and forcing of barriers, of course. But it would probably be much more difficult than in Marienbad, my ideology is firmer, my experiences more vast. What was then a thread of separation is now a wall or a mountain, or better yet: a grave."

11. It should be recalled that he abandoned *Amerika* one night and with no mind to take it up again (except to write the last chapter in Oct. 1914 and perhaps also, at the same date, the episode of Brunelda) when he reread the 400 pages he had already written and could not regrasp its *truth as a whole*.

MERIDIAN

Crossing Aesthetics

Library of Congress Cataloging-in-Publication Data

Blanchot, Maurice.
[Amitié. English]
Friendship / by Maurice Blanchot ; translated by
Elizabeth Rottenberg, 1997.
    p.   cm.
ISBN 0-8047-2758-9 (cloth) — ISBN 0-8047-2759-7 (pbk.)
1. Arts and society.   2. Politics and culture.
I. Rottenberg, Elizabeth, 1969–   .   II. Title.
NX180.S6B55813   1997
700'.1'01—dc20   96-38201   CIP

⊗ This book is printed on acid-free, recycled paper.

Original printing 1997
Last figure below indicates year of this printing:
06 05 04 03 02 01 00 99 98 97